Risk Management Handbook

A practical guide for financial institutions and their advisers

S8

AF754719

Risk Management Handbook

A practical guide for financial institutions and their advisers

DERMOT TURING

Partner, Clifford Chance

Butterworths
London, Charlottesville, Dublin, Durban, Edinburgh, Hong Kong, Kuala Lumpur, New Delhi, Singapore, Sydney, Toronto, Wellington
2000

United Kingdom	Butterworths, a Division of Reed Elsevier (UK) Ltd, Halsbury House, 35 Chancery Lane, LONDON WC2A 1EL and 4 Hill Street, EDINBURGH EH2 3JZ
Australia	Butterworths, a Division of Reed International Books Australia Pty Ltd, CHATSWOOD, New South Wales
Canada	Butterworths Canada Ltd, MARKHAM, Ontario
Hong Kong	Butterworths Asia (Hong Kong), HONG KONG
India	Butterworths India, NEW DELHI
Ireland	Butterworth (Ireland) Ltd, DUBLIN
Malaysia	Malayan Law Journal Sdn Bhd, KUALA LUMPUR
New Zealand	Butterworths of New Zealand Ltd, WELLINGTON
Singapore	Butterworths Asia, SINGAPORE
South Africa	Butterworths Publishers (Pty) Ltd, DURBAN
USA	Lexis Law Publishing, CHARLOTTESVILLE, Virginia

© Reed Elsevier (UK) Ltd 2000

All rights reserved. No part of this publication may be reproduced in any material form (including photocopying or storing it in any medium by electronic means and whether or not transiently or incidentally to some other use of this publication) without the written permission of the copyright owner except in accordance with the provisions of the Copyright, Designs and Patents Act 1988 or under the terms of a licence issued by the Copyright Licensing Agency Ltd, 90 Tottenham Court Road, London, England W1P 0LP. Applications for the copyright owner's written permission to reproduce any part of this publication should be addressed to the publisher.

Warning: The doing of an unauthorised act in relation to a copyright work may result in both a civil claim for damages and criminal prosecution.

Any Crown copyright material is reproduced with the permission of the Controller of Her Majesty's Stationery Office.

A CIP Catalogue record for this book is available from the British Library.

ISBN 0 406 92956 4

Typeset by Doyle & Co, Colchester
Printed by Selwood Printing, Burgess Hill

Visit us at our website: http://www.butterworths.co.uk

Preface

Risk management has changed. All the risks taken on by a financial institution must be managed, and senior management will be accountable to regulators and shareholders if there are lapses. What is being demanded of the risk managers of a financial institution is a much wider grasp of the business than when 'risk management' first became a buzz-word. Being able to compute market price predictions is not enough. Not only do risk managers have to have all-encompassing understanding of their company's aspirations and operations, as well as understand their failings, but everyone in a senior position has to understand what the risk managers are up to.

Something more than mathematical models is needed to provide adequate support for management. Modelling might tell you the magnitude of a potential loss, but it won't help with how you control it, the pros and cons of competing control strategies, or the potential risks which are introduced by a control technique. So this book is not about Value-at-Risk and contains no algebra. There is a chapter on risk measurement, but the focus is on risk management.

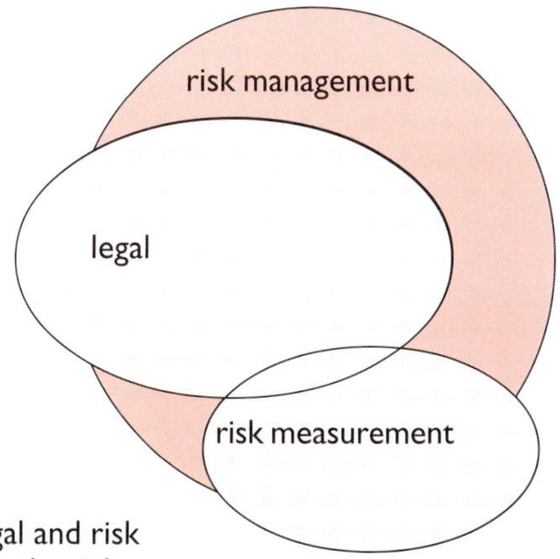

The respective roles of legal and risk measurement in relation to the risk management function

The legal department inevitably gets bound up in this process. Traditionally, there has been no area of legal practice which shadows the risk management function of a financial institution, yet that is what in-house counsel are asked to do much of the time. On both risk and legal sides there is a danger that impenetrable jargon puts up a barrier to effective communication. But though there may be little overlap between the mathematical wizards and the legal boffins they are both serving the same risk-manager master. Lawyers are good at identifying solutions to 'what if . . . ?' problems, which tend to come up in a risk management context. So there does need to be such a thing as a risk management lawyer, who has to have a wider grasp of the general issues facing a firm than those which arise on a particular product line.

But this book is not a traditional legal textbook. The emphasis is on practicality, not prose. No attempt has been made to introduce legal purism: please do not expect this book to treat any part of the subject exhaustively or to mention all the qualifications, ifs and buts. The idea has been to use layman's terms to describe the mathematical and legal concepts, to give a basic introduction and explanation and to provide some illustrations, but not to be a definitive treatise. But beware of the danger in relying on checklists and snapshots of current practice. Practice evolves. Even the best checklist cannot manage to be comprehensive *and* stick to the key points.

Risk management in practice

No money was made without risk taking. But not by being foolhardy.

Each risk is associated with an event or circumstance of some description. Some events are good: the price goes up, we win the lottery, the new IT system comes in under budget. Some are bad: the price goes down, we lose the lottery investment, the project cost twice what we budgeted. Some are catastrophic: the keen guy on the fifth floor has been defrauding the firm for years, the bank has gone bust with all our money in it, all our customer records were wiped out when the computer crashed. Risk management is about risk selection: choosing the good ones and cutting out the bad.

Risks also interrelate. A method for controlling one risk usually introduces other risks. The risk manager needs to have these connections in mind when advising on risk strategy.

Finding guidance on how to make the choice is difficult. Most guidance in printed form is either too high level (appoint a risk committee) or too detailed (written in Greek letters). Yet people are being asked every day to make these choices and to put in place systems and controls which will keep the bad risk events bound and gagged. Whether to do it is an easy decision, but how to do it is tough. This book tries to give some starting points on the how.

Law and practice is stated as at 30 September 1999 although a few changes have been incorporated at the proof stage.

Dermot Turing

October 1999

Acknowledgments

I have drawn heavily on the patience and support of many in bringing this idea to print. Clifford Chance provided the medium in which the idea grew and I am extremely grateful to my partners in the Risk Management and Financial Institutions Group in London for their support.

Much of the source material is papers written by the Basle Committee, IOSCO and ISDA. This material is invaluable to anyone interested in the subject, and I urge the reader to go to the primary sources identified in the text.

Liz Cramb and Louise Desborough have not only supported the concept but given immense amounts of time in reviewing drafts and offering helpful criticism. Special thanks are due to them. Liz also read the proofs, a task of unparalleled tedium and far outside the call of duty. Lynda Wright provided invaluable research skills, ideas and other help. Sarah Robinson, Shefali Choksi and countless others have also contributed to bringing it to fruition.

My family have also been surprisingly tolerant. I hope that Nicki, James and Beryl found some wry amusement, and John some competitive inspiration, in the notion that Dad was writing a book. But to all of them a thank you for not objecting to the evenings and weekends at the computer when other things would have been more fun.

The efforts of all these people will not have saved this book from having the idiosyncrasies, and no doubt errors, which are all mine.

Dermot Turing

Contents

1

Types of risk

1.1 THE UNHOLY TRINITY OF RISKS

There are three main categories of risk.

1.1.1 Market risk

- Synonyms Replacement risk, price risk.
- Varieties Foreign exchange risk, interest rate risk, basis risk, reinvestment risk, liquidity risk.
- Event or circumstance to be managed Adverse price movement.
- Basle Committee definition The risk to an institution's financial condition resulting from adverse movements in the level or volatility of market prices.
- IOSCO definition The risk that movements in prices or values will result in loss for the firm.
- GARP definition Risk of loss resulting from adverse effects of movements in markets/rates/prices/changes in spread, or from breakdowns in observed correlations between instruments, products, currencies or markets.

1.1.2 Operational risk

- Synonyms Operations risk.
- Varieties Model risk, legal risk, reputational risk, business interruption risk, control risk, systems risk, disaster risk, regulatory risk, political risk.
- Event or circumstance to be managed Human error, lax management controls, IT systems failure, transaction booking and processing error, terrorism, employee fraud, external crime, breach of legal and regulatory requirements, failure to meet customer expectations, supplier failure, model failure, pricing error, change in law or taxation practice, change of government, natural disaster, payment system breakdown, market disruption (to name but some).

- **Basle Committee definition** The risk that deficiencies in information systems or internal controls will result in unexpected loss (though see below).
- **IOSCO definition** The risk that a firm will suffer loss as a result of human error or deficiencies in systems or controls.
- **GARP definition** Risk of loss resulting from errors in the processing of transactions/ breakdown in controls/errors or failures in systems support.

Commentary

The Basle Committee states that there is no universally agreed definition, and notes that many banks define operational risk as everything other than market or credit risk. Operational risk is not really one risk but many: it's a sweep-up term covering everything which doesn't fall neatly into one of the other two main categories. Essentially anything that is decided on by management, but does not occur, or anything that is not decided on by management and does occur, can be classified as an operational failure. Certainly it is not limited to 'back-office failure' as some firms perceive it.

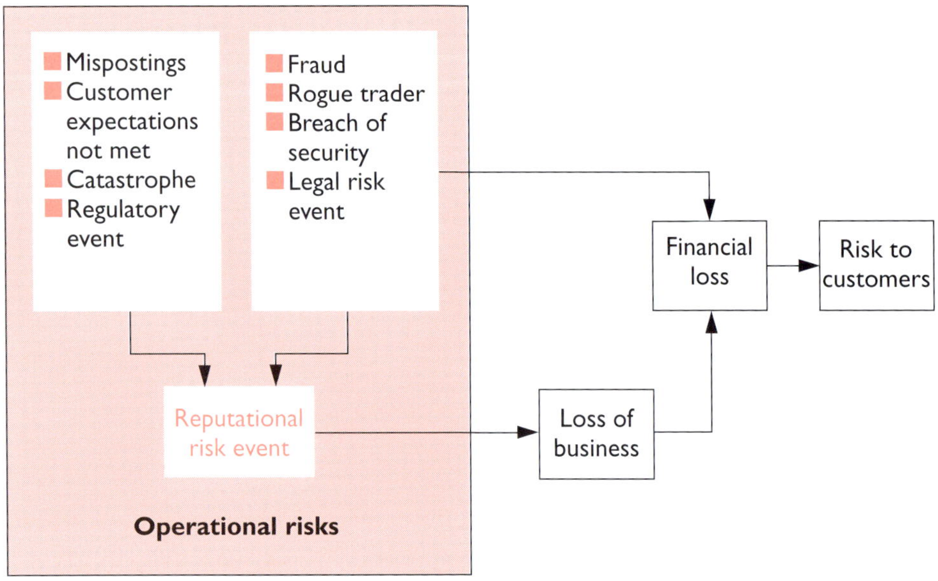

Relationship between operational risks

One operational risk event can lead to another. Some operational risk events cause financial loss directly. Others lead only to reputational damage since the problem can be fixed before direct financial loss occurs. But reputational damage is itself an operational risk event, which can lead to financial loss. Financial losses can put customers' interests at risk, which is why regulators are concerned with reputation as well as the causes of reputational damage.

1.1.3 Credit risk

- **Synonyms** Default risk, credit equivalent exposure.
- **Varieties** Settlement risk, pre-settlement risk, delivery risk.
- **Event or circumstance to be managed** Failure to pay (or deliver) on time or at all.
- **Basle Committee/IOSCO definition** The risk that a counterparty will fail to perform on an obligation.
- **GARP definition** Risk of loss resulting from counterparty default.

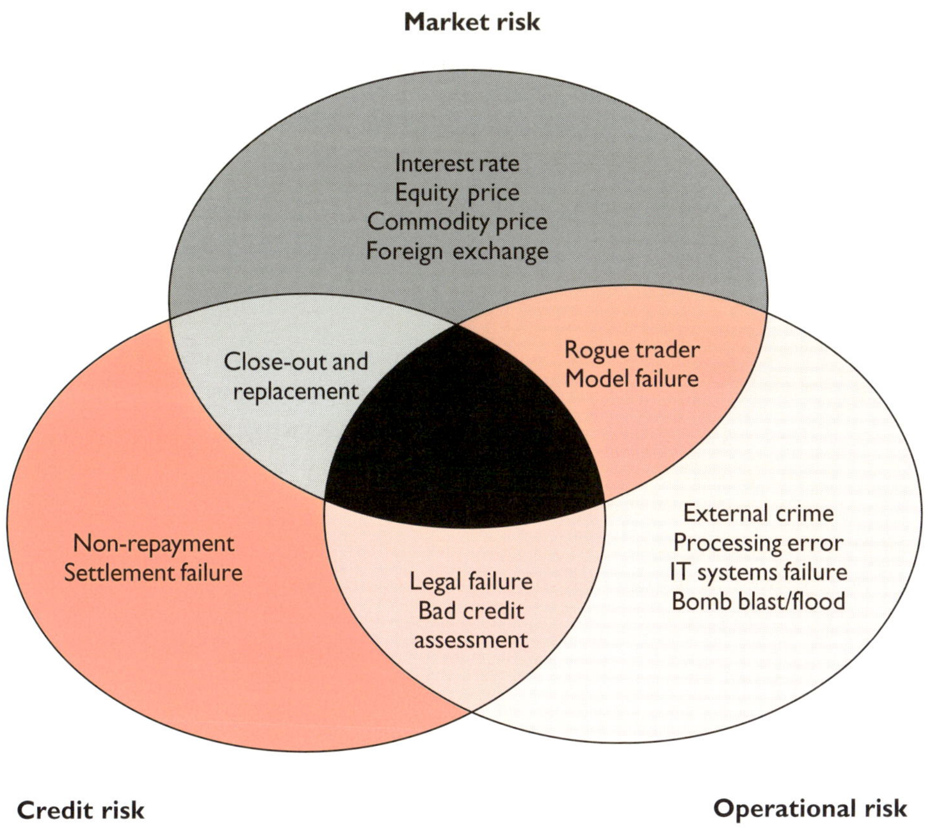

Relationships between risks

1.2 THE OTHER DEVILS, GHOULS AND OGRES

Other types of risk frequently mentioned:

Basis risk

- Event or circumstance to be managed Prices of two different products are not linked in the manner supposed (also called Correlation Risk)—arbitrage activity involves betting on basis risk.

Concentration risk

- Event or circumstance to be managed Lack of diversification increasing susceptibility to other risk events (eg market risk where over-exposed in one instrument, foreign exchange or political risk where over-exposed to counterparties based in one region, credit risk where over-exposed to counterparties active in the same industry sector).

Counterparty risk

- Event or circumstance to be managed Failure by counterparty to pay or perform (usually owing to legal risk event or credit risk event).

Event risk

- Event or circumstance to be managed Unexpected external occurrence (fire, flood, terrorist attack, earthquake etc). Some definitions may include market disruption, political change, legal change, payment systems failure.

Legal risk

- **Event or circumstance to be managed** Inability to enforce or rely on obligations or rights in event of default or dispute.
- **Basle Committee/IOSCO definition** The risk that contracts are not legally enforceable or documented correctly.

Liquidity risk

- **Event or circumstance to be managed** Inability to find a seller or buyer (in practice, at a convenient price). For banks, there is an acute form of liquidity risk in that the bulk of assets are loans which cannot be called in or sold quickly, whereas liabilities are primarily deposits repayable on demand; liquidity risk is a risk of being unable to meet obligations owing to inability to obtain liquid funds, and is therefore given special treatment by bank supervisors.
- **Basle Committee definition** The risk that an institution may not be able to, or cannot easily, unwind or offset a particular position at or near the previous market price because of inadequate market depth or because of disruptions in the marketplace; also the risk that the institution will be unable to meet its payment obligations on settlement dates or in the event of margin calls.
- **IOSCO definition** The risk that a lack of counterparties will leave a firm unable to liquidate or offset a position (or unable to do so at or near the previous market price).
- **GARP definition** Risk of loss resulting from lack of market liquidity preventing quick or effective liquidation of positions or portfolios, and limiting access to funds; also 'prudential liquidity risk', i.e. risk of loss resulting from inability to maintain minimum liquidity ratios.

Model risk

- **Event or circumstance to be managed** Mathematical technique for predicting price movements is ineffective.

Performance risk

- **Event or circumstance to be managed** Failure to deliver a product or service (other than cash) on time or at all (non-cash equivalent of credit risk, which converts to a credit risk on calculation of damages).

Reinvestment risk

- **Event or circumstance to be managed** Inability to obtain the same rate of return for the sum invested (usually arises on premature repayment).

Reputational risk

- **Event or circumstance to be managed** One's own failure to perform as expected by counterparties, customers or the public (or a perception of this, eg 'guilt by association').

Settlement risk

- **Event or circumstance to be managed** Failure by counterparty to pay or deliver notwithstanding full payment or delivery by oneself (lack of PvP or DvP).

- IOSCO definition The risk that a firm will not receive funds or instruments from its counterparty at the expected time.

Systemic risk

- Event or circumstance to be managed Failure of one market participant causing failure of others ('contagion', 'domino insolvencies').

1.3 SECRET LIVES OF RISKS

It is always fun to enquire into the nature of relationships between those who are closely related. But this sort of tabloid investigation is unlikely to lead to many clues in how to manage one's own life. So this section is short: you do not learn much about risk management from academic analyses.

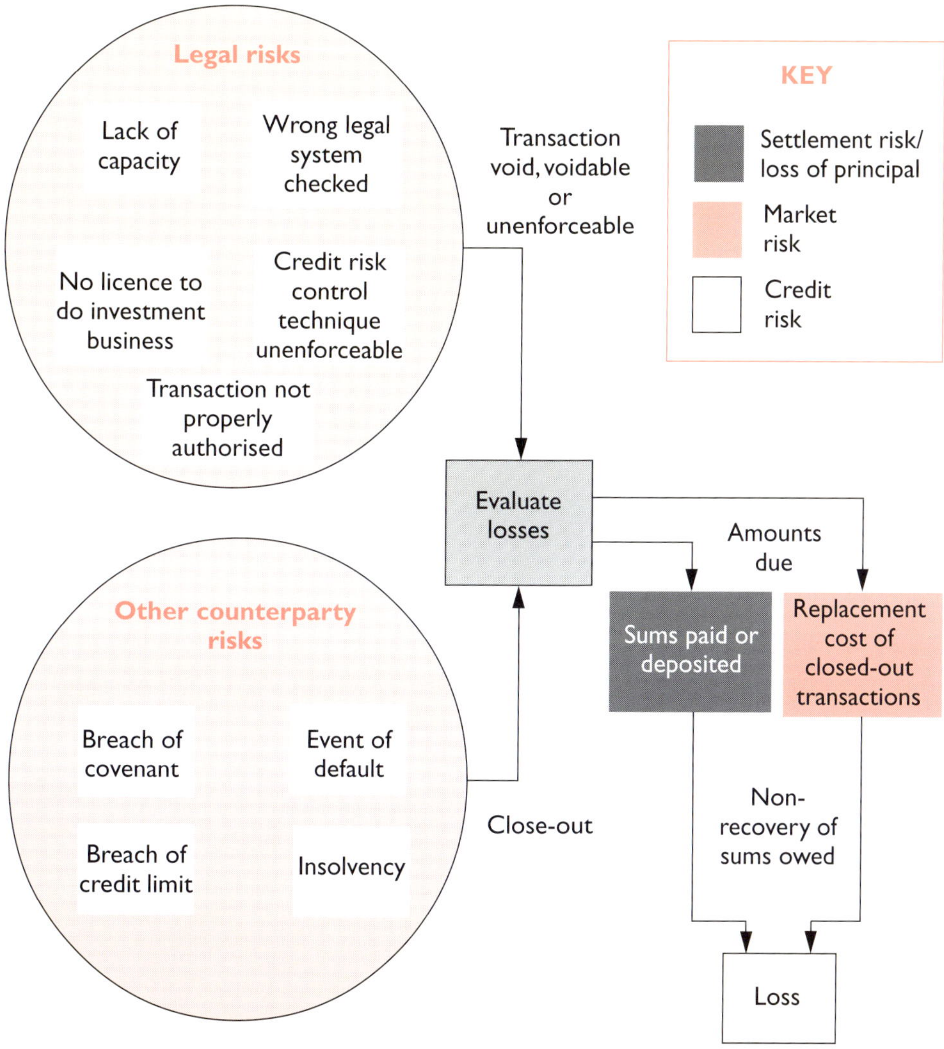

Relationship between legal, counterparty and credit risks

Legal and counterparty risk events come in various guises; any of them can stop the counterparty having to pay. The losses, which give the size of the credit risk, may be replacement costs or loss of principal.

Risk management is about converting unacceptable risk into acceptable risk: either by reducing the exposure to risk (not doing that kind of business, or limiting the extent to which you do it), or by converting one form of risk into another.

- On closing out an in-the-money open position you turn market risk into credit risk.
- On taking collateral to cover credit risk you convert credit risk back into market risk.
- By deciding to take collateral for all your credit exposures you convert credit risk into operational, as well as market risk.
- By participating in industry-wide schemes to combat systemic risk you convert systemic and operational risks into legal, market and credit risks.
- Trying to eliminate human error by computerisation is replacing one form of operational risk with another.
- Keeping control over a firm to whom you have outsourced some IT operations reduces operational risk of one kind at the cost of another (effectiveness of controls) and a combination of performance (ie a species of credit) risk, legal risk, regulatory risk and more.

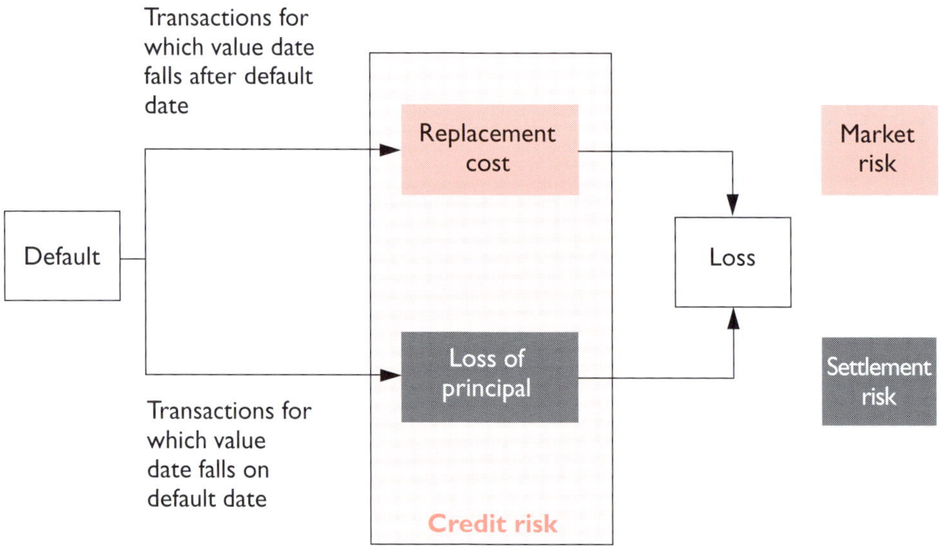

Relationship between market and credit risks upon counterparty default

Market risk can turn into credit risk on default of the counterparty. An in-the-money hedge represents a replacement cost; an in-the-money position represents a potential gain; either way, if the counterparty defaults, the value is lost, though the amount at stake is the replacement cost of the trade. If the counterparty defaults on the settlement date, the amount at stake can be the whole principal value of the transaction, since the non-defaulting party may have paid in full before receiving anything in return. For more on credit and settlement risks, see section 7.8.

Risks interrelate in all kinds of ways. Descriptions of risk overlap. What sort of risk it is, and how you tackle it, depends on which end of it you are looking at. For example, my operational failure is potentially your credit risk or, if you bought shares which I issued, your market risk. If you have managed these risks badly our collective problems could lead to systemic risk. One cause can have many manifestations.

The emphasis must therefore be on understanding each risk. What would the consequences be if there were a risk event? How do you resolve the fundamental equation of risk management (*cost to firm = probability of risk event* x *consequential losses*)? What steps can be taken to reduce the probability of a risk event or contain consequential losses? Are these steps cost-effective?

FURTHER READING

- 'Guide to Risk Management: A glossary of terms' Chase/Risk Magazine, May 1996

GLOSSARY

American option	Options come in various shapes and sizes. American ones are exercisable at any time up to expiry date.
ARCH	Auto-regressive conditional heteroscedasticity. Let's try that again without Greek. Scedasticity: the tendency of things to wander about in a random walk. Heteroscedasticity: what happens when things don't conform to the accepted rules of random walks. Regression is to do with the difference between observation and a fixed point. ARCH is thus measuring volatility and correlation.
Asian option	Options come in various shapes and sizes. Asian ones are (okay, let's face it, this is complex) where the average price of the commodity, currency etc (the underlying) between deal and strike is calculated, compared with strike price, and a cash payment reflecting that difference is paid.
Back-testing	Testing out a model by feeding historical data into it and comparing with real, observed results.
Backwardation	See section 5.5.3.
Basle Committee	The Basle (or Basel) Committee on Banking Supervision (formerly called the Cooke Committee) is organised under the auspices of the Bank for International Settlements and provides frequent seminal guidance to banking supervisors on regulatory policy. Notable achievements are its initiatives on regulatory capital, levelling the playing field between banks operating internationally. More recently the Basle Committee has produced volumes of good sense on all kinds of aspects of risk management.
Black-Scholes	Fischer Black and Myron Scholes cooked up a whizzy formula in 1972 which has ever since enabled options traders to predict the price of the option. Black and Scholes (inevitably) assumed various things, notably that options move around randomly from where they start: they do a 'random walk'. This gives a very useful starting-point for understanding of option price behaviour but should not (like any prediction of the future) be taken too seriously.
CAD	The Capital Adequacy Directive, which sets capital requirements for investment firms and the investment business of banks (see section 2.11).

Clearing house	Futures and options exchanges, and some stock exchanges, enable their members to manage counterparty risk on trades by having a central party which guarantees the performance of the trade. The central party would find this a miserable experience without taking margin from the market members. Typically a central counterparty will become party to the trades (seller to the buyer and buyer to the seller) and manage its own risk by taking collateral from each market member. These counterparties are referred to as 'clearing houses'. Confusingly, some securities settlement systems, which provide for their participants' settlement obligations to be offset against each other (A has to deliver 100 to B; B has to deliver 50 to C; C has to deliver 20 to A; so A puts in 80, B receives 50 and C receives 30) as 'clearing houses'. Worse, some firms which are members of either of these types of system and provide facilities for their customers which provide indirect access to the systems can call themselves 'clearing' houses ...
Close-out	The end of a transaction initiated by another party, eg upon an event of default. Various methods are available: termination, plus ascribing a value to the terminated transaction—this might involve doing a transaction with a third party, to evaluate your replacement cost or loss; or entering into an equal and opposite transaction (which is hard, because it's difficult to force a counterparty to take a position, especially when they're insolvent).
Collateral	I have a credit exposure to you (ie you owe me something, or you might). If you give me some securities or cash to hold against that exposure, on the understanding that you will get it back if the exposure goes away, you are giving me collateral.
Confirm(ation)	The document exchanged on entering into a derivatives transaction which confirms the particulars of the trade agreed and often includes detailed legal provisions relating to it.
Contango	See section 5.5.3.
DNS	Daily Net Settlement. See section 7.8.3.
DvP	Delivery versus Payment. Let's face it, you won't pay unless you know you'll get the goods you've paid for. Nor will firms. They will expect to get simultaneous payment and transfer of property ... but will they get it?
European option	Options come in various shapes and sizes. European ones are exercisable only on their expiry (strike) date.

FSA	Financial Services Authority. This is the UK's new super-regulator (but not until the Financial Services and Markets Act takes effect—in the meantime, the old regulators still operate, though they are using the FSA to carry out most of their functions).
G30	Group of 30 senior individuals from investment banks, academia and elsewhere which debate and drive thinking on issues of current interest to the financial sector.
GARCH	Generalised ARCH. See ARCH (sorry about that): it's a modelling technique looking at volatility and correlation, which works by estimating two variables: how the underlying changes, and how volatility changes.
GARP	Generally Accepted Risk Principles—by Coopers and Lybrand. Also the Global Association of Risk Professionals.
Haircut	The value of your securities may go down instead of up. Even the securities you hold as collateral. So you might want to reflect the market risk inherent in them in the amount of collateral you take, ie cut a bit off the value of the collateral to reflect the risk. Haircuts are often crudely calculated by reference only to the securities in question, or even (?!) the counterparty, rather than the period for which the collateral is held and its likely depreciation during that period.
Hedge	A hedge is a transaction which is intended to mitigate risk, typically market and credit risk, on another transaction.
Hedge fund	There are as many definitions as people reading this glossary. But here are some features: hedge funds tend to invest in 'risky' products, ie where the gearing is very high (small price shift in the product has massive effect on the return on investment); they tend to be dependent on loan, rather than share, capital; they tend to be unregulated but yet to specialise in financial sector products.
Herstatt risk	Bankhaus Herstatt gained a claim to fame by going bust. Having traded in the FX markets. And having received what it was due (in Deutschmarks) before complying with its own payment obligations (in US dollars), it filed for bankruptcy with consequences which live with us still in the world of settlement risk.
Holding period	The expected gap between declaring your counterparty in default and definitively calculating your loss. If the counterparty defaults at 4pm on Maundy Thursday, and even if you get to hear about it within the hour, it's probably not till Tuesday in Easter week you can re-establish your hedges and so forth ... so how long should you reckon to cater for market risk in a position which you have taken?

Initial margin	The amount of collateral required to cover the expected difference between the prices on default and actual realisation of losses.
IOSCO	International Organisation of Securities Commissions.
ISD	Investment Services Directive—see section 2.2.1.
ISDA	International Swaps and Derivatives Association, Inc.
Lamfalussy standards	The Bank for International Settlements issued a key report on interbank netting schemes after deliberation by a committee chaired by M. Alexandre Lamfalussy. The report includes a list of criteria which should be met by aspiring systems—see section 10.5.3
London Code of Conduct	Legal bit: s 43 of the Financial Services Act 1986 allows firms which engage in wholesale market activity to be treated as 'exempt' from the requirement to obtain an investment business licence in respect of that activity. But those firms do have to sign up to a light-touch regulatory system overseen by the FSA. The London Code of Conduct is the rules of this club. The regime will not survive the UK regulatory reforms, though aspects of the code are likely to be revived in the conduct of business rules for wholesale activity in the new regulatory rulebook once the Financial Services and Markets Act takes effect.
Margin	If you and I have entered into a contract, from one day to the next the value (to you or to me) of the contract will vary; that difference will represent a loss or a gain which suggests one of us will ultimately owe the other something on the contract. If one of us requires the other to provide collateral to cover that gain/loss, the collateral provided would be called 'margin'. The term is typically used in the futures markets and may encompass both 'initial' (or 'original') margin and 'variation' margin.
Marking to market	The process of evaluating value (calculated by reference to market prices) of a financial product.
Master Agreement	If you do a whole stack of transactions but you want them all to be governed by a standard set of terms, you don't need to write out the terms in full each time. You can have them put down in a master agreement incorporated by reference in each deal. Some master agreements will work by creating a 'single agreement' including all transactions as well as the standard set of terms, which can give rise to all sorts of legal issues.

Model	Formula for calculating expected prices (or other variables).
Monte Carlo	A computer-intensive technique for predicting prices by looking at zillions of variables.
Netting	I have done various transactions with you. If you go bust, I want to be able to say 'forget all that, let's put a price on each transaction we did, as at today's market prices, tot it all up, subtract the losses from the gains and see where we come out'. That's netting.
Normal distribution	Gaussian. Bell-shaped. The curve shown in section 3.2.1. The Normal distribution curve shows the deviation of prices (or other variables) from the average: the chances are that the price will move to something close to the average; the chances (likelihood) drop off if the price differential (compared with the average) you are worried about rises; but there is a sting in the tail since the chances don't go away altogether, however extreme the price movements are.
OTC	Over the counter: ie when you are talking about a trade, the notion that it was not done on an exchange (and so did not bring with it all the baggage of exchange-traded deals, such as standard terms, standard pricing, counterparty risk management and so forth).
Potential future exposure	I have (in my wisdom) done a derivatives trade with you. You are doing rather well: currently it is worth money to you (because, if it goes all the way to maturity, the expectation is that you will have gained overall and I will have lost). This is reflected in the 'replacement cost' of the transaction to you: if the transaction were to disappear, it would cost you money to persuade one of my competitors to enter into a lookalike deal. But there's more to it than that: you hope to go on doing rather well, so that next week you will be profiting even more. Over the lifetime of the transaction you have a potential credit exposure based on these projections. A potential future credit exposure.
PvP	Payment versus payment: ie absence of interval between settling the opposing payment obligations which arise under a foreign exchange transaction.
RATE	Risk Assessment, Tools of supervision and Evaluation: the process originally devised by the Bank of England and now operated by the FSA for supervision of banks in the UK (see section 2.4.1).
Repo	Sale and repurchase transaction; A sells to B; B agrees to sell the same thing, or something like it, back to A later on.

RTGS	Real Time Gross Settlement. See section 7.8.3.
SFA	Securities and Futures Authority. This is the UK regulator responsible for securities firms, until it is replaced under the Financial Services and Markets Act by the FSA.
STP	Straight through processing—see section 6.2.4.
VaR	Value at Risk—see section 3.2.2.
Variation margin	The amount of collateral required to cover the difference between yesterday's and today's prices.

USEFUL WEBSITES

ONLINE UPDATES

www.butterworths.co.uk	Updates to this book when the new UK Financial Services and Markets Act comes into force

RISK MANAGEMENT SITES AND TRADE ASSOCIATIONS

www.csfp.csh.com	CreditRisk+
www.isda.org	ISDA
www.risk.ifci.org	International Finance and Commodities Institute
www.jpmorgan.com	RiskMetrics, CreditMetrics
www.pw2.netcom.com	Value at Risk bibliography
www.turtletrader.com www.contingencyanalysis.com	Risk Management Glossaries
www.garp.com	Global Association of Risk Professionals
www.group30.org	Group of 30
www.isma.org	International Securities Market Association

REGULATORY AND GOVERNMENTAL AUTHORITIES

www.ny.frb.org	Federal Reserve Bank of New York
www.bis.org	Bank for International Settlements (Basle Committee)
www.fsa.gov.uk	Financial Services Authority (FSA)
www.iosco.org	IOSCO
www.cftc.gov	CFTC
www.sec.gov	SEC
www.ecb.int	European Central Bank
www.hm-treasury.gov.uk	HM Treasury
www.bankofengland.co.uk	Bank of England

CLEARING AND SETTLEMENT

www.ecsda.com	European Central Securities Depositories Association
www.cedelinternational.com	Cedelbank
www.euroclear.com	Euroclear
www.lch.co.uk	London Clearing House
www.crestco.co.uk	CREST
www.nscc.com	National Securities Clearing Corporation

2

The regulatory framework

2.1 REGULATION AND RISK

Risk managers need to understand regulation. In many firms the risk management and compliance functions are integrated. This is in part because the objectives of risk managers and regulators coincide: avoidance or control of unwanted risk which might threaten the profitability or solvency of the firm. But there are important differences between the objectives of regulators and a firm's management. In particular, regulators are concerned with systemic risk, which is a practical issue for only a few firms. Where there are no systemic implications, regulators are more likely to focus on investor protection issues, which tend to focus on maintenance of capital and conduct of business rules.

2.1.1 Objectives of regulation

The three principal objectives of regulators are generally:

- Prudential supervision Managing the risk of failure, in the interests of the market and consumers, by ensuring that firms operate their businesses prudently. This will comprise maintenance of capital and compliance with rules relating to risk management. There is considerable overlap with both the systemic risk management and conduct of business objectives of regulation.
- Systemic risk management Where a firm's failure can spread to other firms, the social costs of failure exceed the 'private' costs. Ring-fencing failures and prevention of 'contagion' is a prime objective of bank regulators in particular.
- Consumer/investor protection Unsophisticated consumers need to be protected when buying complex financial sector products. Consumer protection concerns are a prime objective of investment firm regulators in particular, owing to the greater complexity of investment decision-making, suggesting a need for conduct of business rules.

2.1.2 Objectives of regulation in the UK

The Financial Services Authority will have statutory objectives under the new Financial Services and Markets Act:

- maintaining confidence in the financial system;
- promoting public understanding of the financial system, in particular promoting awareness of the benefits and risks associated with different kinds of investment or other financial dealing, and the provision of appropriate information and advice;
- the protection of consumers;
- the reduction of financial crime.

The FSA's stated high-level aims also include:

- Protection of consumers of financial services
  - to set, promote, monitor and enforce high standards of integrity, financial soundness, fair dealing and competence, in order to protect and secure fair treatment for consumers;
  - to ensure that consumers receive clear and adequate information about services, products and risks;
  - to acknowledge consumers' responsibility for their own decisions while aiming to ensure that they are not exposed to risks they should not reasonably be expected to assume.
- Promotion of clean and orderly markets
  - to promote fairness, transparency and orderly conduct in financial markets;
  - to take action where standards are inadequate or ineffectively enforced.
- Maintenance of confidence in the financial system
  - to set, promote, monitor and enforce high standards of financial soundness and probity;
  - to ensure that the failure of individual financial institutions does not undermine the overall stability of the financial system.

IOSCO states:

> 'The basic role of regulators regarding risk management is to seek an assemblage of rules and requirements that may, at the lowest possible cost, effectively contribute to prevent an isolated failure or a crisis of small proportions from becoming a systemic problem threatening the market as a whole. In other words, the best solution for the trade-off referred to ... too much regulatory requirements mean an excessive burden for financial firms, crippling their activities and making them less efficient (and also the market); but a lack of regulatory requirements may jeopardize the safety of the financial sector.'
>
> 'Traditionally, regulators have focused their job in the following main areas, with regard to risk management:
>
> - market surveillance, with a special attention on large positions and aggregated cross-market supervision

- setting levels of capital reserves
- disclosure of data and information about market value of financial instruments and risk policies ...
- auditing of firms' books and financial registers and internal controls, integrity and soundness of the models and segregation of accounts
- cooperation and exchange of information between regulators both at domestic and international level ...
- development of emergency procedures ...'

2.1.3 The UK backbone

Despite the huge complexity of it, and a large number of carve-outs, financial services regulation in the UK is built around only a few statutory basics:

- **A licensing rule** To do financial sector business, a licence is needed. If a licence ('authorisation') is granted, the firm will become subject to the detailed rules of prudential regulation specific to the industry sector in which the licence applies and, in some sectors, conduct of business rules. Failure to obtain a licence before carrying out regulated activity is an offence. For what regulated activities can include, see 'What requires to be regulated?' at section 2.2.1.

- **Advertising and cold-calling rules** To advertise financial products a licence is needed, or the advertisement must be approved by an authorised person. To make unsolicited calls without a licence to potential consumers of financial services is an offence.

- **Fair market rules** To mislead the market is an offence. In particular it is an offence to make a false or misleading statement in order to induce a person to enter into an investment agreement, and it is an offence to indulge in insider dealing. Legislation to cover other species of 'market abuse' such as cornering of markets (controlling supply or demand in order to affect prices through a dominant position) and artificial transactions (influencing prices by creating an illusion as to demand) is being included in the Financial Services and Markets Bill.

- **Money-laundering rules** To fail to implement anti-money-laundering controls is a criminal offence. Unfortunately the only device which the law has come up with to control it is procedures for verifying the *customer* (not, you will note, the money or its origins).

- **Public offering rules** Prospectuses offering securities to the public must comply with strict disclosure requirements.

REFERENCES

FSA's high-level aims
FSA *FSA—An Outline* (October 1997).

IOSCO statement re role of regulators
IOSCO Emerging Markets Committee *Financial Risk Management in Emerging Markets* (November 1997).

Licensing requirements
- **Deposit taking** Banking Act 1987, s 3.
- **Investment business** Financial Services Act 1986, s 3.
- **Insurance** Insurance Companies Act 1982, s 3.

Advertising and cold-calling restrictions

- **Investment firms** Financial Services Act 1986, ss 56, 57; Common Unsolicited Calls Regulations (Securities and Investments Board).
- **Banks** Banking Act 1987, s 32, Credit Institutions (Protection of Depositors) Regulations 1995 (SI 1995/1442), reg 48; also Consumer Credit Act 1974, ss 44, 46; Consumer Credit (Advertisements) Regulations 1989, SI 1989/1125.

Money laundering laws

- Money Laundering Regulations 1993, SI 1993/1933; Prevention of Terrorism (Temporary Provisions) Act 1989, ss 11–13; Drug Trafficking Act 1994, s 52; Criminal Justice Act 1988, ss 93A–93D.

Fair market laws

- Financial Services Act 1986, s 47.

Public offering requirements

- Public Offers of Securities Regulations 1995, SI 1995/1537.

Client money regulations

- Financial Services Act 1986, s 55; Financial Services (Client Money) Regulations 1991, (Securities and Investments Board).

Insider dealing restrictions

- Criminal Justice Act 1993, Pt V.

2.2 REGULATION—THE LAW

2.2.1 What is regulated?

Various financial sector activities are likely to require a licence. The specifics vary from place to place, but the headline activities likely to require a licence are:

- taking deposits;
- lending, but only in a few cases such as small consumer loans and, under the new regime, mortgages;
- writing policies of insurance;
- selling securities, derivatives and other investments;
- advertising investments;
- fund management.

In particular, a UK investment business licence is needed if the following tests are satisfied:

- carrying on investment business from one's permanent place of business in the UK; or
- engaging in investment business in the UK if this constitutes the carrying on of a business in the UK.

Essentially then: if you set up shop in the UK, and you do 'investment business' out of it, the first test is satisfied; if you don't set up shop, but you are doing 'investment business' in the UK and this is a business rather than a hobby, the second test is satisfied. This test will catch distance-sellers of financial services. The tests for what constitutes 'carrying on a business' are complex and legal advice should be sought. There are also numerous exceptions and exemptions, in particular an exemption for overseas persons which applies in some circumstances. As to the Internet, distance-selling and related issues, see section 6.5.6.

Building on these basics a huge edifice of regulatory provisions in Acts of Parliament, statutory instruments and regulators' rules has been constructed. It is intricate and confusing. Part of the problem is the overlay of EU Directives which approach the same problems from a different direction. Trying to master it is something of a fool's errand because the UK Government has (quite rightly) decided to reform the whole set-up. What is worth knowing is where the boundaries which the EU imposes lie.

As well as determining what activities require a licence, the law and practice of regulation impose restrictions and rules on various related matters:

- money-laundering (see section 2.6);
- protection of client assets (see section 2.7);
- insider dealing (see section 2.8);
- market discipline and 'market abuse' (see section 2.9).

What requires to be regulated?

NB: different systems have different ideas about what constitutes an 'investment'. The basic list is provided in the Investment Services Directive:

- (a) Transferable securities.
  (b) Units in collective investment undertakings.
- Money market instruments.
- Financial futures contracts, including equivalent cash-settled instruments.
- Forward interest rate agreements.
- Interest rate, currency and equity swaps.
- Options to acquire or dispose of any such instruments, including equivalent cash-settled instruments. This category includes in particular options on currency and on interest rates.

Investment Services Directive

To comply with the ISD, all EU member states should have licensing requirements covering the 'core investment services'. Member states are not required to subject other typical investment banking activities to licensing requirements, eg foreign exchange business, commodity and commodity derivative business, although a number of member states have done so.

If you carry out core services, once you have got a licence in your home state covering that activity you can do them (and non-core services covered by your licence) in any member state; but if your licence covers only non-core activities then you are ineligible to do so outside your home country.

Core services

- (a) Reception and transmission, on behalf of investors, of orders in relation to investments ('arranging deals').
  (b) Execution of such orders other than for own account.
- Dealing in investments for own account.
- Managing portfolios of investments in accordance with mandates given by investors on a discretionary, client-by-client basis.
- Underwriting in respect of issues of investments and/or the placing of such issues.

Non-core services also mentioned in the Directive

- Safekeeping and administration in relation to investments.
- Safe custody services.
- Granting credits or loans to an investor to allow him to carry out a transaction in investments, where the firm granting the credit or loan is involved in the transaction.
- Advice to undertakings on capital structure, industrial strategy and related matters and advice and service relating to mergers and the purchase of undertakings.
- Services related to underwriting.
- Investment advice.
- Foreign exchange services where these are connected with the provision of investment services.

Second Banking Coordination Directive

- Acceptance of deposits and other repayable funds from the public.
- Lending.
- Financial leasing.
- Money transmission services.
- Issuing and administering means of payment (eg credit cards, travellers' cheques and bankers' drafts).
- Guarantees and commitments.
- Trading for own account or for account of customers in—
  - money market instruments (cheques, bills, CDs, etc);
  - foreign exchange;
  - financial futures and options;
  - exchange and interest rate instruments;
  - transferable securities.
- Participation in share issues and the provision of services related to such issues.
- Advice to undertakings on capital structure, industrial strategy and related questions and advice and services relating to mergers and the purchase of undertakings.
- Money broking.
- Portfolio management and advice.
- Safekeeping and administration of securities.
- Credit reference services.
- Safe custody services.

Note that UCITS (collective investment schemes) and insurance are covered by different directives.

2.2.2 UK: specific requirements

In the UK various activities fall within the scope of the Banking Act 1987, the Financial Services Act 1986 and the Consumer Credit Act 1974 and thus require a licence:

Banking Act 1987

- Deposit-taking.
- But *not* lending.
- Also consider special rules relating to:
  - advertisements and cold-calling;
  - use of banking names (which may not survive the reforms);
  - whether activities constitute insurance business rather than banking (ss 2, 16 of the Insurance Companies Act 1982) (again, these rules may not survive the reforms).

Financial Services Act 1986

- Dealing in investments (either as principal or agent).
- Arranging deals in investments.
- Safeguarding (custody of) investments.
- Managing investments.
- Giving investment advice.
- Establishing, operating or winding up a collective investment scheme.
- Providing infrastructure supporting the financial services industry.
- Also consider special rules relating to:
  - cold-calling (s 56);
  - issue of investment advertisements (s 57).

There is a complex web of exceptions and exclusions-to-exceptions on which legal advice should always be sought.

Consumer Credit Act 1974

- Lending small sums to individuals.
- Selling on credit or hire-purchase.
- Issuing credit cards.
- Arranging credit.
- Advising on debt.
- Debt collection.
- Credit reference agency.
- Credit advertising.

2.2.3 UK regulatory reforms

The shape of regulation is changing. Shortly after coming to power in 1997, the UK's new Government announced its intention to carry out a root-and-branch reform of the UK regulatory system. The process will be gradual (and that means that for some years the system will be in flux), but at the end the following changes will have been implemented:

- The statutory basis of regulation will have been replaced with a new framework Act, the Financial Services and Markets Act, and secondary legislation which will add in the details. To a greater or lesser extent the existing regulatory statutes such as the Financial Services Act 1986, the Banking Act 1987 and the Insurance Companies Act 1982 will go. Separate regulation of consumer credit will probably remain, with the possible exception of mortgage broking.
- New areas of activity are to become regulated, including the sale of underwriting capacity in the Lloyd's insurance market and, potentially, mortgage broking.
- The multiple separate regulators of banks, securities and investment firms, and insurance companies (and other firms with similar functions to these) will have been merged into the FSA.
- A single rulebook will apply to all firms, though different parts will apply according to the activities carried on by the firm.

Despite the differences between the businesses which are regulated, various functions of regulators in different parts of the financial sector are converging. Approaches to regulation include:

- Institutional mode This looks at each legal entity separately, regardless of the types of business it does. The argument is that controlling the consequences of insolvency is the aim of regulation, and insolvency strikes at legal entities not at businesses (for flaws in this, see the discussion of large groups later in this chapter). Historically, regulation has been of this type.
- Functional model This looks at the business types, regardless of which legal entities are involved. Regulation has historically followed this model as well as the institutional model, allowing a plethora of regulators to grow up in each jurisdiction, with multiple reporting by a single firm to numerous regulators.
- Objective-based model This seeks to find the best system to meet the objectives of regulation—this model seems to be being developed in the UK and elsewhere, with the growth of super-regulators. Other countries moving to objective-based systems with fewer regulators include Australia, Denmark, the Netherlands, Singapore and Sweden.

2.2.4 Which jurisdictions are relevant?

Although there is cross-border co-operation between regulators in the form of Memoranda of Understanding and there are EU directives which allow regulated firms a passport to carry on regulated activities in other states, it is still difficult to know what activities are subject to regulation and by whom. It is not simply a matter of looking at where the firm has branches. Licensing rules may require a licence to be obtained:

- in places where the activities are carried on;
- in places where consumers are located.

It may be possible to overcome the need for a local licence by appointing a local agent who is already licensed, if this works under the law of the place where the activity is to be carried on.

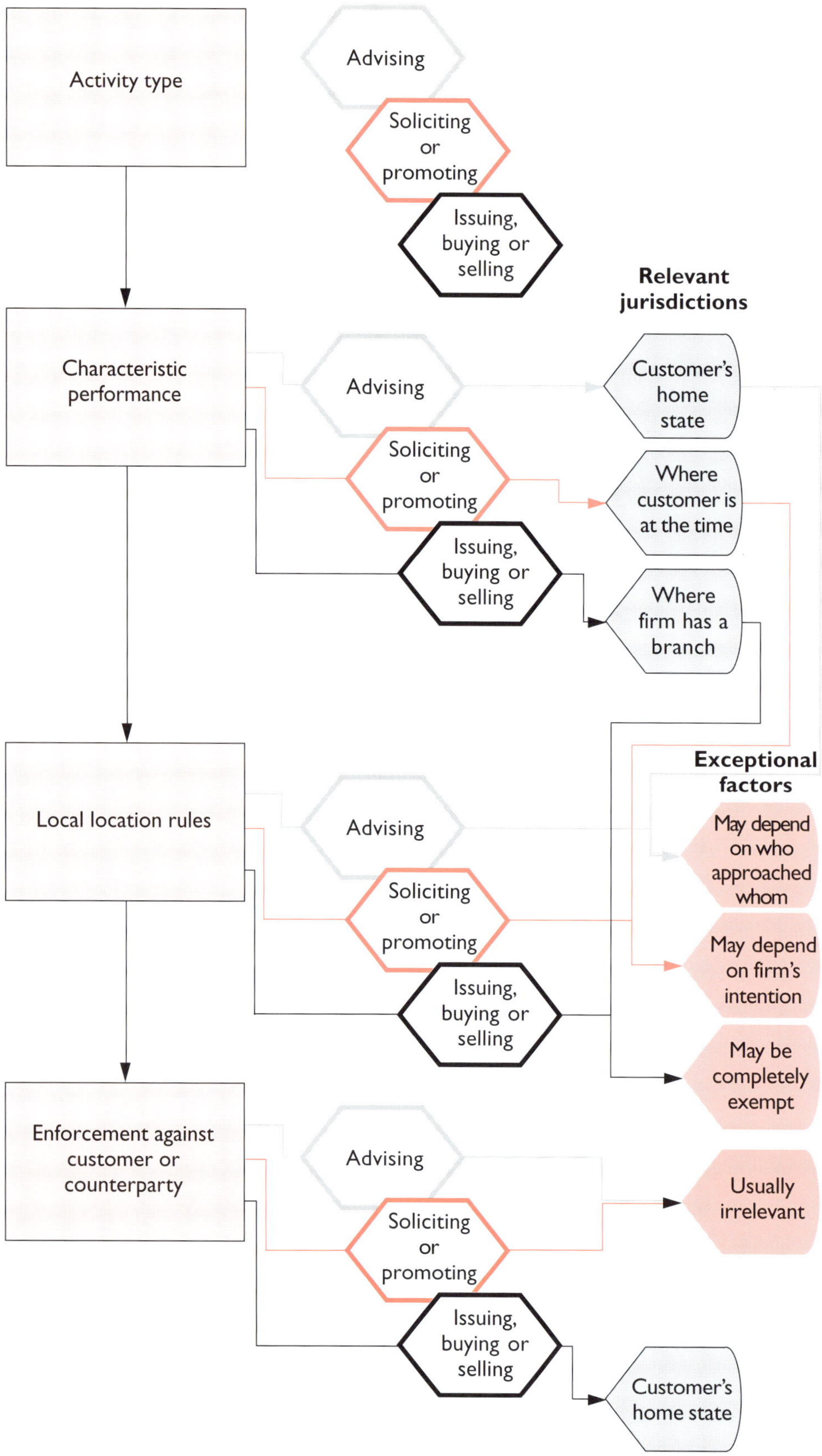

Which jurisdictions are relevant?

To work out which regulatory systems might apply, first consider the activities which might fall under the regulator's spell. The rules which apply (and the countries which are relevant) will differ with different business areas. This diagram looks at advising, gaining new business and selling investments. In the EU, the next step is to identify where the 'characteristic performance' of the activity takes place; then look at any rules in the firm's own locality, because there may be exceptions to the basic rule; and finally, look at whether it is necessary to take any steps against the customer, since the place the firm may need to do so may have its own rules which complicate the picture.

Where are regulated activities 'carried on'?

Where financial sector business is carried on should be analysed from the viewpoint of the regulator. The answer may depend not only on the type of business (investment advice, purchase of securities, operating an information service, deposit-taking, writing a policy) but also the reason why the activity is regulated.

- Systemic/prudential/stability rationale for regulation suggests that the place where the firm is incorporated or organised or has its head office may be relevant.
- Consumer protection rationale for regulation suggests that the place where the consumer is when he is induced to enter into the contract, or where the contract is to be performed, or possibly the place of the consumer's domicile (or where he is incorporated or organised or has his head office) may be relevant.
- Market integrity rationale for regulation suggests that the place where the market is managed may be relevant.

Possible opponents therefore include not only regulators but also customers or other parties to financial contracts and overseers of markets, settlement systems and so forth.

The EU Commission suggests that the place where the 'characteristic performance' takes place, which would be (rebuttably) presumed to be where the firm, rather than the counterparty or customer is located, is the place where investment business is carried on. This suggestion has not been followed in all EU member states. 'Characteristic performance' means the subject matter of the contract which is special to that type of contract-but not the payment of money. So: for sale of goods = the seller is the characteristic performer; banking = the banker is the characteristic performer; advice on financial services = the adviser is the characteristic performer. This looks fine so far, and is less unsatisfactory than other tests, but what about contracts for differences/swaps/credit derivatives etc where the performance is nothing more than the payment of money on either side?

Regulatory problems with the Internet

- The first issue is whether a licence is needed to transact the business:
  - some jurisdictions require a licence if local customers are to be approached;
  - some jurisdictions link need for a licence to whether business is carried on from a base in the jurisdiction;
  - some jurisdictions look at the 'characteristic performance' of the transacted business to see 'where' it is located.

  In the UK the whole issue is inextricably linked to marketing to customers.
- The other main issue is whether marketing activity can be carried out:
  - the FSA has issued guidance on the difficult issue of material accessible by UK investors but which is not intended to be accessed by them;
  - in the UK the question is whether an investment advertisement has been issued in the UK – it will have been if the advertisement is directed at people in the UK;
  - relevant factors in deciding whether an investment advertisement was issued in the UK will include:
    - whether the web site was located on a server outside the UK;
    - whether the service or investment being marketed was available in the UK; and
    - the steps taken to exclude UK persons from the site or the service;
  - disclaimers and warnings help to establish whether a site is directed at UK investors;
  - disclaimers may not be completely effective to eliminate the residual risk.

Consequences of failure to get a licence

In view of the uncertainty of ever getting it right a pragmatic approach is needed. Consider the possible consequences of not getting regulated in a jurisdiction where there is a requirement to do so:

- criminal offence;
- civil action (eg injunction to restrain business);
- loss of other licences/access to settlement or other systems;
- invalidity of contracts.

Even if none of these factors is likely to be problematic, consider the indirect and reputational issues:

- vicarious liability could be pinned onto officers and directors, making it dangerous to travel to that country;
- foreign regulators could complain to the home state regulator, jeopardising reputation or home state licence;
- memoranda of understanding between regulators and market supervisors could allow information flow, jeopardising reputation in other markets;
- contracts could be regarded as invalid in a place where enforcement of contractual rights is sought.

But host state regulators will often be unconcerned with activities outside their jurisdiction. Market supervisors would generally not be concerned unless the activity is taking place on the market in question.

Passporting

The Investment Services Directive and the Second Banking Coordination Directive allow a firm authorised in one EU member state to make use of its home state authorisation to carry on authorised activities in other member states, provided that the firm notifies its home state regulator of the intention to do so and the other states in which it will be carrying on the business. The home state regulator then has to pass on the notification to the local regulators concerned.

- Different states have different definitions of investment business: a passport may have holes in it. For example, if custody business requires a licence in state X but not in state Y, a firm based in state Y may not be able to rely on its home state licence to carry on custody business in state X.
- EU firms only can take advantage of the passport. So an American firm obtaining a licence in EU state X will need an additional licence to carry on the same business in EU state Y.
- Passporting only applies to prudential supervision, not conduct of business regulation where applicable.
- Some host-state reporting requirements have survived the passporting rules—for example, liquidity monitoring of banks has not been reserved to home state banking supervisors by the Second Banking Coordination Directive, so a bank licensed in state X may be required by the banking supervisor in state Y to file regulatory returns on the liquidity of its branches in state Y.
- The directives give little help on 'where' activities are carried on, so different regulators may interpret their jurisdiction more widely than expected.

REFERENCES

EU guidance on where business is carried on

– EU Commission Interpretative Communication *Freedom to Provide Services and the Interest of the General Good in the Second Banking Directive* 97/C209/04 (1997).

2.3 REGULATION IN PRACTICE

2.3.1 Principles of regulation

In order to keep the system flexible the FSA has expressed a preference for operating under broadly expressed high-level 'Principles' rather than detailed rules. Some things will of course require rules, such as regulatory capital provisions, client money provisions, compensation schemes and risk-disclosure requirements. The principles which have been put forward are:

1. A firm must conduct its business with integrity.
2. A firm must conduct its business with due skill, care and diligence.
3. A firm must take reasonable care to organise and control its affairs responsibly and effectively, with adequate risk management systems.
4. A firm must maintain adequate financial resources.
5. A firm must observe proper standards of market conduct.
6. A firm must pay due regard to the interests of its customers and treat them fairly.
7. A firm must pay due regard to the information needs of its customers, and communicate information to them in a way which is clear, fair and not misleading.
8. A firm must manage conflicts of interest fairly, both between itself and its customers and between one customer and another.
9. A firm must take reasonable care to ensure the suitability of its advice and discretionary decisions for any customer who is entitled to rely upon its judgment.
10. A firm must arrange adequate protection for customers' assets when it is responsible for them.
11. A firm must deal with its regulators in an open and co-operative way, and must tell the FSA promptly anything relating to the firm of which the FSA would reasonably expect prompt notice.

Infringement of these principles can give rise to disciplinary action as if a more detailed regulatory rule has been broken. In addition to the principles there will of course be detailed rulebooks, with specialist sections applicable to different financial industry sectors. These will tackle areas such as the application processes for obtaining authorisation; regulation of a firm's finances, prudence and capital adequacy; regulation of individuals, including senior management; conduct of business rules, in relation to both consumers and other market participants; discipline, enforcement and appeals arrangements; and other miscellaneous matters such as client money and asset protection and more specialist material applicable to particular types of financial industry activity such as the Lloyd's of London market. There will also be 'guidance' which is intended to interpret the basic rules.

The high-level principles provide the basic level of expectation from firms. It is not surprising that the principles for individuals carrying out key functions in a regulated firm (approved persons) such as senior managers are broadly similar (see section 2.5.2).

Although these principles will apply to all firms, the FSA proposes to apply only those which relate to *prudential* matters to banks, perpetuating the distinction between banks and other firms that banks are not subject to conduct of business regulation. This makes sense in principle, so long as you believe that banks only offer products to customers which are easy to understand and involve no long-term lock-in.

2.3.2 Style of regulation

The FSA identifies five themes:

- **Risk-based approach** Intended to reflect the nature of the business activities concerned, the extent of risk within particular firms and markets, the quality of firms' management controls and the relative sophistication of the consumers involved.
- **Senior management responsibility** Boards and senior management will be personally responsible (with liability) to ensure financial soundness, proper conduct of business, act with prudence and integrity, develop and operate effective governance structures, systems and controls, and ensure staff are competent.
- **Promote high standards** Throughout firms and markets.
- **Consistency in authorisation** Across the range of businesses to be regulated by the FSA.
- **Enforcement** To secure remedial action and discipline.

These are more or less consistent with (if distinct from) its four expected statutory objectives under the new Financial Services and Markets Act:

- maintaining confidence in the UK financial system;
- promoting public understanding of the financial system (including benefits and risks of investment and financial dealing);
- securing consumer protection;
- reducing financial crime.

The two main themes which will frame the future development of financial sector regulation are risk-based supervision and senior management responsibility for risk management.

REFERENCES

FSA principles for business

– FSA *Principles for Business* Post-consultative version (October 1999).

FSA's five themes for style of regulation

– FSA *FSA – An Outline* Chapter III (October 1997).

Statutory objectives of the FSA

– Financial Services and Markets Act.

2.4 RISK-BASED SUPERVISION

Rigid rules make little sense in a rapidly changing environment, but impose a sizeable compliance burden on firms. Rules-based supervisory techniques have also failed to prevent financial sector collapses. Regulators recognise these criticisms and are responding:

- Regulation is not about preventing financial sector insolvency at all cost, or providing 100 per cent protection to investors and depositors. Firms have to take responsibility for their own solvency; investors have to take some care in selection of investments and who they deal with. The regulator's function is not to shoulder these responsibilities.
- Firms are best placed to manage their own businesses and to assess the risks which they take.
- Nevertheless some minimum level of intervention by supervisors is required to ensure that firms carry out this assessment with the requisite degree of diligence.

Hence, risk-based supervision. The G30 wants the concept to be developed so that firms take responsibility for their own risk management, relying in the first instance on their internal audit function, though subject to oversight by external auditors and regulators. The supervisor's role should be to make qualitative judgments about organisational culture, the ethical climate in the firm, recruitment practices, evaluation of risk-takers, and remuneration practices. They would also offer guidance and incentives to good practice, including differential capital requirements, differential degrees of supervisory reporting and interference, differential fee levels, less detailed rules for good performers, and penalties for poor performers. Moreover, this should be done on a global, rather than national, basis.

2.4.1 Bank supervision

The new ethos for banks subject to UK supervision is 'RATE': Risk Assessment, Tools of supervision, and Evaluation. Risk assessment will be done according to the CAMEL-B and COM factors. These accord closely with similar initiatives by the US Office of the Comptroller of the Currency and Federal Reserve Board.

Business Risk Factors	Control Risk Factors
Capital **A**ssets **M**arket Risk **E**arnings **L**iabilities **B**usiness factors	**C**ontrols **O**rganisation **M**anagement

The stated objective of the RATE framework is to improve the supervisory effort by cutting out 'routine supervisory work' and focus on:

- explicit identification of the risks facing a bank and whether these are increasing or decreasing;
- setting clear objectives for supervision of the bank;
- a risk-based supervisory action plan;

- communication of the risk analysis and supervisory plans to the bank.

A helpful degree of detail on the factors which the FSA looks for under each of the CAMELB and COM factors is provided and detailed descriptions of the supervisory cycle have been issued. Risk ratings will be secretly assigned to banks in order to ensure appropriate allocation of supervisory resources. If the FSA has serious concerns, it will seek remedial action from the bank; action it may take includes increasing the bank's capital requirement, ring-fencing the bank from the rest of its corporate group and formal supervisory action using its statutory powers (eg by restricting the bank's business, or even revocation of its authorisation). The 'tools of supervision' include accountants' reports (see section 2.4.3); a visit from the FSA's Traded Markets Team, which focuses on the bank's treasury areas, and their risk management, systems and controls; a visit from the FSA's specialist Credit Review staff; liaison with overseas regulators; and meetings with senior management of the bank.

The FSA has plotted its supervisory response against 'business' and 'control' risks. From this diagram it appears that business risks require only to be 'monitored', but control risks need to be 'remedied'.

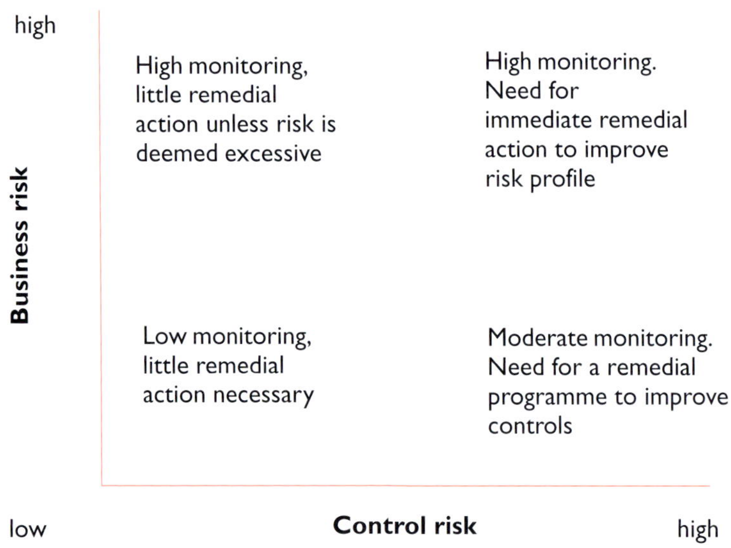

The FSA's matrix of risks and supervisory responses

This is a long way from the old-fashioned capital-adequacy-and-cup-of-tea approach to banking supervision of the Bank of England before the Barings collapse; it is closer to the model of regulation of investment firms in the UK and the US; it is likely to infuse the culture of regulation right across the financial sector.

2.4.2 Investment firm regulation

For other types of firm the trend is similar. Further consequences can be expected when the FSA assumes all the functions of the other UK financial sector regulators. Factors which regulators are likely to heed are:

- financial stability;
- internal controls;
- business quality;

- supervisory complexity;
- personnel;
- management.

This enables regulators to give risk-ratings to firms, which will determine the degree of surveillance attention given to a particular firm. To achieve a low-risk rating a firm must achieve a low score under all heads. The emphasis is on a review of high level controls inside a firm to ensure that the regulator understands why the firm is in business, if it is successful, how well it is managed; all in order to put surveillance work into context.

The better a firm can satisfy its regulator that it is managing risks prudently, the lower the external compliance burden. It is a further move towards self-assessment. But regulators still need to be sure that the self-assessment machinery is robust. This is a responsibility which is being pinned firmly onto the board and senior executive management.

2.4.3 Accountants' reports

Under the new Financial Services and Markets Act, when in force, all firms (not, as now, just banks) will, if the FSA so requires, have to commission reports from accountants or other professionals on a particular aspect of the management or affairs of the firm. For banks, these reports increasingly focus on the following:

- The supervisor's understanding of an institution's control culture has become an important component in forming its view on the general prudent conduct of the business by the institutions.
- The primary responsibility for establishment and maintenance of controls rests with senior management, who should determine the nature of the institution's risk profile and ensure the adequacy of the systems for identifying, monitoring and managing the risks.

2.4.4 Satisfying the regulator

Regulators are not going to oblige senior management by providing detailed rules and enabling compliance to be shown by box-ticking against detailed prescriptions in a rule-book. Less certainty is the flip side of risk-based supervision. Where the supervisor has not sufficient expertise to assess the quality of the firm's risk management, outside professionals will be called in. The agenda is much broader than compliance with financial and conduct-of-business rules:

- **Regulators focus on internal controls** Firms need to be able to show regulators that they are controlling risks and how they are doing so. Demonstrating that there are effective internal procedures is important.
- **Risk management is no longer solely about market-risk models** Risk managers have to demonstrate a thorough grasp of all the implications of the business they are managing, ranging from credit and market risk assessments to anything which has implications for the viability of the firm.

There is published guidance on risk control and reporting systems suitable for financial sector businesses (see section 4.2.2). Regulators will wish to be satisfied that the risk control system is comprehensive and effectively implemented. Where might the consultants or in-house risk management team have missed something?

- **Traditional financial reporting** Focusing on the end-of-period balance sheet will miss a huge area of risk, namely off-balance-sheet transactions.
- **Reporting an control systems** Look at operational risks, in particular personnel risks—to reduce the risk of a rogue trader, of processing errors, and so forth.
- **Independent consultancy** The danger of missing something is more acute when a firm relies on its own staff to identify internal weaknesses, but a consultant's report may not go into areas which lie outside the consultants' expertise. It does not follow that risk analysis should always be left to mathematicians who are expert in VaR modelling or accountants who are expert in financial projections.

Regulators are more likely to be satisfied where they can be convinced that:

- risk control systems have been objectively prepared;
- there is a culture that does not regard discussion of risk management issues, changes to operational procedures and expenditure of resources on risk issues as an intolerable burden on the business;
- there is a procedure for audit of risk management, to check on implementation in different areas, with frank and objective discussion of the audit report.

In practice this will mean that a firm should be able to produce:

- a written risk management plan showing who has responsibility for which areas of risk;
- evidence that the plan has been certified by someone objective;
- regular audit reports prepared by someone objective with expertise in the risk areas reported on.

Which risks count?

Howard Davies, when Deputy Governor of the Bank of England, said:

> '[Regulators can ask] firms about the full range of risks they face (including those—like reputational and settlement risk—that they would often rather ignore); pointing out to complex groups the extent to which their managerial and organisational systems have moved away from their legal structure; spotting signs of fraud or money laundering; and revealing gaps in management's understanding of new financial instruments.'

REFERENCES

G30 recommendations on risk-based supervision

– Group of 30 *Derivatives: Practice and Principles* (July 1993).

RATE Paper

– FSA *Risk based approach to supervision of banks* (June 1998).

Other regulators' risk-based supervisory approach

– SFA Briefing, Issue No 13 ('FIBSPAM') (July 1996).

Accountants' reports

– Banking Act 1987, s 39.

2.5 SENIOR MANAGEMENT RESPONSIBILITY

2.5.1 Ancient history

It has been long recognised in financial services legislation that the integrity of financial sector business is bound up with the integrity of the senior staff who run it. So both in the banking and investment firm sectors managers' personal backgrounds are relevant to the licensing question. The SFA requires key personnel to register with it in order that it may obtain jurisdiction over their dealings. The FSA will have similar powers under the Financial Services and Markets Act to require key personnel to be 'approved' by it.

2.5.2 FSA guidance

The standard of conduct expected of senior management by UK regulators appears to be much higher than the corporate law duty to exercise reasonable care and skill (see Checklist: Legal Duties of Senior Management for legal duties).

As part of the regulatory reform process the FSA has been working on a code of practice for senior managers. Under the new UK regulatory regime senior managers (as well as those who deal direct with customers or their property, will need to be vetted—ie become 'approved persons'—much in the way that 'managers' of banks and 'registered representatives' of securities firms (to pick just two examples) have previously been vetted by their firms' regulators. Under the proposed new model for senior managers:

- Who is a senior manager?
  - A person who can exercise a significant influence on the conduct of the firm's affairs in relation to a regulated activity, including if you are legally a director (or equivalent), partner, member of the committee of management or equivalent.
  - A person who exercises significant control over the firm's resources and commitments.
  - A person responsible for ensuring that the firm's records and controls comply with regulatory, accounting and legal requirements.
  - A person responsible for functions which could expose the firm to serious operational risk.
  - A person responsible for business units, including branch offices, which have a significant impact on the financial resources of the firm.
  - A person responsible for business and sales units dealing directly with customers using the firm's services in relation to regulated activities.
  - A person responsible for functions where individuals have control over customer funds.
  - A money-laundering reporting officer.
  - A person who sets the firm's policies in relation to recruitment, training and remuneration.
- What eligibility criteria apply to senior managers?

- Senior managers have to be fit and proper persons—which means they must have honesty, integrity and reputation; competence and capability; and personal financial soundness. The FSA has guideline lists of what it considers relevant under these headings.
- Other personal factors may be taken into account if they are relevant (such as the nature of previous convictions or habits such as substance dependency).
- The functions which the person will perform and the firm's activities will also be relevant.

■ **What rules of conduct apply to senior managers?** The new FSMA will give the FSA power to issue Statements of Principle applicable to all approved persons together with a Code of Practice, breach of which is evidence of breach of the Statements of Principle. The Code of Practice is full of guidance on conduct which would be regarded as unacceptable. Senior managers are subject to additional Statements of Principle. The proposals are broadly:

- Principles applicable to all approved persons
  - Individuals must act with integrity.
  - Individuals must act with due skill care and diligence.
  - Individuals must observe proper standards of market conduct.
  - Individuals must deal with regulators in an open and co-operative way.
- Additional principles applicable to senior managers
  - Senior managers must take steps to organise the business so it can be controlled effectively.
  - Senior managers must exercise due skill care and diligence in management.
  - Senior managers must ensure their business complies with regulatory requirements.

These principles echo the Principles for Business suggested by the FSA (see section 2.3.1).

■ **Do the rules apply to senior managers of non-UK firms?** Firms authorised in another EU state which are passporting into the UK should not need to worry about the UK's requirements in relation to passported activity (see section 2.2.4). Non-EU firms do have to consider the rules. If the manager is based in the UK, the full regime will apply; if the manager is based outside the UK the FSA will consider the manager's fitness and propriety as part of the firm's application, or continuing eligibility, for authorisation.

■ **What are the consequences of breach?** It does not follow that a regulatory breach automatically leads to disciplinary action against senior managers; but senior management is collectively responsible; and if an 'approved person' is responsible for the area of activity and ought to have dealt with the problem, discipline may be appropriate. Discipline can be applied for deliberate breaches of the Statement of Principles and for cases where the manager's behaviour was below a reasonably expected standard for a person managing a particular business or part of it, taking into account its size and complexity.

Historically the FSA has identified ten points of guidance for senior management. These remain valid as a guide to best practice. The main ideas boil down as follows:

■ Decision-making structures should be designed with the objective of protecting investors and managing risk.

- Information flow to management must be effective.
- Staff policy must be effective: staff must be of good quality, understand the business areas for which they are responsible and be sensibly remunerated.
- Lines of accountability must be put in place.
- Robust supervision and control systems must be in place.
- Failures of systems and controls, and losses to customers, must be rectified immediately and redress provided where appropriate.

These guidelines should be backed up with a 'management statement' which would show how responsibility is distributed throughout the firm.

Checklist: Legal duties of senior management

General duties

- To exercise skill and care
- To act in good faith in the company's interest (not necessarily the parent company's interest)
- Not to act for personal or collateral purposes
- To disclose interests in contracts and shareholdings in other companies
- Not to deal in share options issued by the company or its parent
- Not to borrow from the company (unless the company's ordinary business includes lending)
- Where required, to obtain shareholder consent for transactions with the company

Also to be considered

- Contract of employment
- Cadbury, Greenbury, Hampel codes of conduct
- Requirements of listing authorities (eg stock exchange yellow-book)

Extra duties if solvency is in question

- To avoid loss to creditors
- To avoid entering into voidable transactions (such as preferences, transactions at undervalue, etc)

Risks faced by directors

NB: whether or not designated a 'director', senior management may be subject to the following:

- Vicarious criminal liability for offences committed by the firm
- Personal liability for the company's debts for 'wrongful trading'
- Disqualification for unfitness under the Company Directors Disqualification Act 1986
- Accountability before a statutory inquiry
- Disciplinary action by regulators (such as a fine, or prohibition on employment)
- Loss of approved person 'status' for want of fitness and propriety

The detail of UK rules about senior managers of investment firms at present includes a requirement that the senior executive officer understands the firm's business, takes responsibility for junior staff compliance and ensures (amongst other things) that:

- lines of responsibility are clearly delineated;
- there are effective controls to manage risk and segregate duties;
- information systems are in place to provide him with risk-related information;
- warning signs are acted on.

These themes are developed further in the section on internal controls (section 4.2).

The Financial Services and Markets Bill proposes to give the FSA a power to fine approved persons for breach of the high level principles applicable to approved persons or requirements directly imposed by the legislation. This will represent a major change to the way in which senior managers are regulated in particular sectors of the finance industry.

2.5.3 Disqualification of directors

The Company Directors Disqualification Act kicks in only after the event: an order can be made disqualifying a person from holding office as a director if (amongst other things) he has been convicted of certain offences, has engaged in wrongful trading under the Insolvency Act 1986, or for persistent breaches of the companies legislation; but the tough part of the Act is the ability to disqualify for 'unfitness'. This applies in cases where the company in question has gone into an insolvency procedure. The insolvency office-holder is obliged to file reports on the directors with the DTI Insolvency Service. The Insolvency Service reviews the reports and decides whether to take action. If it does, the court can make a disqualification order if the director's conduct makes him unfit to be concerned in the management of a company. (Proposals to streamline the process are being considered.) There is a statutory list of factors which the court must consider, which include the extent of the director's responsibility for the insolvency.

In the case of the Barings directors, the court gave some guidance on the application of this provision in a financial sector situation:

- The question for the court was not whether the conduct of the director fell below some accepted practice in investment banking but whether he acted incompetently.
- The court does not need expert evidence on questions of competence.
- The fact that a director has a wider role within the group of companies does not lessen the extent of the managerial responsibilities placed on him as a director.
- The fact that the director has properly delegated certain functions does not relieve him of the duty to supervise and monitor the discharge of those functions.
- Failure to investigate 'warning lights', to investigate exception reports, to enquire whether positions were being reduced in accordance with directions, to investigate unrealistic profitability figures, were all indications leading to a conclusion that the director had borne a heavy responsibility for the insolvency of the company.
- Likewise, failure to report limit breaches, shielding junior staff from enquiry into aberrations, turning a blind eye to compliance issues and failure to introduce a system for monitoring risk limits were similar indications for another director.

2.5.4 Fitness and properness

Financial sector legislation requires senior management to be fit and proper to carry out the task. 'Fitness' connotes competence and 'properness' or 'propriety' tests integrity and suitability. Fitness therefore goes towards formal, paper qualifications; properness goes more towards personal qualities and can only be objectively assessed by reference to absence of convictions, financial position, civil debt actions, ejections from professional bodies and so forth.

REFERENCES

Senior managers – proposed new rules

- FSA *The Regulation of Approved Persons* Consultation Paper 26 (July 1999).

Disqualification of directors

- Company Directors Disqualification Act 1986, ss 6–9.
- *Re Barings plc and others (No 5)* [1999] 1 BCLC 433.

FURTHER READING

- FSA *Senior Management Arrangements, Systems and Controls* Consultation Paper 35 (December 1999).

2.6 MONEY LAUNDERING

2.6.1 Rules about money laundering

There is a motley collection of rules and laws on money laundering. For regulated firms the important point is that there should be controls to combat it:

- firms need procedures to know their customers;
- firms need to implement record-keeping procedures;
- firms need to train staff to spot the signs;
- firms need to appoint a Money Laundering Reporting Officer.

See further section 2.1.

2.7 CLIENT ASSET PROTECTION

2.7.1 Client money

Brokers dealing with customers' money must, where the client money rules apply, hold the 'money' on trust. (In some cases the client money rules do not apply—for example, where the broker is a bank; and where the client has requested to opt out of the protection of the rules.) Of course money is rarely held as cash; more often it is in the form of bank deposits. So some of the peculiarities of the client money rules appear immediately:

- Client money must be held in an account at an 'approved bank'.
- Some things like cheques are treated as 'client money' even before they become bank deposits.
- Once the client money is drawn from the account at the approved bank, and spent, it ceases to be client money and therefore ceases to be impressed with the trust in favour of the client.
- Where money is passed onto third parties, such as other brokers engaged on the client's behalf, the claim which the firm has against the third party is impressed with the trust in favour of the client even though the money itself is clear of the trust.
- If the approved bank or the third party goes bankrupt, there is no obligation (in the absence of a special agreement) on the firm to top up the shortfall.
- Provided that the firm ensures that no money is disbursed from the client account unless the client put it there, there should be no risk of a shortfall on the client account if the approved bank remains solvent, even if the firm itself is bankrupt.
- If the firm disburses funds from the client account in expectation of receiving a payment later in the day, which never materialises, a shortfall on the client account can arise; it is the firm's responsibility to top up such shortfalls and if the firm cannot do so (because it is insolvent) the clients share the losses pro rata.

2.7.2 Other client assets

In the UK, client money protection applies only to client money, not to other assets held by insolvent firms. Even in countries where protection applies to non-money assets there may be risks which will be similar to custody risks (see section 7.10.3).

The SFA has various rules relevant to safe custody. One provides a checklist for firms checking out custodianship for customers:

- expertise and market reputation of the custodian and his performance of services to the firm;
- arrangements for holding and safeguarding of investments;
- insurance;
- custodian's capital;
- custodian's credit rating;
- extent to which the custodian is regulated;
- other activities of the custodian and its affiliates.

SFA rules also provide for (limited) pooling of customers' assets on broker insolvency: where securities cannot be identified by separate certificates and there is a shortfall which cannot be reconciled, the customers may share in the shortfall pro rata. In cases where the broker is not insolvent, any such shortfalls are to be made good by the broker.

REFERENCES

Client money rules

- Financial Services (Client Money) Regulations 1991 (Securities and Investments Board); SFA Rules, Chapter 4.

Safe-keeping rules

- SFA Rules, rules 4-100 to 4-116.

2.8 INSIDER DEALING

2.8.1 Rules about insider dealing

The UK rules about insider dealing are limited in some respects and controversially wide in others:

- only individuals can commit the offence;
- only 'securities', not other products, are within the scope of the offence;
- dealing, encouraging others to deal, and tipping off, are caught;
- the individual has to have inside information from an inside source (essentially an employee of the issuer of the securities or a person who got the information by virtue of his employment).

The legislation is complicated and there is little in the way of official interpretative guidance. The new 'market abuse' regime is likely to add significantly to the law in this area (see further section 5.6).

REFERENCES

Insider dealing

Criminal Justice Act 1993, Pt V.

2.9 MARKET DISCIPLINE AND MARKET ABUSE

2.9.1 Rules about market discipline

Traditionally organised exchanges have had (and have been obliged to have) rules to prevent market users being ripped off. Prices which are quoted to market users have to be fair; market users should be treated uniformly; products which are too illiquid should not be traded; cornering and other forms of price manipulation should be controlled; taking advantage of secret knowledge should not be allowed. Some of these principles are fuzzy at the edges (all trading depends to some extent on better knowledge than others have; all trading is bound to affect prices to some degree, etc) and require a more flexible approach than is typical in the rules-driven regulatory world.

Yet as well as exchange rules there are rules in the London Code of Conduct about dealings in the wholesale money markets; there is the general law of contract which tells you not to misrepresent things to your counterparty; and there are provisions in the Financial Services Act to combat misleading statements which induce people to buy investments. The new UK financial services legislation will contain provisions allowing fining of regulated and unregulated persons for behaviour which amounts to 'market abuse' (see section 5.6).

There are also specific rules for some well-known problem areas:

- stabilising the price of securities newly issued to the market;
- trading away from the market price;
- insider dealing (see section 2.8).

REFERENCES

Market discipline rules

– **Stabilisation** SFA Rules, rule 5–47 and Appendix 16.

– **Off-market prices** FSA, London Code of Conduct, paras 50–52.

2.10 LARGE AND INTERNATIONAL GROUPS

2.10.1 Structure of large groups

Regulation has typically divided financial institutions up along strictly legal lines, looking at the exposures and capital of particular legal entities in a corporate group, without recognising that business units are often spread across corporate as well as geographical boundaries. The factors which shape the way a group is structured legally are not those which motivate regulators. The legal structure of a group is distinct from its business and management units, though there is some overlap since a subsidiary's board of directors must answer to its shareholder/parent company for the subsidiary's performance.

Regulatory Concerns	Group Architecture Drivers
Systemic risk Market stability Consumer protection	Tax Ring-fencing business units/profit centres Need for local regulatory/business licence Cost of establishment

This is to some extent recognised by regulators: consolidated supervision and reporting is possible; lead regulators can be appointed to oversee a whole group; intra-group exposures can be disregarded for large exposure (concentration risk) purposes; capital adequacy can be demonstrated by looking at capital injected into other corporate entities where consolidation is allowed. But there are shortcomings with treating groups as single integrated units:

- insolvency is generally administered on a company-by-company basis;

- intercompany obligations can cause trouble in one subsidiary to spread to others;
- liability for other companies' debts can be imposed on insolvency (corporate veil may be pierced);
- one company may act as another group company's agent;
- intra-group transactions which are not on arm's-length terms may be vulnerable to attack;
- a parent company's assets are normally holdings in, and loans to, subsidiaries, which may be worthless; so a parent company guarantee may add nothing by way of credit support.

Inasmuch as regulators are concerned with the effects of insolvency of a regulated firm, consolidated supervision will be inappropriate. Looking at the legal entity stand-alone rather than the whole group is important for management of counterparty risk as well as regulation.

Other issues which make large groups complex to supervise include:

- non-financial sector businesses with different business needs being carried on in the group (Sainsbury's bank; IT offshoots of financial sector firms);
- merger and acquisitions activity;
- consolidated accounting;
- different accounting conventions in different countries, eg as to what is on or off the balance sheet;
- distinctions between cross-border recognition of conduct-of-business and prudential supervisory rules and categorisation of rules into these pigeon-holes;
- matrix management;
- running the group as if the businesses and assets were in the parent company, when in practice it is usually a funding vehicle through which capital and profits are piped;
- a complex web of intercompany debts and obligations, not only arising out of current activities but also from historical events such as past acquisitions.

2.10.2 International regulatory issues

Background themes to international regulation:

- Regulation is still mainly organised on a national basis.
- In the financial sector it is much more common than in other sectors for firms to set up branches, rather than subsidiaries (separately incorporated legal entities), when they wish to start business in a new country. This is encouraged by EU Directives implementing the 'freedom of establishment' concept in the financial sector.
- Electronic means of communication are making cross-border financial sector business much easier. Exchange controls and other barriers to international financial sector business are being dismantled world-wide. E-commerce is seen as a means of making money in new areas and from an expanded customer base. These trends are encouraging more firms to engage in business on an international basis.

- Regulators are concerned about the systemic implications of cross-border payment and settlement systems, which could allow a problem in one country to infect firms in other countries.

The G7 finance ministers came up in 1998 with ten principles for removing information exchange barriers in supervising financial firms: these focus on removal of laws and practices (such as the need for formal written requests or agreements) which impede information flows.

2.10.3 The lead co-ordinator concept

Regulators acknowledge that supervision of financial conglomerates cannot be fully effective if organised on a firm-by-firm (solo) basis. But with differing standards and objectives of regulation in different countries, and even between different business sectors within a single country, global supervision is still some way off. In the meantime what has grown up is the concept of a single supervisor selected from among a multinational multiproduct firm's regulators to carry out a central (and primarily administrative) role as 'lead co-ordinator' of the group's supervisors. (Another term for it is 'lead convenor'; 'lead supervisor' is perhaps misleading at present.)

The role of the lead co-ordinator is to assess the capital adequacy of the group, to make other supervisors aware of developments which might affect the viability of the group, and to co-ordinate 'supervisory action' involving more than one regulated entity when this is called for. Individual regulators could still take action on their own and how differing philosophical approaches to crisis management (rescue versus allow failures) would be reconciled among supervisors is unclear.

The primary features of lead co-ordination are:

- The focus of lead co-ordination is assessment of a group's overall capital adequacy rather than other aspects of supervision. This will include considering whether capital is available in the appropriate parts of the group, and ensuring that 'double gearing' is avoided wherever possible (eg where financial resources of a parent company can be counted as capital by two or more trading subsidiaries in the group, so that the total financial resources are less than the sum of the requirements). Capital may be assessed on a 'consolidated supervision' basis or a 'solo-plus' basis: *consolidated supervision* focuses on the parent company (and makes assumptions that the group's consolidated financial statements are a useful guide to the group); *solo-plus* looks at individual entities within the group and takes a more qualitative look at their interaction in the whole group.
- Other prudential information may be shared, but regulators still have to contend with local secrecy laws and other obstacles such as cultural differences.
- Intra-group exposures are important: the current approach is to tackle them as an element of solo supervision. At the group level, large exposures pose a difficulty because there are widely differing regulatory standards. Lead co-ordination is intended to free up information flow between regulators on external exposures.
- Legal structure is another focus of concern. Who is the true controller of the regulated entity, and does a complex legal structure impede effective supervision? Groups may also contain unregulated entities. Information about them may be crucial to an understanding of the affairs of the group and the lead coordinator may be expected to obtain and share this knowledge.

The G30 considers that these arrangements, which do little more than group together bundles of national regulators, could be improved by eliminating duplication and replacing national rules-based regulatory systems with global risk-based supervision.

Minimum Standards for Supervision of International Banking Groups

(Basle Committee, July 1992)

- All international banking groups and international banks should be supervised by a home country authority that capably performs consolidated supervision.
- The creation of a cross-border banking establishment should receive the prior consent of both the host country supervisory authority and the bank's and, if different, banking group's home country supervisory authority.
- Supervisory authorities should possess the right to gather information from the cross-border banking establishments of the banks or banking groups for which they are the home country supervisor.
- If a host country authority determines that any one of the foregoing minimum standards is not met to its satisfaction, that authority could impose restrictive measures necessary to satisfy its prudential concerns consistent with these minimum standards, including the prohibition of the creation of banking establishments.

REFERENCES

G7 principles on large groups

– G7 Finance Ministers *Financial Stability—Supervision of Global Financial Institutions* (May 1998).

Lead co-ordinator concept, supervision of international groups

– Tripartite Group of Bank, Securities and Insurance Regulators *The Supervision of Financial Conglomerates* (July 1995).

– Bank for International Settlements *The Supervision of Cross-border Banking* (October 1996).

G30 report on large groups

– Group of 30 *Global Institutions, National Supervision and Systemic Risk* (1997).

2.11 CAPITAL ADEQUACY

2.11.1 What is capital adequacy?

Capital adequacy is a fundamental regulatory tool. It purpose is to evaluate the ability of financial institutions to meet their commitments. If an institution loses its assets, can it still pay its creditors? The answer depends on whether it has other financial resources which do not compete with creditors' claims. Although assessments of capital adequacy are based on fairly crude risk measures, the computation of adequate capital is far from straightforward and imposes a heavy compliance burden.

Actually capital adequacy is of limited use. A firm can spend the capital invested by its owners in a very short space of time. Adequate capital is no guarantee of prudent management. The amount invested in a firm is a poor guide to its ability to pay its creditors. Arguably a firm's profitability is as good a guide-though paper profits sometimes do not manifest themselves as cash (a mismatch which should always bother senior management).

So why use capital? The original objectives of the Basle Committee, when setting a single capital standard, were to increase solvency and to reduce competitive inequalities. The plan was to make regulatory capital more sensitive to differences between banks' risk profiles, take off-balance sheet exposures into account, and lower the disincentives to holding liquid low-risk assets. Perhaps also capital is a convenient means of keeping an eye on things, because you can easily measure it and it remains reasonably static. Other measures, such as VaR, are open to even more objections. And because capital adequacy, as the basic tool of financial sector regulation, was invented by banking supervisors to address the relatively simple risk profile of commercial banking (that borrowers might not repay). And, above all, it forces the shareholders of the institution to think hard about corporate priorities: the more capital a firm must have for a given amount of business, the lower the return will be for shareholders.

Capital adequacy has numerous disadvantages if relied on slavishly as a sign of good health:

- the rules become so complex in order to meet the challenges of modern financial sector activity, that they are open to manipulation;
- regulated status and counterparty risk-weights are no guide at all to the credit of the counterparty;
- capital is here today, gone tomorrow, with today's business profiles in the financial sector;
- arcane procedures are needed to convert assets which do not primarily involve credit risk into credit equivalents in order to fit them into the capital adequacy regime.

Some firms—primarily those which regulators perceive are not expected to have counterparty exposure (such as non-trading brokers and advisers, and service providers assisting the market)—have a different 'capital adequacy' regime. For these firms cash or liquid resources have to be sufficient to meet a given number of months' expected liabilities. Yet this regime is also applied to some entities (such as central clearing houses) which do undertake counterparty exposure.

Other objections to capital adequacy as a guide to regulatory health include:

- counterparty risk weighting and evaluation of assets form the basis of capital adequacy calculations, but liabilities and operational risk events cause collapses;
- operational risk requirements are crude and arbitrary;
- counterparty risk weights are arbitrary: historically a corporate entity has been unable to achieve lower than 100% whereas a government security may be as low as 10% even though it may be about to default;
- haircuts for market risk are based on historical volatilities;
- no account is taken of correlations between risk, whether good or bad;
- nor is recognition given for diversification;

- uplifts for market risk models are arbitrary and take no account of the success of the model;
- pigeonholing transactions allows for arbitrage and leads to anomalous differences in treatment of new products with similar economic effects, not to mention regulatory arbitrage ('it's more like a letter of credit than a credit derivative');
- different supervisors use different approaches.

Capital adequacy rules have also attracted criticisms that they encourage banks to invest in the poorest-quality (highest return) assets within a risk-weight band, and that they encourage banks to adopt a policy of reducing lending at times of dips in the economy (because it is hardest to raise capital then) thereby exacerbating the situation.

2.11.2 How capital adequacy is calculated

A company's published accounts are a poor guide to its financial health. So special regulatory rules have been devised to determine whether the company has enough capital.

What the capital rules try to do for banks is to ensure that depositors (unsecured creditors) get paid in full before liabilities owed to capital providers. The leap of faith here is whether the bank has any assets that can be realised to pay off the depositors. A bank which is solvent on a balance sheet test (assets minus liabilities leaves net amounts due to capital providers) should allow this. Capital 'adequacy' does not, however, ensure solvency. Nevertheless the basic capital rules are called 'solvency ratio' rules in the EU Directives, which set out this approach:

- credit risk is the primary source of risk;
- on the whole liabilities are ignored;
- credit risk of assets is reflected in a risk-weighting percentage;
- total risk-weighted assets are compared to capital.

With investment firms the idea is pretty similar to banks: the emphasis is not on depositors but customers of the firm and completion of their bargains. (Capital adequacy does not address the risk that the firm may make off with the customer's money or other assets—this is tackled through other rules.) Completion of the bargain requires, as a primary step, solvency; but it also requires liquid assets. Solvency is dealt with by similar methodology as for banks, and adjusted to cater for illiquid assets:

- market risk is the primary source of risk;
- illiquid assets are deducted from capital completely;
- on the whole liabilities are ignored;
- market risk, counterparty risk and large exposures risk factors for transactions are reflected in percentage tables;
- a capital requirement for each transaction is built up of these elements;
- total capital requirement is compared to capital.

With either approach the idea is that assets will be used to repay short-term liabilities before providers of capital; both approaches assume that the investment made by the providers of capital has been converted into assets, not spent on wine, women and song.

There are two parts to the typical assessment for a firm with exposures to customers and counterparties:

- How much capital does the institution need (its financial resources requirement)?
- How much capital does the institution have (its 'own funds' or financial resources)?

2.11.3 Financial resources requirement

Since implementation of the Capital Adequacy Directive, in the EU almost all firms have to split their activities into 'banking' and 'trading' books to which different rules apply. Something falls into the Trading Book if it is:

- a proprietary position in an instrument held for resale or short-term benefit in differences between buy and sell prices;
- a position taken to hedge another part of the trading book;
- an unsettled transaction, a free delivery, or an OTC derivative, a repo, stock-loan or reverse repo, provided that certain conditions are met;
- a fee, commission, interest, dividend or margin on an exchange-traded derivative.

If it fails all these tests it is in the Banking Book.

The FSA summarises the approach as follows:

- Is the instrument a 'financial instrument' as defined in the Investment Services Directive?
- If so, is it held for trading purposes?
- If not, is it hedging a position in the Trading Book?

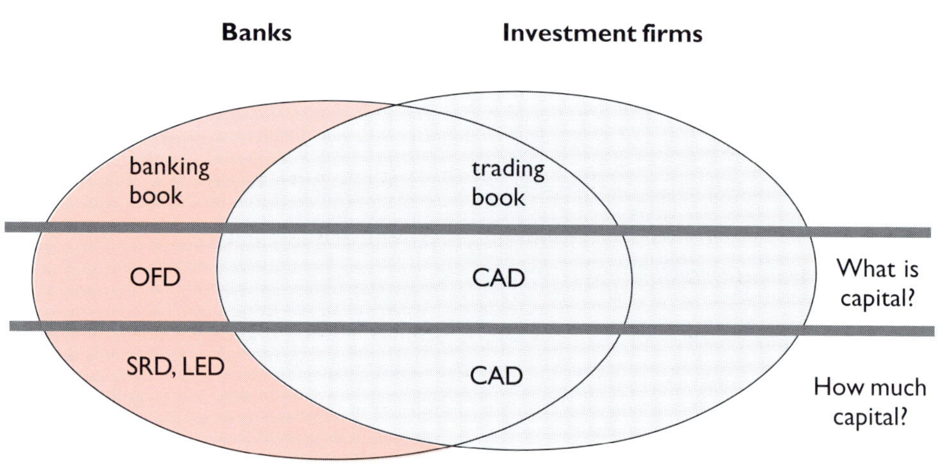

The EU Regulatory Capital Directives

- Banks' business is divided into banking and trading books. Trading book activity is basically the same as activities carried on by investment firms.
- Banking book activity has different capital directives from trading book activity.
- Banking book activity is governed by the Own Funds Directive, the Solvency Ratio Directive and the Large Exposures Directive.
- Trading book activity and measurement of capital of investment firms is governed by the Capital Adequacy Directive.
- Each of the directives has been amended on various occasions.

Banking Book

The Solvency Ratio Directive lays down the financial resources requirements for assets in the Banking Book.

- The starting point is that institutions must maintain capital of at least 8 per cent of the value of each asset (called the 'solvency ratio' or, in England, 'risk asset ratio').
- Assets are, however, risk-weighted to reflect credit risk: they are grouped into categories of 0%, 20%, 50% and 100% (called the 'counterparty risk weight').
- Off-balance sheet items are subject to further weighting: grouping into 20%, 50% and 100% categories (called, in England, the 'credit conversion factor').

Then, to compute the capital requirement:

financial resources required = [size of exposure] x [risk asset ratio] x [counterparty risk weight] x [credit conversion factor].

Where items for which a capital requirement arises do not have an obvious measure of exposure, national rules usually prescribe how the notional exposure is to be calculated.

Trading book

The Capital Adequacy Directive lays down the financial resources requirements for assets in the Trading Book.

Requirements are set out for:

- Position risk (market risk) For a debt or equity instrument this breaks down into components for specific risk—the risk attributable to the issuer of the instrument: and general risk—the risk attributable to movements in interest rates or (in the case of equities) broad equity—market movements unrelated to the positions of individual securities.
- Settlement and counterparty risk There are separate requirements for settlement mismatches (delivery before payment and vice versa), repos and stock-lending, OTC derivatives and fees (the last two of which get calculated in accordance with the Solvency Ratio Directive). Counterparty risks are risk-weighted as under the Solvency Ratio Directive.
- Foreign exchange risk A requirement of 8% x [excess of net FX position over 2% of own funds] is imposed.
- Large exposures There are separate requirements for net exposure to a client in respect of instruments issued by the client, net underwriting exposures and exposures arising under the heading 'settlement and counterparty risk'.

The rules under each heading are complex and one transaction may attract a financial resources requirement under more than one heading.

2.11.4 Financial resources

The Own Funds Directive (for banks) and the Capital Adequacy Directive (for investment firms) lay down the requirements for national rules as to what constitutes financial resources (capital).

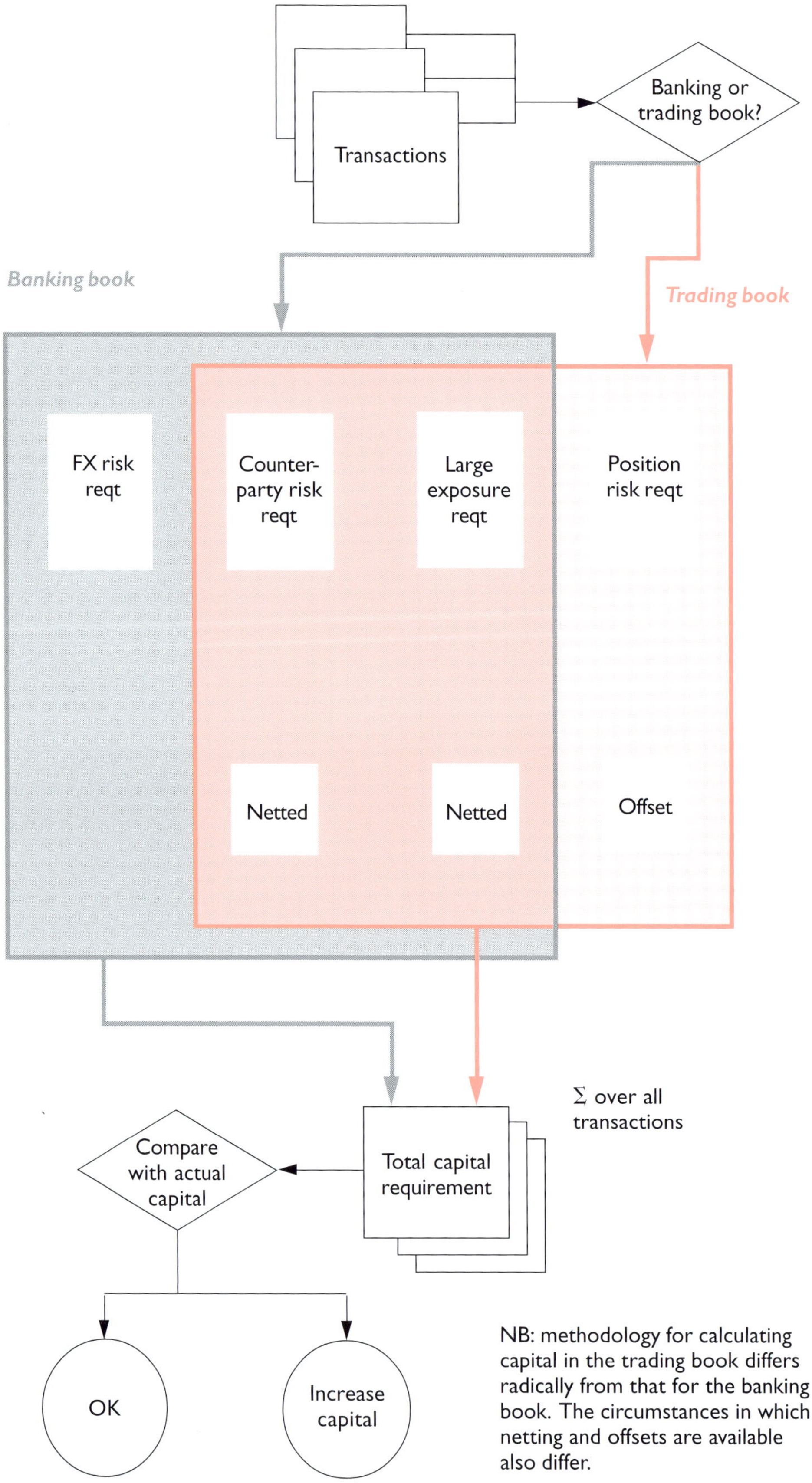

Calculating regulatory capital

Step 1 is to decide whether a transaction falls within the banking or trading books. Different rules apply to these 'books' although the criteria against which capital is assessed have some similarities. Both banking and trading book business have rules about credit risk ('counterparty risk') and large exposures, though these can differ in the detail. A separate calculation is done for each risk factor in the box and these are added together (the 'building block approach') to get the capital requirement.

The Own Funds Directive allows share capital, reserves, fixed term cumulative preference shares, subordinated loan capital and certain adjustments and other items to be treated as capital. Various items have to be deducted from capital, such as shareholdings or other capital holdings in other financial institutions, and certain intangible assets. In order to qualify, subordinated loans must rank behind other creditors' claims, have maturity of at least five years, and be incapable of repayment before maturity except on winding-up.

The degree to which revaluation reserves, cumulative preference shares and subordinated debt can be regarded as capital is restricted. These items are referred to as 'Tier 2' capital in the UK.

The Capital Adequacy Directive starts from the same basis as the Own Funds Directive, but allows the EU member states discretion to include additional items as financial resources ('Tier 3 capital' in the UK) and requires illiquid assets to be deducted from financial resources. The Tier 3 capital items are net trading book profits and subordinated loans of maturity of two years; the amount of subordinated loan capital which can be relied on by a firm is restricted.

2.11.5 Reforms of the capital system

The Basle Committee has published plans for an overhaul of the Capital Accord which has been adopted by the EU and bank regulators worldwide as the model for capital adequacy. The changes proposed include:

- Risk weightings may be based on rating agencies' assessments rather than arbitrary classifications; so highly rated corporates may be allowed a 20% counterparty risk weight.
- Risk weightings could exceed 100% and OTC derivatives counterparty risk weight could exceed 50%.
- Capital charges for interest rate and operational risks.
- Improved recognition of credit risk reduction techniques such as guarantees, collateral, on-balance sheet netting and credit derivatives.
- Regulators to have power to impose super equivalent minimum capital ratios.

REFERENCES

Reforms of the Capital Accord

– Bank for International Settlements *A New Capital Adequacy Framework* Consultative paper (June 1999).

FURTHER READING

– IOSCO *Objectives and Principles of Securities Regulation* (September 1998).
– Financial Services Authority *Meeting our Responsibilities* (August 1998).
– Bank for International Settlements *Capital Requirements and Bank Behaviour: The Impact of the Basle Accord* (April 1999).
– International Swaps and Derivatives Association *Credit Risk and Regulatory Capital* (March 1998).

3

Risk measurement

3.1 INTRODUCTION

Much literature is devoted to the science of market risk measurement. 'Risk management' is sometimes regarded as a fancy name for measurement of market risk. This reflects the fact that market risk is (relatively) easy to model and therefore to predict. Credit and operational risk events have, in general, lower probability than market risk events. That means the data are scarce, so modelling credit and operational risk has been more difficult. It is easy to focus on what you can do (because you are good at it) and put off what is more tricky. For regulatory, and increasingly, business reasons, risk measurement is no longer only about market risk. If you model your market risk badly, you are negligent and stand to lose your bonus/profits. If you model your credit or operational risks badly, you are reckless and stand to lose your whole company.

Some assessment of the probability of the risk event is needed, otherwise we would all be worried sick about the possibility of the moon crashing into the earth next week. Some risks may not need managing because they are too remote. The art of the risk manager is to identify those low-probability events which need to be managed, then he can turn his attention to how. Part of this process, whether for market risk or lower probability risks, is sizing the risk.

3.2 MARKET RISK

3.2.1 Modelling

Measurement of market risk is easy. There are lots of data. Models can be formulated and tested against observable price movements. This means that models have become increasingly accurate and complex. Modelling has developed a rich vocabulary (see glossary at end of chapter 1).

Models are glamorous, and can earn lots of money, but they are not as clever as you would like them to be:

- Complex accurate models are slow. A model is no use if all it can tell you is what you ought to have done but too late to act on it.

- Models can become replacements for risk management strategies. Risk management is more than complex algebra—the qualitative element may be more important than the quantitative element.
- Models are only models, they are not real life. Markets may not behave as they 'should': traders are humans, not models.
- Modelling jargon is useful as a succinct way of dealing with complex ideas. But it may be a mask for woolly thinking. A modeller who cannot explain his model in layman's terms to management is as much of a risk as a trader without a position limit.

Never use a model unless you know why you are using it, what its limitations are and what assumptions were made in developing the model. (Common assumptions underlying value-at-risk (VaR) models are given in section 3.2.2.) Things to watch out for include:

- The predictions of models are expressed with a confidence interval: that is, that the modeller is satisfied that there is a 95% chance (or whatever confidence threshold is chosen) that the prices will move within a particular range.
- The predictions of models are based on previous market data. Small samples in: garbage out. Irrelevant data in: garbage out. Low-volatility data in: low volatility prediction out.
- Markets do not follow Normal distributions. Price rises do not occur to the same degree in opposite conditions to price falls. Extreme deviations from the average are more prevalent than predicted by Normal distributions (the tails of the bell-shaped curve are fatter than expected—see diagram). Complex models can factor in these oddities, sometimes at the cost of other simplifications; simpler models may not.
- Fat tails are well understood and often written about. They are not the only way in which models may mislead. The deviations which are unusual and unexpected will be unpublicised; but they may cause the worst losses. These risks may be unsuitable for everyday VaR modelling and may need a different approach to control (see, for example, sections 6.5.3 and 4.2.3).
- What is the objective of your model? Is it intended to tell you what (on reasonable assumptions) you might lose if markets move within expected parameters, or is it intended to cater for market shocks? Regulators, concerned with systemic risk, may expect models to do the latter; institutions, concerned with profits, may find the former more beneficial. Regulatory requirements do not necessarily imply best practice.

VaR modelling has come in for more critical examination since the market shocks at the end of the 1990s: models did not predict the Russian debt crisis or the Asian market collapse. But they were not designed to do that. Extreme market turmoils are unlikely to be covered by VaR models which work efficiently in everyday situations. Even after you devise the best model imaginable it cannot predict what kind of market crunch is going to occur or when. You cannot expect your model to predict things which even leading economists disagree about. An approach devised for operational risks is going to be more appropriate than reliance on a VaR model for these kinds of event. It is the role of senior management to provide the sort of reality check which allows for unmodellable factors to come into the equation. This is the objective of scenario analysis (see section 3.2.4).

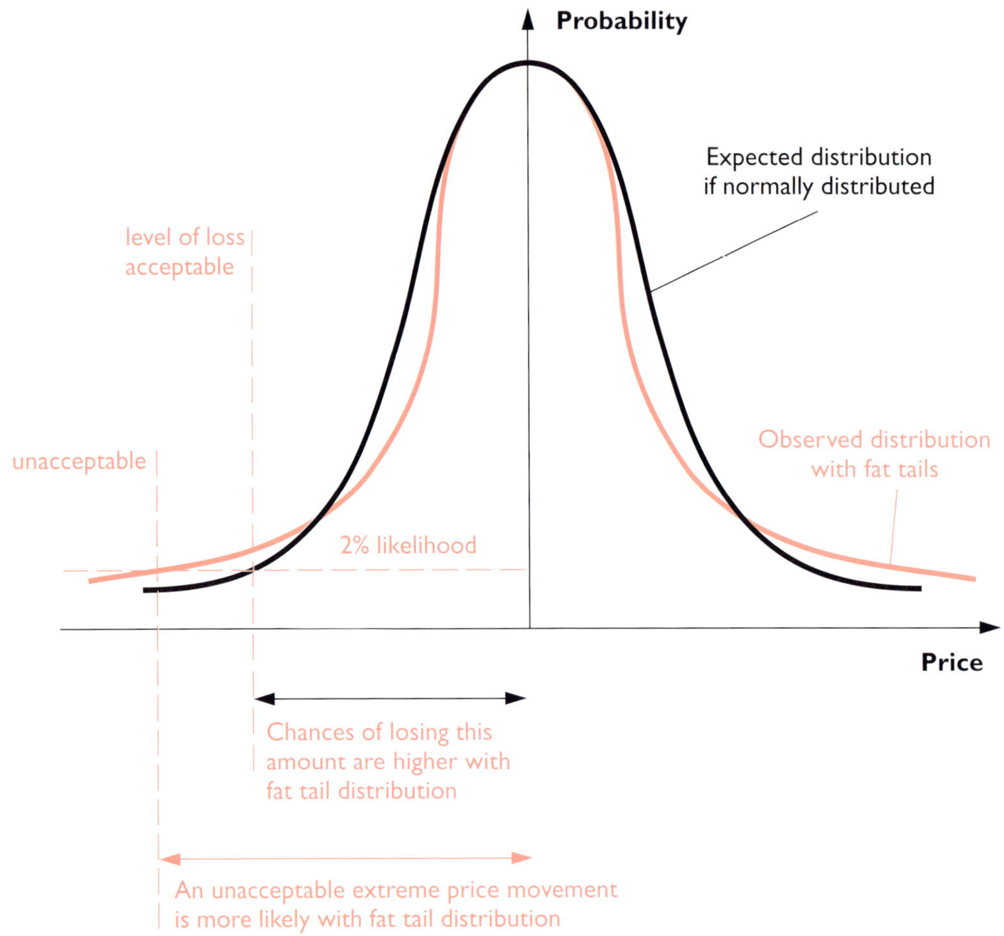

Normal distributions and fat tails

OK, this is the maths diagram. But you can't visualise a fat tail without a picture. What the graph shows is the likelihood of the investment having a particular price. High probability, near the top of the chart, means the price is very likely to be around this figure. Probability theory suggests that prices are 'normally' distributed around the mean (average) price. Real life on the trading floor tells you that an unexpectedly large number of prices are 'too far' from the mean—they don't fit the theorists' predictions. The 'fat tails' are the tail ends of the 'observed distribution' graph. So if the risk appetite of the firm is to risk only a certain fall in price, relying on the theorists could lead to an underestimate of the chances of such a loss.

3.2.2 Value at risk

Contrary to expectations, VaR modelling does not tell you how much you stand to lose. What it tells you is the *probability* that you might lose a certain amount; and even then the measure of probability depends on the *assumptions* made and the *reliability* of the model.

Probability

Historical data allow you to make predictions. Within limits, past behaviour of prices allows for prediction about future behaviour. If prices behave in statistically sensible ways, then a statistical (parametric) model can be built. Statistics are based on probability. The model can then tell you what the likely deviation from today's price might be: in a given time frame it is much more likely that the price will move to something close to today's price than a long way from it. A movement in prices to a level miles away from today's prices is so improbable that we can ignore it. Anything with less than 5% likelihood (say) is too improbable to be worth worrying about.

The starting point for using a VaR model is to work out this 'confidence interval'—the level of improbability which you are going to disregard. It is inherent in VaR modelling that you *disregard* extreme price movements. (And, of course, because it is known that the behaviour of markets in these extreme cases disobeys the predictions of models, there is a particular risk in relying too heavily on models, rather than scenario analysis, when thinking about anything other than everyday movements in markets.)

Where this gets you is that the VaR model tells you the price deviation corresponding to 5% probability, ie the chances are 5% that you could lose that much money *or even more*. VaR modelling does not tell you the cap on your potential losses. With some kinds of instrument, such as options written by the firm, there may be no cap at all short of the firm's capital.

Assumptions

All models rely on assumptions about how prices might move. Some of the more important ones may include:

- The variable which is being modelled is Normally distributed about the mean (average) of the variable, ie the chances of a price being far away from the average of the sample on which you are basing your forecasts fall away as on the bell-shaped graph (see below).
- The mean and standard deviation (breadth of the bell-shape; variance is the square of the standard deviation) remain constant over time, ie that prices, over time, do not tend to go up or down, and that volatility does not vary either. Or it may be assumed that these things vary in a particular way, eg according to another variable which is itself Normally distributed.
- A variable's change over time is proportional to the square root of the time expired.
- Variables move about in a 'random walk', ie they behave like molecules in a gas, bouncing off each other in an unpredictable way, so that tomorrow's price movement is wholly unrelated to today's. This assumption is central to Black-Scholes option pricing theory and to the Garch approach to modelling of volatility.
- Gaps in the data which form the basis of the model or slowness may be overcome using interpolations, approximations and shortcuts.

Reliability

How you extrapolate from the historical data to soothsay about the future is the clever bit. This book is not by a mathematician and it does not try to explain how models are engineered. But a few pointers can help the non-specialist influence the way the assumptions shape the model.

- **Does the model rely on the *variance-covariance* technique?** This assumes that the risk is captured by the variance (deviation from average price movement) of the sample. Each factor which influences price will have a variability. Some models (putting it crudely) tot up the variances. Some factors can be assumed to move in tandem rather than independently, so their covariance can be plugged into the model. But assumptions about correlations can break down—for example, as to the relationship between equity prices and bond prices during the Asian market turmoil of 1997-98.
- **Does the model rely on *historical simulation*?** This technique tries to eliminate the risk of fat tails or other prediction errors which creep in by assuming price movements vary Normally. Instead the recent past is assumed to be the best guide to the future. But often that is just as misleading—for example, where prices are subject to annual peaks and troughs; eliminating these by scaling down or scaling up the size of the sample introduces other oddities into the results.

- **What is the *observation period*?** This is the period over which data are gathered with a view to finding the pattern from which future market prices are to be predicted. The difficulties of this are obvious, particularly when volatility has changed suddenly.

- **What is the *theoretical basis* for the model?** The temptation to squeeze a variable into a *Normal distribution* (by using a logarithm of a Normal distribution or some other mathematical massage) is overwhelming, because statisticians know how Normally distributed variables behave and therefore they can make predictions. A statistician who cannot make predictions is not earning his salary and therefore needs to do this. But there can be an exercise in blind faith here: there may be no theoretical justification for the mathematical processing which enables the Normal curve to be fitted to the data. How well the equation fits the graph of real data, and that alone, may be what justifies it.

- **How were *fat tails* dealt with?** Various mathematical devices can be used to squash the shape of the Normal distribution curve to make its tails fatter. But how realistic are these? There are fewer data on the unusual events which cause these extremes of price movement, so the reliability of modelling is reduced. Some statistical techniques completely eliminate 'outliers' as freaks, so as to preserve the purity of the model; this approach may in ordinary circumstances be more appropriate than trying to include them.

- **Does the model *apply* in the market it is being used to measure?** It is tempting to use a model which works well to capture market risk in one market to address risks in similar instruments in a different market, or different instruments in the same market, but the model may not be effective to do this; on the other hand it may be better than nothing.

- **Does the model capture *specific risk*?** Specific risk is the element of price change which is determined by factors peculiar to the issuer of the instrument: a bond issued by company X will be priced differently from one issued by company Y because they carry different default risks.

- **How has the *holding period* been determined?** The amount of money you might lose depends not just on the volatility of the market or where you are when you decided to close out your position, but on the length of time before you can actually close the position out. This interval is called the holding period. Its length depends on the liquidity of the market. And holding periods differ according to the type of instrument. One of the dangers of reliance on models for anything other than everyday market conditions is that liquidity in anything except rock-solid developed-world Government debt can evaporate in times of market stress, lengthening real holding periods. See further section 7.5.5 for special considerations which arise when determining the holding period for collateral.

- **Were *close-out costs* taken into account?** In illiquid markets bid-offer spreads widen. Depending on the purpose for which the model has been constructed, it may be appropriate to build in conservative assumptions.

- **How was the model *validated*?** Back-testing is usually used to validate a model: what did the model predict, and how did it measure up against what actually happened? Systematic errors can creep into how back-testing is done, in the same way as they creep into the data that are used to shape the model in the first place.

3.2.3 Regulators and modelling

Regulators now accept that models are useful predictors of losses and will allow models to be used by firms in calculating their capital adequacy ratios.

But regulators have also required that the predictions of value at risk computed by models be multiplied up (by a factor of threeP) for this purpose. The Basle Committee has put forward the following explanation for the multiplication factor. The factor is to compensate for weaknesses in the modelling process. Identified weaknesses are: fat tails, the inadequacy of the past as a guide to the future; models which do not take account of intraday risk; failure to capture 'event risk' arising from exceptional market conditions; and simplifying assumptions. While describing these concerns as 'prudential', at least two of the factors suggest that the Committee was worried about the exceptional market movements (such as the 1987 stock market crash, the exit of currencies from the European exchange rate mechanism in 1992 and the Asian market disruptions of 1997–98). What happens outside the confidence limits really concerns regulators—this is because this is where the systemic risks lie. Many institutions would not expect their models to capture these risks and would regard the multiplier as a crude and unreliable way of catering for them.

Detailed regulatory requirements for models are being imposed in Europe through CAD II (the Directive revising the Capital Adequacy Directive). By inserting Annex VIII into CAD, this will allow firms to calculate capital requirements for position risk, foreign exchange risk and commodities risk (each a species of market risk) using their own internal models, if recognised by their regulator. Capital can then be calculated on the basis of the higher of the previous day's value-at-risk and the average of the previous 60 days' value-at-risk. Recognition will require models to have at least the following characteristics:

- proven track-record of reasonable accuracy;
- frequent and rigorous stress testing;
- back-testing: the multiplication factor of three will be increased if there are five or more overshootings in the last 250 business days;
- VaR must be calculated daily, with 99% one-tailed confidence interval, ten day holding period, one-year historical observation period, and three-month data set updates.

Specific requirements are imposed in relation to particular variants of market risk:

- **Interest rate risk** The yield curve must be modelled using a generally accepted approach, divide the yield curve into at least six maturity segments and the model must capture the basis risk of less than perfect correlation between different yield curves.
- **Foreign exchange risk** Models must 'incorporate risk factors corresponding to gold and to the individual foreign currencies in which the institution's positions are denominated'.
- **Equity risk** A separate risk factor must be used for each market in which the institution has significant positions.
- **Commodity risk** A separate risk factor must be used for each commodity in which the institution holds significant positions, the model must capture the basis risk of less than perfect correlation between similar (but not identical) commodities and maturities, and the model must take account of delivery dates and opportunities for traders to close out positions.

The Greeks

The 'Greeks' are shorthand words used to describe (and model) influences on the price of options. Every option is a derivative of an underlying asset: for example, a call option on a bond is a derivative of that bond. The 'analogy' column is strictly for lawyers and others who have fear of maths. It is far from accurate, and the different analogies do not fit tightly together. It will make all option traders scream – so don't take it too seriously!

Name	Factor measured	Description	Analogy
Delta	Sensitivity of price of option to change in price of underlying asset.	Change in price of option per unit change in price of underlying: eg $100 increase in option price for every $1 increase in underlying bond price. Delta provides only a snapshot of how an option price is moving. Delta is affected by changes in the price of the underlying, volatility, time to expiry of the option, etc.	Delta is like the distance travelled by a can rolling about on the floor of a train. With a nice constant speed the can and a train cover ground at the same rate. Delta shows you a snapshot of the movement of the can relative to the train. To plan where the can ends up you need to know how it will move throughout the trip, not just take a snapshot.
Gamma	Sensitivity of delta to change in price of underlying asset.	Change in delta per unit change in price of underlying. Gamma measures fluctuation in likelihood of exercise of an option. If today the option is out of the money, the likelihood is low, if it is in the money, it is high; but market conditions will change. Gamma captures the expected volatility of the market.	Gamma shows the effect on the can of the accelerator and brake of the train. If the driver hits the accelerator or the brake, the can moves about a lot relative to the train, ie the delta will rise (the option price will become more sensitive to changes in the price of the underlying). An option is more likely to be exercised if the market becomes more uncertain.
Vega	Sensitivity of price of option to change in volatility.	Volatility is another description for the width of the bell-shaped curve which suggests how far the price might move away from the observed average. The higher the volatility the greater the value of the option. Vega decreases if the strike price and the price of the underlying are far apart; also if the expiry date of the option is near.	Vega is like the railway's placement of seats in the carriage. The more obstacles there are, the more likely it is that big changes in the can's positions will be constrained during the journey, regardless of big swings in the train's speed. In other words, vega is measuring change in volatility relative to the price of the underlying.

Beta	Correlation of volatility of asset price to that of general class of assets to which it belongs.	Beta measures idiosyncrasy of the particular option relative to the market average. If an option is more volatile than the market generally, beta >1; if less than the market, beta <1.	Beta is like what makes a beer can different from soft-drink cans.
Theta	Sensitivity of price of option to decrease in time left to expiry.	Theta shows the time decay of the option price: the effect on price of getting another day closer to the expiry date. As the expiry date approaches, theta falls. If theta is positive then gamma is usually negative.	Theta tells you how the can's movement changes over time. Will the can get to the other end of the carriage before the journey ends? Is it going fast enough? As the train slows right down it gets less and less likely.

There are also rules about management of risk within an institution, including audit and policy, which must be complied with. Modelling can also be used for the specific (issuer) risk component of market risk associated with traded debt and equity positions.

Checklist: Factors for regulators when evaluating firms' models

- Position sensitivities
- Market risk volatility and correlation assumptions
- Holding period
- Confidence interval used
- Historical sample period (observation period)
- Method of estimation
- Approach to non-linear risk (fat tails and the like)
- Approach to specific risk

3.2.4 Stress testing and scenario analysis

VaR is best suited to 'ordinary' market conditions where variables change within fairly usual limits. But firms need to be able to manage the rarer events, when markets move dramatically. Stress testing and scenario analysis are designed to provide information about these types of event. Stress testing is more quantitative than scenario analysis, but both involve analysis of 'what-if' imagined scenarios.

Stress testing

This kind of test can allow a firm to predict how much is at risk as a result of certain kinds of market shock. Movements in particular market variables—eg an increase in UK interest rates of 2%—are used as the basis for revaluing the firm's positions. This enables potential losses or gains to be assessed. The difficulties with stress testing include: identifying the firm's particular sensitivities; choosing the appropriate stresses to work through; working out what assumptions have been made in the revaluation exercise (eg as to liquidity of markets or correlation of variables); and knowing what to do with the results. Often actual market movements (eg the exit of sterling from the European exchange-rate mechanism) are used as the scenarios for stress-testing.

Scenario analysis

These tests do not really allow a quantitative approach but are intended to ensure that a creative approach to shocks is developed in the firm. What would be the consequences of a major political, geological or economic event? What about operational disasters? Which markets would it affect and how? What steps could be taken now, or after the event, to minimise its impact?

The US Office of the Comptroller of the Currency has given guidance on some of the factors which should be explored when conducting a stress test:

- Historical worst case scenarios Eg the drop in equity prices in 1987, the spike in US interest rates in 1994, the flight to quality in 1998.

- **Changes in liquidity** Eg the widening of bid-offer spreads during periods of volatility. Time horizons should be adjusted to reflect the potential for disorderly market conditions making it difficult to liquidate or hedge positions.
- **Changes in correlations** During periods of low market confidence, markets which would otherwise show little correlation become more closely correlated and the benefits of diversification are reduced.
- **Portfolio-specific characteristics** Huge movements are not necessarily the best test. The test should reflect the actual instruments in which the firm is exposed. For example, only small market movements are needed to give rise to large losses where the firm has written some types of barrier option.

3.2.5 Extreme value theory

Extreme value theory is one possibility for dealing with the unusual. Its development lies outside the world of finance: it has been used primarily for dealing with environmental problems like exceptionally high tides. In relation to financial risk management it may help to deal with the amount at risk as a result of rare risk events. Extreme value theory allows the modeller to form some sort of idea as to the amount at risk from rare scenarios. For example, there is a certain fall in the stock market which should be exceeded on average only once every *x* number of years. Previous years' data can be used to enable the modeller to predict this. Because of the need for historical data, only certain kinds of low probability event can be modelled in this way. These numbers may be useful to feed into stress testing.

REFERENCES

Basle guidance on models

- Bank for International Settlements *Overview of the Amendment to the Capital Accord to Incorporate Market Risks* (January 1996).

OCC guidance on stress testing

- Office of the Comptroller of the Currency *Risk Management of Financial Derivatives and Bank Trading Activities* (January 1999)

3.3 CREDIT RISK

3.3.1 Guises of credit risk

Credit risk comes in various shapes and sizes. The measurement technique to use depends on the source of the credit risk. One particular feature of 'credit risk measurement' is *whether*, rather than how, to measure it. For example, foreign exchange settlement risk has historically not been measured because banks were not aware that there was a significant credit exposure worth measuring. Whether you classify this as an operational risk issue (failure to identify significant risks) or a credit risk issue is up to you. But firms will often find that there are unmeasured (and uncontrolled) credit risks in ordinary trading relationships-for example, in a simple securities business where the customer's order will not be settled for several days and the firm is left taking the market risk on the securities ordered if the customer fails to pay. Another example: the Basle Committee now considers that regulators should monitor intra-group transactions and credit exposures.

Type of credit risk	Features	Measurement?
Loan made	• On balance sheet • Pre-loan due diligence may have revealed credit risk information • Account relationship managers may be unaware of this information	• Probability of default • Amount at risk in event of default (effect of security and other credit enhancements or subordination)
Guarantee given	Contingent	• Probability of call • Amount at risk in event of call (recourse to principal or collateral)
Bond bought	On balance sheet	Model
Default of derivative counterparty	Pre-settlement v settlement risk	• Pre-settlement risk: model amount, but not counterparty-specific aspects • Settlement risk: as loans, but see Basle Committee guidance issued in July 1999

For derivatives, a number of factors affect the measure of credit risk. The easiest to model is the amount of pre-settlement exposure. If the counterparty defaults today, assuming that the contractual arrangements with the counterparty allow for immediate close-out of the position, the credit exposure is the amount by which the position is in-the-money *plus* the amount by which the position might move further into the money by the time it is replaced. Then there is 'potential future credit exposure' which is how this number might change between today and the actual default date. The potential future credit exposure can be modelled using market risk modelling methods. But this is only the 'relatively easy part' of the modelling process discussed below: it only tells you (with all the usual caveats about market risk modelling) how likely it is that you will be running a large credit risk at a certain date.

Derivatives exposures may be subject to a margining arrangement which alters this profile, by bring in-the-money positions up to the money every so often. Margining arrangements may give a false sense of security because it may be assumed that they work efficiently—the vagaries of collateral valuation, settlement risk, and the delay since the last occasion of marking-to-market may all need to be factored in before the real credit exposure can be worked out.

3.3.2 Credit risk models

New software products are available which model credit risk in similar fashion to VaR models for market risk. Old-fashioned bankers are sceptical about these models because they tend to be portfolio-based: bankers know that a true assessment of a customer's credit involves intimate knowledge of the customer's affairs coupled with a business judgment about the customer's ability to sidestep the common pitfalls of commercial life. The similarity of credit risk models to market risk models shows where the weaknesses may lie.

- they are based on historical default probabilities of debtors;
- models developed by investment banks are likely to be more suitable for investment banks than for other types of financial institution;
- probability data are only available for certain kinds of debt instrument which are traded in sufficient volumes for a databank to be built-basing forecasts on a databank which has too broad a range of credits in it can be just as unreliable as one which has too little data;
- much credit exposure is on other sorts of instrument;
- traded debt ≠ syndicated loans ≠ unsyndicated loans ≠ securitisable retail debt ≠ wholesale counterparty risk;
- default data are scarce, information on recovery rates even more so—banks in general did not historically collect information on which statistical analyses can be run;
- there is no universally accepted methodology for choosing and weighting the risk factors which underpin many credit risk models;
- applying a risk weighting to a debt issuer may depend on the issuer's publicly reported financial data—which may be out of date and subject to well-known distortions in the form of 'creative accounting';
- holding periods have to be very long to reflect recovery times—with credit risk the holding period is the period from default to recovery rather than default to close-out of a position; debt is illiquid so recovery may not be achievable through sale;
- observation periods have to be even longer to reflect economic cycles;
- general economic data (such as trends in real estate prices) may be underweighted in importance relative to the type or concentration of exposure in an individual institution's credit portfolio;
- lack of liquidity in the debt actually held may invalidate assumptions on which the model is based;
- backtesting, and thus model validation, may be much more difficult.

There are various different approaches to credit risk modelling. Where there is a relatively homogeneous pool of debt (as encountered in securitisations) there may be a large enough number of debtors to eradicate the usual problem of credit risk modelling: low probability risk event x serious consequence of risk event if it happens. The difficulties referred to in the list above would not normally arise in such cases.

Other portfolios of credit risks do not enjoy this luxury. So some sort of estimate of the default and recovery rate of each credit in the portfolio needs to be made. And then an estimate of how this might change over time: this involves predictions about volatility (upgrades, downgrades and default). And of course you need to know the sizes of the exposures (that should be the relatively easy part). And then you need to make the assumption that any given credit in the portfolio will not behave differently from expectations except in accordance with a known statistical pattern such as a Normal distribution. Some credit exposures are contingent in nature, for example undrawn loan facilities: they need to be factored in. To do all this may necessitate assumptions which are peculiar to credit-risk modelling: that senior and junior debt issues behave similarly; that recovery rates are statistically distributed; that the holding period is one year; that credit behaves like an option to repay granted by the creditor to the debtor, and can be modelled in that way; that there is a correlation between likelihood of drawdown of loans and weakness of credits in the portfolio. Added to this are the modeller's bugbears: in particular, credit distributions do not match the shape of the Normal distribution curve (they tend to be skewed and to have fat tails), so they can only be modelled empirically by statistical sampling.

Perhaps more fundamental is the modellers' approach to credit risk events. You can choose between the following approaches:

- a credit risk event is a change in market value of the debt;
- a credit risk event is a default;
- credit risk events are pre-ordained by economics, so they will be correlated with certain factors (eg increase in price of fuel will affect solvency of airlines);
- credit risk events are the result of mismanagement by the debtor, which is essentially random once management has convinced the firm's credit committee of its soundness.

Notwithstanding the difficulties, a credit risk model may still be suitable, eg to provide a more realistic assessment of the risk/potential return of a portfolio than the crude approach of regulatory capital risk-weightings. But it depends on the nature of the institution's business. A bank which is primarily involved in trade finance or commercial lending secured on property will have different credit-assessment needs from an investment house which is principally exposed in the bond markets.

3.3.3 Credit risk assessment without portfolio-based models

Banking regulators have been categorising credit risks for years. Capital adequacy ratios depend on crude assessments of creditworthiness. Objections to this approach are easy to list: the breadth of risk-weight categories, the arbitrary 8% ratio of capital to risk-weighted assets, the equally arbitrary net-to-gross ratio method for calculating future exposure on derivatives, the relative unimportance of maturity of exposures and the (absence of) recognition of benefits of taking security or of diversification, to name some of the most commonly cited. For more on capital adequacy, see section 2.11. Regulatory acceptance of VaR-style credit risk models is still some way off.

Rating agencies also spend a good deal of time trying to assess the relative standing of credit obligations.

Banks may instead assign their own ratings or risk categories to debt types. This may be used to feed into portfolio-based models. Credit scoring is typically easiest in compiling data on high-volume business such as retail banking business (credit cards, mortgages, car loans and such like).

The Standard & Poor's approach to ratings

Standard & Poor's gives 'issue' credit ratings which reflect S&P's current opinion of the creditworthiness of the obligor with regard to a specific obligation, taking into account credit enhancement and currency (eg where the obligor has assumed an obligation in a foreign currency). Debts are divided into long- and short-term categories with different rating scales.

Ratings are based on:

- likelihood of payment in accordance with the terms of the obligation;
- nature and provisions of the obligation;
- robustness of the obligation in bankruptcy or reorganisation of the obligor.

Ratings are expressed in terms of risk of default; they pertain to senior obligations; junior obligations will be rated lower to reflect reduced ranking of the debt on insolvency and may thus not conform to the strict descriptions otherwise applicable to the rating. The ratings set out below are long-term ratings; ratings below 'BBB' suggest a speculative investment.

AAA	extremely strong capacity to meet financial commitment
AA	very strong capacity to meet financial commitment
A	strong capacity to meet financial commitment but somewhat susceptible to adverse effects of changes in circumstances and economic conditions
BBB	adverse economic conditions or changing circumstances more likely to lead to weakened capacity to meet financial commitment
BB	major ongoing uncertainties or exposure to adverse business, financial or economic conditions which could lead to inadequate capacity to meet financial commitment
B	adverse business, financial or economic conditions are likely to impair capacity to meet financial commitment
CCC	in the event of adverse business, financial or economic conditions, obligor not likely to have capacity to meet financial commitment
CC	highly vulnerable to non-payment
C	bankruptcy petition has been filed or similar action taken, but payments continue to be made on the obligation
D	obligation is in payment default
+ or -	reflects relative standing within these categories
r	reflects significant non-credit aspect of obligation (eg equity-linked instrument)
credit watch	rating may be raised or lowered, if the credit watch designation is positive or negative respectively; or raised, lowered or affirmed if it is developing

3.3.4 Non-debt obligations

Obligations other than mere payment obligations may need to be sized into credit risk calculations. Some obligations assumed by counterparties are performance, rather than payment obligations. For example, the counterparty may be obliged to deliver particular securities or to build a piece of computer software. If a counterparty fails to perform on time or at all, the non-defaulting party has been put into a similar position to a payment default, except that there is the added factor of managing the need to replace the missing property or service. Provided that there is an alternative source of supply (ie provided the liquidity risk can be managed) the problem is a combined credit and future market risk problem: so long as the credit support is sufficient to allow purchase of a replacement product, the default can be contained. Where the market is illiquid (or the exposure is long term and there is a risk that illiquidity might develop), credit support may have to be increased to cater for the extra risk.

REFERENCES

Basle guidance on intra-group transactions and exposures

- Bank for International Settlements *Intra-group Transactions and Exposures – Principles for Supervisors* (July 1999)

Basle guidance on credit exposure

- Bank for International Settlements *Principles for the Management of Credit Risk* (July 1999).

Standard & Poors approach to credit risk

- *Standard & Poors CreditWeek*, weekly, inside back cover.

FURTHER READING

- Bank of England 'Credit Risk Modelling' *Financial Stability Review* (June 1999).

3.4 OPERATIONAL RISK

3.4.1 Why bother?

If the problem of low probability risk event x serious consequence of risk event if it happens is bad for credit risk it is virtually insuperable for many operational risks. This makes people think that operational risk is unmodellable and therefore unmeasurable.

Another difficulty of 'operational risk' is the diversity of sources of risk. Arguably, measurement of operational risk is a pointless exercise: if you are unaware of the risk, you won't know it needs measuring; if you are aware of it, you should be controlling it. The Basle Committee described methods for measuring operational risks in September 1998 as 'relatively simple and experimental, although a few banks seem to have made considerable progress in developing more advanced techniques for allocating capital with regard to operational risk'.

Yet we hear received wisdom such as this, quoted from an author writing in *Risk* magazine in August 1998: 'One thing about risk that has not changed is the importance of recognising and measuring it [*fair enough*]; it remains true that you can only manage what you can measure' [*arrant nonsense*]. This is just one quotation from a forest of similar views. Of course you can manage risks you cannot measure; much of the chapter in this book on operational risk control is about management of unquantifiable operational risks.

Received wisdom is based on these factors:

- Risk measurement is sometimes regarded as equal to risk management, particularly where market risk is concerned.
- Traditional software solutions do not work for many types of operational risk, so software suppliers are tempted to say there is no solution.
- Risk factors are frequently internal: measurement is measurement of the effectiveness of a firm's controls. As controls vary between firms, there is no sensible universal model for quantification of the residual risks.

Enlightened risk managers regard measurement as a useful tool but one which, when unavailable, has to be replaced with others. Data gathering (risk measurement by another name) is just as important for management of operational risk as for other types of risk:

- You need to be able to assess which risks to manage, which involves information gathering, if not the statistical analysis of historical events typical of a VaR approach to risk measurement.
- To do this you need to be aware of the risk and to form a judgment as to its degree of seriousness (probability as well as impact of risk events), and for this accurate data on the risks and the control structures to be put in place are a crucial part of the risk management process.
- Firms typically list risk factors which contribute to or reduce operational risk, such as volume, complexity, error rate, gross profitability, and try to score risk in each business segment.

Some operational risks are rare in occurrence, so that no statistically reliable data are available: exposures, for example, to concealed frauds of rogue traders; to the dangers of participating in settlement systems; to the risk of IT systems failure. How can these be measured so the firm knows whether it is devoting sufficient (or excessive) resources to it?

Various methods rely on historical data to ascribe some sort of number to operational risk. For example, if the known influences of market and credit risk can be stripped out mathematically from fluctuations in a business area's income, what volatility in that income remains is presumably attributable to operational matters. Such an approach may not, however, tell you much about the sources of risk, or enable appropriate risk-mitigating behaviour to develop. An alternative approach is to identify a list of potential sources of risk, to rank them in terms of business impact if there were to be a risk event, and to try to put probabilities on them. The exercise itself probably identifies a number of control and other weaknesses in the firm's risk management system, so even if the end-product is some rather arbitrary numbers there may be some benefits.

3.4.2 Risk-adjusted return on capital

Some firms have developed data-sets which enable them to attempt full-scale quantification exercises for particular types of risk. The approach works for risks where there are reasonably high-frequency risk events (such as processing error), so that data can be gathered and extrapolated from. Risk of loss estimations can be made actuarially in much the same way that an insurer evaluates the premium on fire or motor insurance policies. Gathering this sort of data could be a very useful exercise in identifying current control weaknesses.

But beware over-reliance on statistical methods of measuring operational risks:

- Data-sets bought in from other institutions will be unreliable, because the frequency of operational risk events is directly related to the effectiveness of that institution's controls (or rather the absence of them). Industry averages may be helpful but they are rough guides only.
- Data-sets from a single institution are unlikely to be large enough to be statistically significant. To get enough data you probably have to go back over many years—can you be sure that the data-capture is good enough, and that the same thing has been measured over the whole sample period (eg that controls did not change)?
- Few (if any) operational risks are sufficiently frequent to be susceptible to this quasi-statistical approach.
- Choosing which parameters to quantify and correlate is almost as hard as getting reliable data-sets.

The designers of methodologies like Bankers Trust's RAROC (risk-adjusted return on capital) model are of course aware of these potential pitfalls. Their systems are designed with hundreds of risk factors and plenty of flexibility to allow the user to mould the different parameters according to their observed behaviour. But still you have to have the data on which to set your model going.

Sharpe Ratios

- The idea behind a Sharpe Ratio is to provide a measure of risk-adjusted return.
- Start with the benchmark profit which should be generated by each business centre.
- Each centre will deviate from the benchmark by so much: call this the 'excess profit' (or loss).
- The return of each centre is divided by the standard deviation of the excess profits.
- These are the Sharpe Ratios.
- A high ratio indicates close-to-target; a low one indicates high risk or bad profitability.
- Sharpe Ratios are crude because they depend on correlation with the benchmark, which may be inappropriately chosen; for example, they could disregard hedging effects if unsuitably applied.

3.4.3 Insurance

Insurance premiums can be a useful guide. Insurance companies can measure some operational risks much better than individual firms, because they see the effects of risk events over a large number of institutions and can therefore aggregate data and calculate probabilities more realistically. Individual institutions, unless they are very large and have very good data capture facilities, are unlikely to be able to do so. Large institutions may prefer to self-insure (ie not insure at all) against some operational risks. Note some of the drawbacks:

- added bureaucracy in gathering information internally about risk events and losses: without data capture you cannot be said to be 'managing' the risk at all and no effective control strategy can be devised;
- staff reluctance to discuss operational failings may be less apparent where some outsider appears to pick up the bill—reporting to an outsider may be perceived by individuals to be less damaging;

- insurance premiums may be priced arbitrarily or competitively and outside insurance may therefore be cheaper for some risks or across a portfolio of risks.

3.4.4 Other aids

A subjective approach to risk evaluation (self-assessment) may be appropriate. Appraisals of this kind also carry dangers: the diligent tend to be highly aware of weaknesses and excessively self-critical; the negligent to be cavalier and self-confident. So you can end up with a completely distorted picture. To combat this an independent review of self-assessments can be done by central risk management, but this requires a completely clear mind free of prejudgments about controls in the business area under review, as well as a thorough understanding of the business itself—a rare combination. Don't forget that control systems can fix the agenda for risk assessment: the objective can become finding the gaps in the controls, rather than envisaging where there is no control system at all.

Other aids to quantification include indexes and rankings given by independent bodies to industry infrastructure, such as the GSCS/Thomson index which seeks to quantify the costs of dealing in different equity markets. This brings in factors like settlement efficiency, income payments, tax, costs of establishment and so forth.

REFERENCES

Basle guidance on measurement of operational risks

– Bank for International Settlements *Operational Risk Management* (July 1998).

Bankers Trust's RAROC approach

– 'Getting the Measure of the Beast' *Risk Magazine* (November 1998).

4

General principles of risk control

4.1 GENERALLY APPLICABLE PRINCIPLES?

4.1.1 Is a universal theory realistic?

Once risks have been identified, it has to be decided which are acceptable and how to manage them. A general formula for management of all the diverse sorts of risk is unlikely to be practical. Different techniques will be needed for different risks, according to their transparency, time-frame for emergence, the amount at stake and the probability of the risk event occurring. But there is still a question whether similar approaches are possible, whether a general science of risk management is possible.

There is a menu of items from which good practitioners choose in setting about managing any risk. You need to choose from the menu; and the choice must be imaginative. Because risk categories overlap and interact, it is dangerous to assume 'it is market risk therefore solution X is correct'. But given sensible choice then the list is probably of general application.

One of the first pitfalls to be avoided is assuming that risks cannot be managed unless they can be measured. The risk of lightning striking tall buildings may be infinitesimal (unmeasurable) but that is no reason not to put a lightning conductor on it. The risk of slugs eating my lettuces may be easily measured but that does not mean I have a ready solution to the problem. And: no money is made without risk-taking; if all the risks are easily measured, there is no opportunity to do a better deal than any other player in the market. Good fortune and good judgment are as essential to profitable business as prudence.

There is also a danger in assuming that all risks should be managed like market risk. Risk measurement is therefore not the same as risk management. Because market risk is the easiest risk to measure, there is a tendency to assume that market risk management techniques must be the preferable way to go. So: manage credit and operational risks by trading and hedging? There may be other, more suitable techniques. Most risk management approaches focus on prevention and risk-event mitigation, rather than measurement and trading-out. There is a lesson here for market-risk managers.

4.1.2 What are the techniques?

- **Identification** If you don't know about it, you can't manage it. Operational risks are the primary group of risks of which management may be unaware, since new operational risks develop every day. But don't forget the latent credit and market risks which grow out of ordinary trading patterns (see section 6.1.3).
- **Limitation** Placing limits on the amount of risk which the firm is willing to contemplate is axiomatic. If a risk is difficult to measure, a numerical limit may be meaningless, but a qualitative limit may still be achievable. For example, only certain individuals may be authorised to carry out particular transactions—this is a form of limit.
- **Diversification** Spreading risks is the first rule of investment. The technique applies well in other areas too: for example, lenders diversify credit risk by taking guarantees.
- **Conversion** Turning one risk into another. Collateral, for example, converts credit risk into market risk. Insurance turns operational risk into credit risk.
- **Reporting and testing** Formulating policy is one thing. But it's no use without a police force who check that the procedures are adhered to, and that the procedures work when they are needed.
- **Enforcement** Cracking down on offenders is often the most effective way of managing operational risks where the acceptable limit is zero—for example security breaches. (For more on enforcement and operational risks, see section 6.6.)

Some of these techniques have common elements which apply regardless of the type of risk which is being controlled. This chapter looks at some of them in more detail.

4.2 CONTROLS

4.2.1 Guidance

For the control of many risks it is essential to have internal systems and procedures which work efficiently. Position limits will not work to control market risk if they are not made known, checked up on and enforced. Credit exposure reductions such as use of collateral will not work if the type of collateral is unacceptable or the requisite documentation is not in order. For many operational risks the only realistic method of risk management is to impose and enforce internal controls.

Understanding the guidance on controls which is available to the industry is therefore essential to the management of any of the three principal spheres of risk. Particularly since the collapse of Barings in 1995 there have been numerous guides to management of risks and a general shift towards recognising the virtues of firm-wide, integrated risk management. Without that, the thinking goes, we could turn ourselves into the next Barings.

Four basic principles of control

1. At senior level formulate a risk management policy. And then enforce it.
2. Measure and report risks to senior management. Set limits. And then take action if necessary.

3 Watch the staff. Carry out double-checks. Double-check on the double-checkers.

4 Review everything. Often. Especially the basic assumptions.

See also section 6.3.

Barings' management's complacency was in part attributable to the fact that things seemed to be going so well. The company was astonishingly profitable. On paper. There is a natural tendency to rake over things thoroughly when they go sour but to congratulate yourself when they go well. Is this a sensible approach to risk management? All deviations from your expectations merit examination, not just the bad news.

GARP

A seminal work developed by Coopers and Lybrand is the list of 89 'Generally Accepted Risk Principles'. These add a lot of detail for financial institutions especially on risk measurement and reporting, and various operational functions. They do not try to prescribe optimal management structures presumably because the diversity of ways of doing things makes it hard to find a structure which is 'generally accepted'.

Arthur Andersen's Ten Commandments

Rather terser (and more fun) are the Ten Commandments of effective risk management developed by Arthur Andersen:

1 Understand your profits.

2 Focus on distance (operational risk increases with distance from head office).

3 Honour the Sabbath (rogue traders have a tendency to work all hours in order to cook the books secretly).

4 Assign key tasks to quality people.

5 Invest with authority (the CEO's imprimatur is essential).

6 Reconcile with diligence.

7 Track the cash (unlike accounting entries, disbursements can't be manipulated).

8 Respect business quality (volume ≠ value).

9 Ensure it adds up (accounting errors mean problems somewhere).

10 Watch your systems.

In all this it is obvious that IT systems play a vital role. IT systems breakdown or design failure can fatally damage a risk management strategy. IT systems risk is a key operational risk (see section 6.5).

4.2.2 Regulatory guidance

The FSA requires a bank to maintain adequate accounting and other records and adequate systems of control of its business and records. The list below sets out what is needed. The FSA has also issued guidance to reporting accountants on the types of control it expects them to check for in banks—see section 6.4.2.

- Records and systems should be commensurate with the institution's needs and the businesses it is carrying on.
- Records and systems must, as a minimum, enable the business to be prudently managed and must therefore reflect the 'prudent conduct' criterion of bank authorisation, including money laundering compliance.
- Other threats to the interests of depositors and potential depositors must be identified and reflected in records and systems.
- Complex branch structures and overseas operations require particular attention.
- New businesses or branches or overseas operations require additional data and information-flow mechanisms for supervision on a consolidated basis.
- The functions and responsibilities of non-executive directors are vital.

The Basle Committee and IOSCO have each issued guidance on internal control systems. The following features are expected in a control system:

- Management oversight: understanding the risks, setting policies, monitoring the effectiveness of controls.
- All personnel should have clearly defined responsibilities and understand their role in the control process.
- Segregation of duties should be enforced.
- Data flow: information should be reliable, timely, accessible, in consistent format; and the right information should reach the right people.
- Electronic information systems should be secure and tested periodically.
- Effectiveness of controls should be monitored; internal audit should report to the board; deficiencies should be reported and addressed.

Regulators are urged by Basle and IOSCO to take action where control systems are found wanting. Supervisors are expected to do the following, either themselves or through reporting accountants' visits:

- decide what the control objectives should be for the types of business which the institution carries on;
- review policies and procedures;
- ask for documentation setting out the control strategy;
- observe how the operating environment fits in with the stated policies;
- test the system in practice;
- order corrective action where needed.

Internal controls

Control culture

- Management must believe in and insist upon operation of strong and relevant controls and demonstrate this in their everyday action. The firm should instil a firm control culture among its staff paying attention in particular to:
  - the importance attached to controls by management;
  - the way staff are assessed and rewarded (including promotion and bonuses);
  - controls training and audit.
- A firm should regularly monitor compliance, test its control systems and undertake and record an annual review of its business to determine the effectiveness of its compliance and monitoring procedures.
- Warning signals of emerging problems should be followed up and customer complaints should be dealt with promptly.
- Management must exercise judgment (having regard to costs and benefits) in determining the scope and nature of control procedures to be adopted.
- Activities which are outside the mainstream should not fall outside the organisational structure and should be given a proper level of management control.
- Firms should ensure that personnel have capabilities commensurate with their responsibilities.
- Officers charged with compliance must be sufficiently independent to be able to perform their duties objectively and must be allocated adequate resources.
- Compliance staff should have appropriate status and independence.

Nature of controls

- Firms should have documented procedures and controls covering all aspects of transaction processing, accounting and reporting. Personnel asked to deviate from documented procedures and controls should question why and be encouraged to report the matter immediately to senior management.
- Segregation of duties should occur in all business areas and should cover in particular authorisation, execution, valuation, reconciliation, custody and recording and systems operation. Non-segregation should occur only in exceptional cases and compensating controls must be established, including close and regular scrutiny by internal audit.
- A robust system for verification and reconciliation of settlements should be maintained, irrespective of whether settlements are in favour of group companies or third parties.
- Relationships (rights and obligations) with all other parties should be determined and appropriate legal documentation should be put in place before trading commences.
- Firms should ensure that transactions have been authorised and are correctly recorded and processed.
- Firms should ensure that access to assets or information is limited to authorised personnel.
- Firms should have operating standards and audit procedures which ensure compliance with money laundering legislation and guidance.
- Firms should have controls over IT infrastructure.
- Firms (particularly those with securities businesses) should have controls to identify the points at which a credit exposure may arise and to ensure that the exposure has been approved before it is incurred. Commitments should be reviewed regularly.
- The risk management function should identify risks, set processes for risk identification, in particular for new products, and review new risks in existing business units.

- Limits should be set for each business which reflect the risks and risk appetite of the firm.

Internal audit

- Internal audit should be a core part of an institution's control systems, should be established or overseen at group level and should co-ordinate its activities with external auditors and communicate key findings to them. The Audit Committee should satisfy itself as to the effectiveness of the internal audit function.
- In preparing internal audit reports, major control weaknesses should be highlighted and a management action plan to remedy weaknesses should be agreed with a timetable.
- Management should implement internal audit recommendations and remedy major issues expeditiously. In the case of major weaknesses, internal audit should plan return visits within a short period to ensure corrective action has been taken. Implementation failures should be reported to the Audit Committee.

4.2.3 What went wrong at Barings

The failure of Barings has caused a lot of debate and much of what has been written since 1995 about risk control has been influenced by the Barings experience. Numerous other instances of rogue trader-induced losses or other control failures have not caused insolvent collapses, so have not caused public investigations and reports: the existence of these materials allow for in-depth study in the case of Barings alone. Because this is a study of one example, it is illustrative only, not an exhaustive analysis of everything that could go wrong.

Barings had a rogue trader. But so do lots of firms. Not every firm with a rogue trader goes bust; some firms with rogue traders have lost far more money than Barings but survived because of stronger capitalisation. Barings' reputation survived well enough for ING, the purchasers of the Barings businesses, to retain the trading name. (For more on rogue traders see section 6.6.2.) But there were structural failings inside Barings which allowed Nick Leeson's activities to go unchecked.

Control failures

The following control failures were identified:

- unclear reporting lines;
- trader had control of back-office, reporting and settlement systems;
- trader treated as untouchable because of apparent profitability of his work;
- no check on cash: how could positions be profitable and require a continuous outward supply of cash margin?
- no reality check on apparent profit levels versus risk undertaken;
- arrogant reaction to warnings.

The senior management errors included the following, which could apply to any organisation, not just a financial sector institution:

- insufficient technical knowledge as to how the profits were generated;
- failure to put in place effective reporting and responsibility lines;

- unlimited authority given to junior staff;
- incorrectly geared incentivisation for employees.

Notwithstanding this catalogue of inadequacy, the SFA found (with the support of leading counsel) that there was insufficient evidence of wrongdoing which amounted to a breach of the SFA's rules as then in force. On the other hand, the DTI obtained disqualification orders against the same individuals under the Company Directors Disqualification Act 1986. To address this absurdity, which became known as the 'Tuckey gap' after one of the unpunished Barings directors, the UK regulators have been racking up the formal duties of senior management (see section 2.5). See also section 6.3.4, for more detail on control failures in the context of operational risks.

REFERENCES

GARP
– Coopers & Lybrand *Generally Accepted Risk Principles* (January 1996).

Arthur Andersen 10 Commandments
– Compliance Monitor 'The Ten Commandments of Effective Risk Management' (February 1998).

FSA guidance to reporting accountants on controls
– FSA *Guide to Banking Supervisory Policy* Chapter R2, s 4.3.

Basle guidance on controls
– Bank for International Settlements *Risk Management Guidelines for Derivatives* (July 1994).

IOSCO guidance on controls
– IOSCO *Risk Management and Control—Guidance for Securities Firms and their Supervisors* (March 1998).

What went wrong at Barings
– The SFA Briefing, Issue 13, July 1996.
– Report of the Board of Banking Supervision Inquiry into the Circumstance of the Collapse of Barings (HMSO, July 1995).

The Tuckey gap
– The SFA Briefing, Issue 15, March 1997.

4.3 MANAGEMENT STRUCTURE

4.3.1 General

Almost all guides to managing risk explain that a good risk management culture is essential if risks are to be effectively controlled. Culture cannot be imposed by management like rules, but without rules which have board approval and day-to-day backing the culture will not develop. For more on 'culture', see section 6.3. From the risk manager's perspective:

- You have got to have the board on side. Nothing gets done unless the board is committed to it. And there has to be a budget to support it. And decent staff to carry it out. Anything else is doomed.
- Risk managers are no longer back-room boffins who understand amazing mathematical models. They are central to the planning of business strategy. So the risk management staff need to be the most business-focused people you can find. This will allow a virtuous circle to develop, as risk managers stop being nuisances and become recognised as strategically relevant.
- Avoid conflicts of interest as far as possible. Not just in segregating back and front offices and how people are remunerated. But think about whether the people who investigate possible breaches of limits or enforce disciplinary rules are ideal to uncover nascent control failures.
- Keep reporting lines simple. Matrix management needs special care—see below. Act on the information which the reporting lines generate. Don't ignore the internal auditors.
- Establish systems for checking and reconciling what goes on. Use people as well as computers. Make sure the people are thinking about what they see. Especially if they are routinely reading long reports of figures and are expected to spot anomalies.

Controls are irritating because they distract staff from the 'main' business of earning money for the firm. Controls delegated to junior levels can be overridden by strong-willed senior staff. Do not allow matrix management to be used as a device to circumvent controls.

These points are of course not legal rules, but senior management are being held increasingly accountable for effective risk management policy. Legal help in drafting written guidelines may become more and more common.

4.3.2 Matrix management

Multinational firms need to split up their management lines along both geographical and business lines. This means that a given individual may report to more than one person: his local head, his product head and, in the case of people in support functions such as risk, compliance, IT and such like, the head of that division. A network of reporting lines rapidly grows up in a structure like this.

A confused management structure is a recipe for control failures. Dual reporting may be necessary (eg where there are geographical and product-related responsibilities which divide up a firm in different dimensions). But it can lead to supervisory underlap, particularly if there is political infighting between managers—in Barings one of the reasons Leeson went undetected was that middle managers with complementary information did not communicate effectively with each other.

It is also important that people know what their responsibilities are. IOSCO states that where a firm has adopted a system of matrix management it should have clearly defined lines of reporting at all levels. Other things to watch out for are: gaps in the structure, as well as overlaps; having a process for resolving conflicts where overlaps are inevitable; reconciling the structure with the legal structure. Directors are answerable to their shareholders and have additional legal duties to creditors and employees of the company. They cannot avoid their corporate responsibilities by pointing to a matrix management organisation chart which suggests some other person is responsible. For more on directors' duties, and the regulatory requirements imposed on senior management, see section 2.5.

Matrix management (1-4)

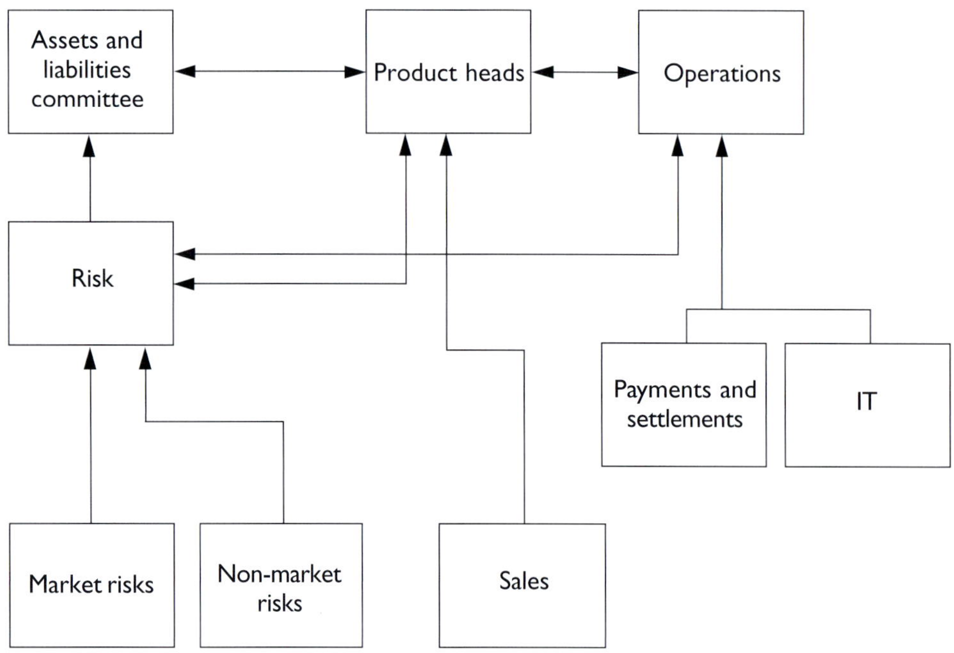

1 Risk management lines

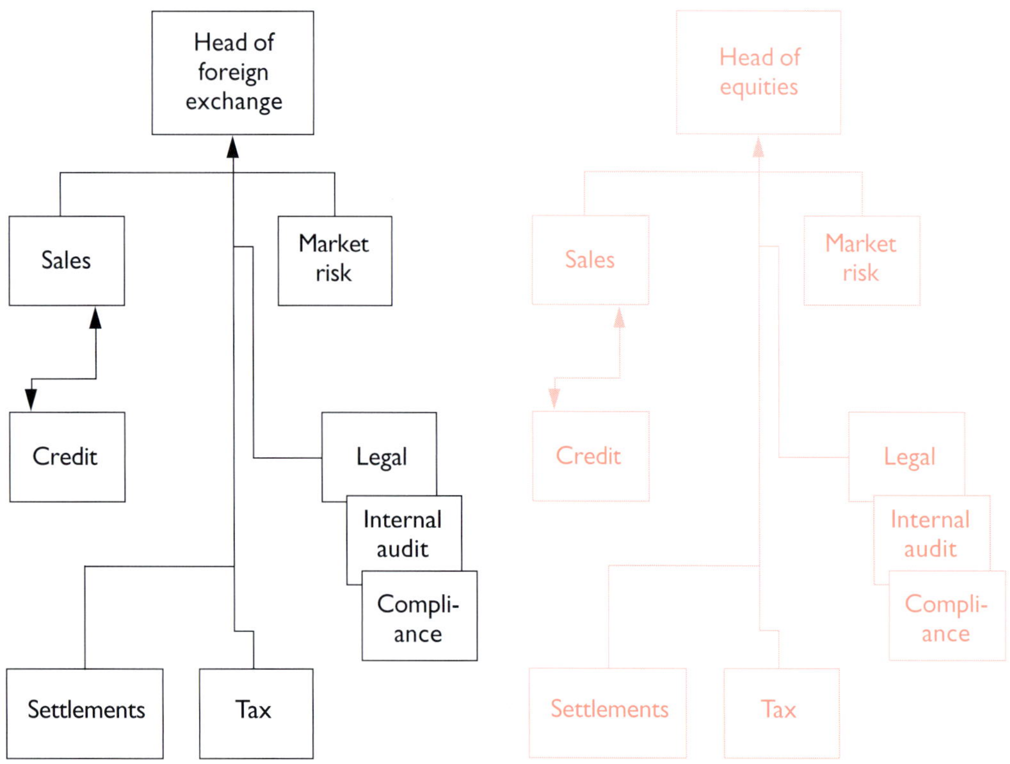

2 Product lines

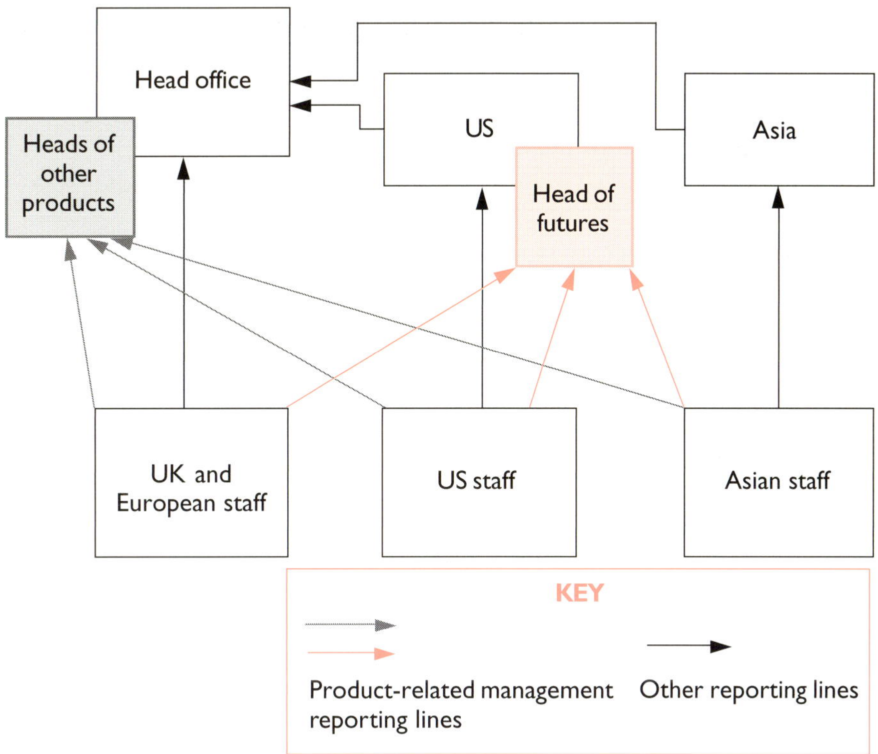

3 Geography

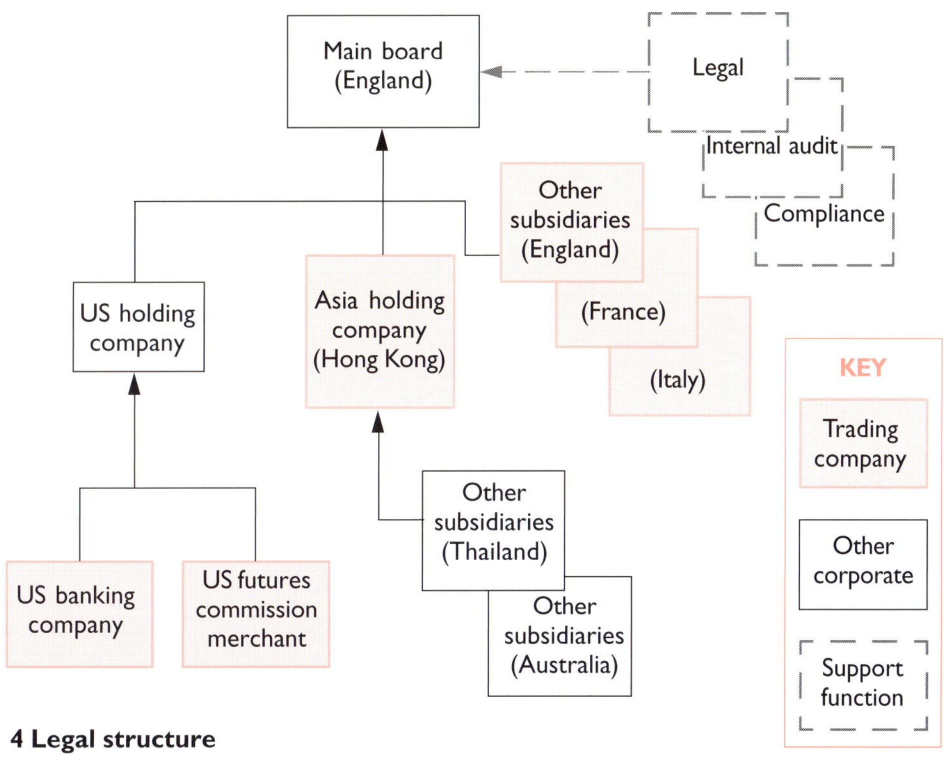

4 Legal structure

Matrix management

Most multinational financial firms have multiple management structures operating together. There is a risk management function which might have all sorts of support and product functions working as a team, possibly reporting to senior level committees. Each product is likely to grow its own reporting lines. Time zones and travel limitations mean that numerous functions, especially staff, back-office, IT and logistics, have to be run locally. And superimposed is a legal structure of companies owned by other companies, with boards of directors answerable to shareholders which may not be in line in any of the other reporting models. There is no right way (although there are probably wrong ways) of doing this, so don't treat the diagrams as showing the ideal approved by regulators. What works for you may not work for another firm—personalities can be as important as products and organograms.

Matrix management

- Top management should collectively understand the broad nature of the institution's material activities.
- Product management should have a detailed understanding of all aspects of the activities they manage, including:
  - risk and potential return of each product;
  - how risk and return relate to each other;
  - type of control systems required to reduce error and fraud to an acceptable level.
- Managers should make visits with reasonable frequency to overseas offices to gain an understanding and feel for the business in order to ask the right questions.
- Management of local (geographic) offices should have a clear understanding of the business conducted locally, notwithstanding other reporting lines based on product type.
- Local (geographic) management should have authority to act to ensure that standards of control prescribed by the organisation are adhered to.
- Matrix, as well as direct, managers who have responsibility for functions which could expose the firm to serious operational risks, or who have responsibility for business and sales units which deal directly with customers, should comply with the FSA's Principles for senior managers, viz:
  - to take reasonable steps to ensure that the regulated business of the firm for which they are responsible is organised so that it can be controlled effectively;
  - to exercise due skill, care and diligence in managing the regulated business for which they are responsible;
  - to take reasonable steps to ensure that the regulated business of the firm for which they are responsible complies with the regulatory requirements imposed on that business.
- Prime responsibility for effective management and control of a firm rests with its Board and in particular with the nominated Senior Executive Officer.
- Clearly defined lines of responsibility and accountability covering all activities must be established, including communication to and acceptance by those responsible. The documented organisational structure should reflect the real and perceived lines of control and influence within the organisation.
- Each individual should have a job description which identifies his or her responsibilities and to whom and for what he or she is accountable.
- All managers and employees must be informed of the reporting structure.
- Firms should maintain an up-to-date organisation chart showing all reporting lines and who is accountable to whom and for what.
- Firms' decision-making frameworks should ensure appropriate:
  - level of delegation;
  - prevention of the firm being committed before approval is given;
  - documentation.
- As well as lines of accountability, firms should have clear reporting lines under which information is freely relayed to management.
- Effective communication between senior managers is essential.
- Information systems should be in place to inform the SEO of the risks to which the firm is exposed.

4.4 CRISIS MANAGEMENT

4.4.1 Need for contingency plans

From time to time the best risk controls may break down. Given the importance for senior management personally, as well as for the survival of the firm, of riding out a storm, it is essential to have in place a procedure which can move swiftly into operation if anything goes wrong. Banks are required by the FSA to have (and to have tested) disaster recovery plans. Crises can occur because of a sudden and major shift in market prices, an internal problem or a counterparty failure. While the detail of the response to these different situations will differ, the need for a plan, and its basic structure, will not. This section deals with some of the common elements; more specific issues related to counterparty defaults and discovery of serious operational failures are mentioned in sections 8.5 and 6.8 respectively.

4.4.2 Basic elements of contingency plans

No two crises are alike. This makes it tempting not to plan at all, because the amount of effort in analysing innumerable possibilities makes it not cost-effective —'we'll have to wing it'. But there are several things which can be done to ensure that any crisis is handled effectively. Those who succeed emerge from crises relatively unscathed; some even manage to profit.

- Have a central response team. There will be a myriad of issues to deal with and events will unfold extremely fast. This means that there needs to be a core team which is kept fully up to date with all that is changing. The team needs to be staffed with competent, experienced and confident decision-makers who will be immune from panic. It is important for the team members to understand not only the needs of the firm but also the likely reactions of other players in the market.
- Empower the central response team to get their job done. They will need top quality information about the problem they have been asked to solve. Some information can be identified in advance of a crisis and systems can be set up so that instant retrieval is possible—for example, in the event of a counterparty collapse, which exposures the firm has and which companies in the respective legal groups are involved. They also need to be seen to have the authority of the topmost level of management to do what will probably be regarded as unusual and possibly threatening things.
- Take the initiative. The picture will change. It may change for the better, so the best course of action sometimes is to do nothing. On the other hand, if opportunities arise, delay can be fatal. Do not assume that because there is a major problem in which a number of official agencies are involved that it is improper to do anything to protect or improve your position—very often self-preservation is not only acceptable, it is required. But do be prepared to take professional advice on what can and cannot be done, since this will vary according to the nature of the problem.

Contingency planning checklist

- **Disclosure obligations to regulators, insurers and other outsiders** In most cases it will be necessary to inform some outsiders, including regulators and insurers. They may be entitled to come in and take control of the problem from you. In other cases you may wish to invite regulators to deal with the problem.
- **Media handling** Settling the party line is difficult; an attempt to ignore the media because one is self-evidently innocent can look like an apparent cover-up and be as damaging as a frank revelation of failings. Professional media advisers are skilled at deflecting the flak.
- **Business viability** As information becomes available to senior management, any effect on the viability of the firm's businesses or even its solvency as a result of liabilities or reputational costs should be considered. Relations with key customers and counterparties may have to be handled if the firm's reputation or viability is perceived to be at risk.
- **Staff relations** Any sort of crisis will threaten the staff. Change will be afoot, regardless of the origin of the problem. Even if everybody keeps their job, working practices will probably be reviewed. Telling the staff what is happening (and dovetailing this to the media handling exercise) will probably require devoted attention of a member of the central response team.
- **Documents, discovery, evidence and privilege** (see further section 6.8.4). Crises bring lawyers and litigation—sorry, but it's true. A word likely to strike fear into the heart of any potential party to litigation is 'discovery'—the process of revealing to one's opponent all relevant documentation (which includes all non-paper materials such as those suggested at section 6.4.3). Do not forget discovery risk: confine potentially sensitive discussions to oral conversations only (not email!). Evidence probably needs to be secured.
- **Recovery** If the firm is the victim of fraud or a counterparty has defaulted, or if the cause of the crisis is some other person's failing, action may have to be taken to redress the position. Investigations and tracing of assets may be necessary. Trails go cold very fast; clumsy attempts to find out whether there is any prospect of success before committing resources usually mean that success is impossible, because they give notice of what could be planned.

4.4.3 Fire drills

Contingency plans need to be tested like any other part of a risk management programme. Dry runs or fire drills are now commonplace for IT failures and bomb evacuations. Less frequently they are used to prepare for market risk events, counterparty failures, or discovery of rogue trading.

The advantage of a fire drill is that it shows up holes in the contingency plan. If the plan requires key personnel to be telephoned, but the emergency contact list is in a part of the IT system which is walled off; or if the plan requires immediate realisation of collateral but the documentation cannot be retrieved from storage in time, the run-through will highlight these deficiencies. Even with the most careful foresight a contingency plan will be a better oiled machine if its prototype has been tested.

FURTHER READING

- Futures and Options Association *Managing Derivatives Risk: Guidelines for End-users of Derivatives* (December 1995).
- Bank for International Settlements *Framework for Internal Control Systems in Banking Organisations* (July 1998).
- London Investment Banking Association *Key Risk Management Issues for Derivatives* (July 1996).

5

Control of market risk

5.1 INTRODUCTION

A market risk event occurs when the price of a product moves adversely and contrary to the expectations of the investor in the product. This can be because the market for that product is volatile, as with the behaviour of European currencies at the time of sterling's exit from the European Exchange Rate Mechanism in 1992. It can be because the market is generally in turmoil, as with the 1987 stock market crash. It can also be because there are specific factors related to the issuer of a product, as with Barings listed notes and bonds when Barings collapsed in 1995.

No perfect strategy for eliminating all these influences exists. But they are mostly well understood and measurable and hedging techniques for protection against the factors to which a firm wishes to avoid exposure are available in most cases. But, because the management techniques differ, it is important to distinguish two types of market risk: everyday movements in prices and exceptional swings such as market crashes. And then you need to think about the other factors at work, such as liquidity risk, which can arise once a market risk event has happened.

5.2 SOURCES OF EVERYDAY MARKET RISK

5.2.1 Ordinary or extraordinary

Even with the best modelling software the prediction of market movements is essentially guesswork based on previous market behaviour. Models are not generally designed to capture the risk of unusual risk events such as a sudden worldwide fall in prices (a crash). Modelling tends to assume a continuation of current market behaviour and/or random changes in prices. Models can therefore only help you plan for everyday market behaviour—assuming that next week will be roughly the same as last. This is extremely valuable but has its limitations. (For more on models, see section 3.2.1.)

Usually we are content to assume that the earth is safe to build on, taking suitable precautions where known hazards such as waterlogged soil or subsidence exist; but from time to time there are earthquakes which cause unexpected and devastating effects. Making predictions about market upheavals is more difficult than surveying: earthquakes in the financial markets are much less well understood than everyday fluctuations in prices. Still controllers of market risk also need to recognise and be prepared for market collapses. Stress testing and scenario analysis, rather than models, will be used to see the effects of major upheavals; the response to the results will probably be rather different from the response to a level of risk revealed by a model.

5.2.2 Everyday factors at work

There are two primary influences on the price of an investment:

- the design of the investment;
- the issuer.

So, the value of an OTC interest rate swap will depend on the movement in interest rates in the selected currencies and the identity of the counterparty to the swap. The counterparty's identity is important: a swap written by me is worthless, because my credit is so poor.

In order to assess the factors underlying market risk, the components need to be split out. Regulatory guidelines on calculation of exposure for capital adequacy purposes rely on this approach with the commoner forms of instrument.

Information is the major influence on prices. Risk management is in part about being successful in what you do. Getting good information is what will enable some firms to profit and cause others to lose out. Exploiting informational asymmetry is what gives sharp players their edge. Recognised UK investment exchanges must ensure that there is proper information to enable persons dealing in investments traded on the exchange to determine their current value. There are legislative provisions which are intended to regulate misuse of information (see sections 2.8–2.9).

5.2.3 Risk measurement is not risk control

This appears to be self-evident, but:

- risk management has meant risk measurement for so long that control techniques can be overlooked because the risk managers are analysing rather than problem-solving;
- there are other control techniques than position limits;
- a control technique may bring in additional risks. Market risk management is generally risk substitution: a hedge may involve additional market risk; credit risk management (collateral) may require management of market risk.

5.2.4 Control techniques

Numerous types of control may be suitable for market risk:

- **Set position limits** Fairly obvious really—but consider how the limits should be fixed. Are models being relied on slavishly? Who has decided the firm's appetite for risk on this type of investment? How was the decision reached? And what factors were taken into account?

- **Review modelling assumptions and methodologies** Yesterday's model may have been brilliant in yesterday's market. But you get your car serviced and sometimes the engineer gives you useful information about what might go wrong in coming months. A programme of reviews and quality control for mathematical models is a good idea. Add in a stress test (see section 3.2.4).

- **Review limit breaches** Without policing, there is no risk management. 'Should have' is not the same as 'did'. In fact 'should have' usually means 'did not', because there was no effective control—the risk manager does not know what actually happened. Barings went bust and near misses at various major houses happened because position limits were honoured in the breach rather than the observance. This is really a question of managing operational rather than market risks. So part of this function includes an anti-Barings check: do the reported profits, the cash flow and the apparent degree of market risk taken by the firm add up?

- **Close out** Cut your losses, if you can. Close-out depends on finding a counterparty willing to assume the risk you wish to escape. This requires at least some liquidity in the market.

- **Hedge** To combat excess positions. But see the particular risks with hedges discussed below. Reliance on hedging involves an assumption that markets remain liquid. And in OTC markets closing out a complex position may not be easy.

- **Enter into a back-to-back contract with the customer** If a customer asks you to take a position in an instrument where you are already at the position limit, you expect to take on no net extra risk because the customer will indemnify you. Is this true though? There are credit and legal risks here.

- **Review new products carefully** New products and new structures, particularly where they involve complex interactions of different components and a variety of counterparties, can expose a firm to unexpected market and credit risks. These should always be reviewed by an experienced team. (Beware of 'sign-off risk': credit wants legal to sign-off first but legal wants operations to sign-off first and so on—in practice everybody signs off as soon as one person does because they assume that the first person to sign off analysed all the risks. Sign-off forms are no substitute for a team discussion.)

5.2.5 How trim is my hedge?

In illiquid markets some forms of hedge may be unhelpful. The right to call for a commodity or security may be useless if the counterparty finds that the commodity or security is unavailable. If the hedge can be cash-settled, that may solve the problem—but: (a) is cash an adequate replacement where a hedge is concerned, for example, the hedger may be under a delivery obligation which cannot be cash-settled so favourably; (b) in an illiquid market, how is the price for cash settlement to be determined?

The purpose of a hedge is to transfer the exposure to someone more willing than you to shoulder that risk. A hedge is no better than the credit of the counterparty. If the counterparty fails to perform, it is no hedge at all.

Mismatched hedges is another area of danger. Instruments which have different maturity dates but otherwise equivalent terms may be equivalently priced at the outset, but as time goes by they will diverge. As time goes by, the mismatch will also become more acute. If a bond used as a hedge reaches maturity and pays out in full, how will the proceeds be reinvested so as to ensure that the protection remains intact? Can this be done at the prevailing market investment rates? The more complicated the product being hedged, the more likely it is that prices quoted for a hedge against it, or to close it out, will be widely divergent. Accepting a vanilla product as a partial hedge may improve pricing but leave the firm exposed to the residual unhedged part.

Dynamic hedges are particularly difficult to unwind. Dynamic hedging involves hedging the portfolio as a whole rather than specific exposures. Not only does this require faith in the model to predict accurately the aspects of the portfolio which represent unacceptable risk, but also the confidence that where a market risk event occurs the unwanted position risk and the corresponding parts of the hedge can be closed out when desired without jeopardising other aspects of the risk management. A dynamic hedge which does not have this functionality reduces the flexibility which a securities firm usually has to manage its positions, namely the ability to close out at any time. Restricting your freedom to do this introduces additional risks: future credit exposure on the counterparties to trades and future expectations about liquidity of markets in particular.

Hedging using exchange-traded products

Where exchange-traded products are concerned, whether as your primary exposure or your hedge, do not disregard the credit risk element of market risk. First, consider whether the exchange or clearing house 'guarantee' applies to you (see further section 8.2.2). Secondly, evaluate the creditworthiness of the true counterparty. Thirdly, consider any systemic risk influences inherent in the structure of the exchange. Fourthly, remember that exchange-based trading requires payment of margin, which may impose cash flow constraints. Finally, do not disregard the credit of the issuer—even if the market is generally stable, the issuer of an exchange-traded product may fail. FT-SE 100 companies go into receivership with tedious regularity.

5.2.6 Opting out

Beware the special risks associated with options. Option buyers are looking only at the price of the option, which is essentially the value of the difference between the strike price and the expected market price on the strike date of the underlying instrument or commodity. Option writers can face uncapped liability if prices move unexpectedly, because they are having to pay for the underlying instrument or commodity at its market price. Closing out an option that you have written depends on there being sufficient liquidity in the market, ie players willing to take the position that you wish to abandon.

5.3 INTEREST RATE RISK

5.3.1 Nature of interest rate risk

Most financial institutions are exposed to changes of interest rates because they are both payers and receivers of interest. Interest rate risk is essentially the risk that interest rates change so that outward interest flows exceed the optimum or inward flows fail to meet the desired level.

The old fixed versus floating mismatch should not be forgotten. In the US markets where floating interest rates were traditionally very stable it was once tempting to pay floating rate interest to investors but receive fixed rate income from debtors. When floating interest rates rose, institutions (thrifts) which had fallen into this trap rapidly went bankrupt since they had no right to raise the interest payable by their borrowers and had to be rescued by state intervention.

5.3.2 Factors to watch

The Basle Committee identifies the following sources of interest rate risk:

- Repricing risk where rate changes are out of synch. Maturities and reset dates should be watched.
- Yield curve risk where longer term expectations of interest rate movements change relative to shorter term expectations, a firm's small exposure to repricing risk can change into a large one.
- Basis risk where correlation between expected interest received and interest payable is unstable or breaks down.
- Optionality where the counterparty can escape from its interest paying commitment, such as in the domestic mortgage market, the inward flow of interest behaves like an option.

Regulators expect firms to measure these risks; they also expect firms to 'define authorised instruments, hedging strategies and position-taking opportunities. Interest rate risk policies should also identify quantitative parameters that define the level of interest rate risk acceptable' (Basle again).

5.3.3 Control of interest rate risk

Interest rate risk is essentially reinvestment risk. Will the market allow reinvestment of a sum received in such a way as to generate the needed returns? Other means of reinvestment than interest-bearing instruments may be a way to manage the risk; though usually greater market risk is borne when switching into other types of exposure.

Regulatory guidance focuses on the need for internal controls over interest rate risk management. In other words, the regulators treat interest rate risk management as an operational matter—it is assumed that the methodology is simple, but the dangers will arise in implementation of policy.

Interest rate derivatives are now a standard part of financial institutions' risk management armoury. Some factors to watch are:

- Documentation issues See section 6.4.3 for the risks of mismatched confirmations, no confirmations, failure to negotiate a master agreement and so forth.
- Settlement arrangements Will payment flows be netted? across branches?
- Tax Will withholding or other taxes apply to flows in either direction?
- Netting and capital adequacy benefits Will netting be legally effective and will regulators recognise it as risk-reducing?

REFERENCES

Basle guidance on interest rate risks

– Bank for International Settlements *Principles for the Management of Interest Rate Risk* (September 1997).

5.4 FOREIGN EXCHANGE RISK

5.4.1 Factors at work

Factors to consider include:

- business done overseas: volume and timing of foreign-currency denominated cashflows;
- need for repatriation of cash (eg to pay dividends to equity investors);
- maturity, mismatch between outward and inward flows, and local reinvestment possibilities before repatriation;
- mismatch between currency of collateral realisation and currency in which credit exposure is calculated.

5.4.2 Control of foreign exchange risk

The obvious control technique is to enter into a forward contract to eliminate the risk. However, good treasury management recognises that this is not invariably the right way to optimise foreign currency resources. Much will depend on the firm's business plans in a particular country, the potential for using foreign currency resources as collateral, local reinvestment opportunities and political risks. Conversion and repatriation will often involve counterparty risk on correspondents and the vagaries of settlement systems.

5.5 COMMODITY RISK

5.5.1 Factors affecting commodity prices

Commodities are unlike purely financial instruments, for two principal reasons. One: their value depends on their quality—rotten oranges are no use. Two: their value depends on where they are—oranges are no use if they are at the north pole. Quality and delivery determine many of the peculiarities of commodity markets.

There are more traps for the unwary. In particular the legal rules about ownership of commodities are different from those relating to securities. On the other hand, goods do not generate income and do not involve voting rights, so some of the complications experienced with securities do not arise.

Do commodities behave like securities?		
Characteristic	**Securities**	**Commodities**
Fungible	Securities of same series generally indistinguishable	Quality and location can vary, though price adjustment can rebase differences
Economics	Value is in income or enhanced value at maturity	Value is in potential for end-use: turn it into chocolate, aeroplanes or bacon
Income and expenditure	Income-producing (usually)	Costs of warehousing and storage
Market risk	Issuer-related features and general economic influences	Supply and demand affect price —supply can fluctuate and be manipulated
Certainty of ownership	Registration system gives high level of comfort	Possession is often key to legal title, but owner rarely in direct possession. No registration system
Settlement	Change the register	Exchange possession of warrants/take physical possession/rules variable according to location of commodity

5.5.2 Quality, delivery and similar factors

Ensuring that quality is reasonably uniform can be difficult. Recognised UK investment exchanges are obliged to ensure that there is a proper market in products traded on the exchange. This requires a certain minimum standard of quality to enable a benchmark price to be set. Because no two parcels of goods will be completely identical though, some tolerance is allowed and will be reflected in price adjustments. Quality checking has to be done before goods can be tendered in satisfaction of an exchange contract. The means of checking differ between exchanges and between commodities (copper can be relied on not to go mouldy but cocoa is less stable). These exchange benchmarks are important underpinning for the OTC markets in commodities. Because of their key role, the consequences of manipulation of the commodity exchanges can be very far reaching. Unfortunately the delivery-related aspects of commodities make manipulation easier than in other markets.

The true value of a commodity is in its worth to the end-user: to be turned into aeroplane wings, chocolate, newspaper or veggie-burgers. Even if less than 5% of contracts go to delivery, without those 5% there would be no market. Delivery, warehousing and transportation are key influences on the commodity markets. Delivery under an exchange contract will typically not require physical delivery of the commodity but transfer of documents evidencing ownership of the commodity (see further section 5.5.5 relating to particular risks of transfer of documents). Inconvenient locations can in theory be factored into price adjustments, but it is harder to say whether a warehouse in Liverpool is more 'inconvenient' than a warehouse in Bremen—it all depends where the end-user is. With exchange-traded commodities, clearing arrangements will typically prevent buyers from knowing where the commodity they are buying will be situated. Exchanges will try to minimise the difficulties that arise by limiting delivery locations. Likewise exchanges will approve warehouses as fit for storage of goods traded on the exchange and carry out quality control checks.

Other factors to be borne in mind are whether rent has been paid to the warehouse where the goods are stored and whether any other charges attach to the goods (eg port duties, taxes or liens). Liquidity difficulties can also arise—where, for example, the amount of commodity to be delivered in satisfaction of all contracts exceeds the total worldwide deliverable stock of that commodity. Exchanges may allow roll-over of delivery obligations to future months in such cases. The rules are complex and differ between commodities.

5.5.3 Price aberrations

Cornering

Control of the supply of a commodity can influence the price. If I hold 90% of the stock of copper (just to pick an example entirely at random) in a deliverable state in approved warehouses then most firms with short positions are going to have to pay me whatever price I dictate in order to fulfil their obligations. Building up stocks in order to force up prices is regarded as abusive, though opinions differ as to the level of control which converts behaviour from legitimate exploitation of a large position into market abuse.

Backwardation and contango

Supply and demand affects commodity prices differently from securities prices. The amount of securities of a particular issue is roughly constant. With commodities things are different: they get manufactured or grown and they get used. Bad harvests or poor mining conditions, or changed demand from manufacturers, may reduce supply. When the amount of commodity available for immediate delivery is low, of course the spot price will be high; the forward price may be lower because the market expects supply to increase. Where this situation prevails (spot price exceeds forward price) there is said to be a backwardation. The converse situation is where the market is in contango. Here market forces will have a slightly different effect. If the forward price is too high, market players will be able to borrow, buy, store and insure the commodity and sell it at the future delivery date and make a profit without risk. This will cause the forward price to fall and even out the aberration. Thus, in markets in contango, the difference between spot and forward prices has factors corresponding to interest rate yield curves built into it, because the cost of borrowing is part of the equation. By contrast, markets in backwardation may not have this feature because the amount of backwardation is primarily due to limitations on immediate supply and the amount of backwardation is therefore constrained only by the willingness of market participants to pay astronomic prices for immediate delivery. Some exchanges take steps to intervene and limit the amount of backwardation.

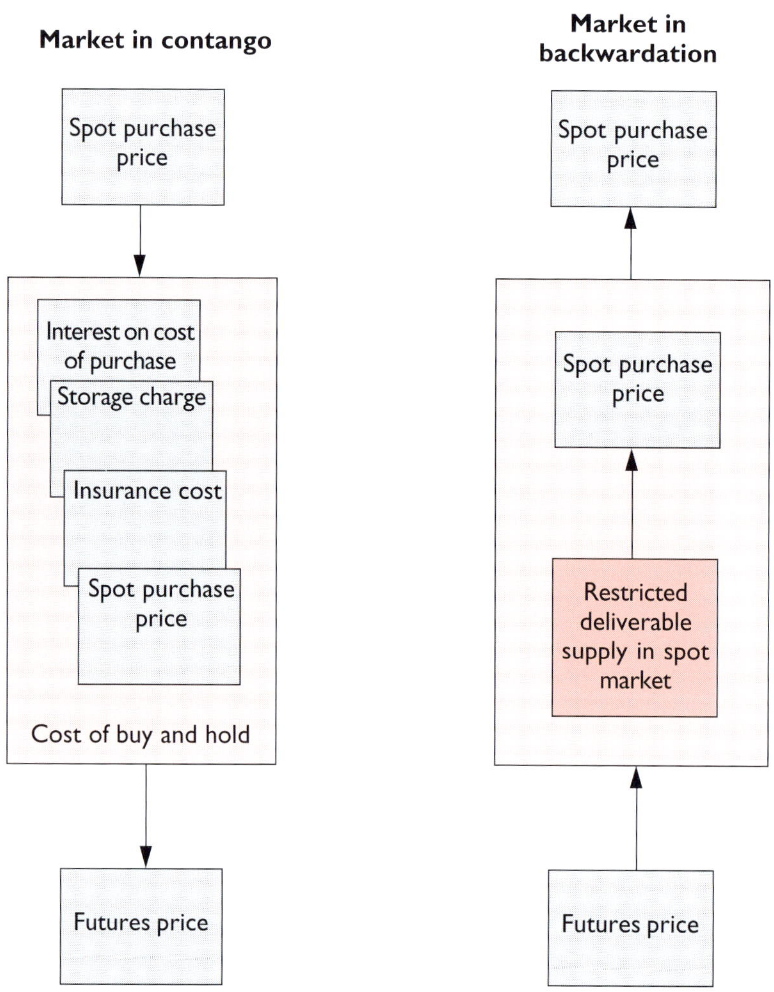

Contango and backwardation

When the market is in contango, the forward price is pushed up by the costs of borrowing, storage, etc. In backwardation these costs are stifled by the shortage of goods available for immediate delivery, which pushes the spot price up to 'artificial' levels. In commodity markets where seasonal and other factors can lead to legitimate expectation that the shortage will ease in the future, the forward price may be lower than the spot price (or the spot price plus expected costs as listed above).

5.5.4 Ownership rules

- Ownership is determined by the law of the place where the commodity is physically located. You may buy a warehouse warrant in London, but if the goods are in the Netherlands then Dutch law is relevant to determine whether you own them.

- Ownership rules differ from one country to another. There is no harmony like there is for securities. Some countries (England) allow for ownership to transfer according to contractual provisions. Others (civil law systems) require transfer of possession (or its equivalent) for ownership to be transferred. Some countries (Germany) require local law documentation for effective transfer of ownership. Some countries (England again) have special rules which allow title to be acquired from non-owners.

- You can't usually own goods which are part of an undivided bulk. There are some exceptions to this, eg if there is an agreement for sale of a specified portion of the bulk. But where there is in fact no separation of your goods from everyone else's, even if the parties agreed that they should be separated, you may not get ownership. All you get is a claim for delivery. This is credit risk, not market risk. Unallocated bullion is credit risk, not ownership of bullion.

- Market practices which treat possession of documents (in particular warehouse warrants) as equivalent to ownership do not bear close scrutiny. Risks to be considered include (a) acquisition from non-owners; (b) other third party rights; (c) whether the warehouse will recognise the claim of the warrant-holder; and (d) whether the warrant-holder has the full range of rights against the warehouse.

5.5.5 Warehouse warrants

Warehouse warrants raise particular risk issues. Commodity financing typically depends on the owner of a commodity raising a loan on the security of the warrants, which are pledged to the lender, but released back to the owner under a 'trust receipt' which gives the lender a proprietary claim on the proceeds of sale. There is usually no indication on the face of the warrants that there is a lender who has an interest in them and so there is risk for lenders or buyers that an undischarged pledge might still attach to the goods. Legal rules give special status to bills of lading which minimises most of these dangers.

There is no particular magic in something being a 'document of title'—even though most people would assume that it means 'possession = ownership'. In strict legal usage the phrase indicates only whether the English law rules relating to acquisition of title from non-owners apply. But other factors can affect whether possession of the piece of paper equates to ownership.

- **Acquisition from non-owners** A typical rule of ownership of goods is that you cannot transfer a better title than you have got. So if you bought them from someone who stole them, or from someone who has pledged them but not taken steps to discharge the pledge, you might get impaired rights. Under English law this risk will often be averted since a sale by a person in possession of a warrant, with the owner's consent, gives clean title to the buyer.
- **Other third party rights** Fraud is not the only danger from third parties. Consider also liens asserted by creditors of previous owners (or of the warehouse) and attachments (legal execution of judgments) obtained by creditors of previous owners (or of the warehouse). Whether these affect buyers who had no knowledge of the third-party claim depends on the local law in the place where the goods are situated.
- **Warehouse recognition of the warrant-holder's claim** In some countries the practice of warehouses to deliver up goods to the current warrant-holder, even though a different person from the depositor of the goods, may not be legally binding. 'Warrants' may have no special status—they may simply be receipts to acknowledge that there has been a deposit of the goods.
- **Rights against the warehouse** The depositor of the goods had various rights against the warehouse, eg the benefit of a duty to take care of the goods. Do transferees of warrants obtain these rights? In England it is usually necessary for the warehouse to 'attorn' to the transferee, ie to acknowledge the transferee as the beneficiary of the storage arrangements ('bailment' in legal jargon).

5.6 MARKET MANIPULATION

5.6.1 Relevance of manipulation

Victims of abuse include all participants in markets. Abusive behaviour on markets is thus a source of market risk. Artificial distortion of prices wrecks the assumptions on which models are based and exposes players to unmanaged risks.

This of course raises the question of what the 'proper' price is. Definitions are generally inadequate unless they go round in circles so nothing philosophical will be attempted here. One of the themes running through any discussion of market abuse will be the difficulty of imposing objective standards of market behaviour, because in any free market economy prices will be set by the participants in the market and it is to some extent artificial to say 'oh yes, well, we only meant the prices quoted by good participants in the market, not the rogues and bounders'.

5.6.2 What is manipulation?

Publication of a draft code of market conduct in the UK has suggested that there is only a limited list of types of behaviour which amounts to market abuse. In each case the perpetrator's objective is to manipulate prices up or down to his own advantage. Abusive behaviour divides into two groups:

Misuse of information

- Giving out misleading information about an investment, its issuer etc.
- Trading on the basis of insider information not available generally. This type of abuse can cover both 'insider dealing' and front-running.
- Tipping off potential investors about insider information.

Transaction-based manipulation

- False transactions which create a misleading impression of position-taking.
- Cornering or squeezing the market (supply-side manipulation).
- Inflating the market (demand-side manipulation), eg buying heavily just before a close in order to influence the level of an index dependent on closing prices.

Some of these activities are more readily carried out in particular markets. For example, cornering is adaptable to commodities markets but it can apply in securities markets where supply of the securities in question is limited.

In organised markets there is an imperative to provide investors who are end-users of the market with some degree of protection that the prices quoted to them reflect the 'true' market price. Some market practices enable off-market price trades to take place, potentially obfuscating the price discovery machinery of the market and putting investors at risk of investing at the wrong price. The FSA issued guidelines on proper trades in relation to on-exchange derivatives in 1993:

- Hedging, investment, speculation, price-fixation, arbitrage, delivery, market-making and executing customer orders which appear to be for one of the foregoing purposes are proper trading purposes.
- A trade must generally be exposed to an exchange's pricing mechanism such as open outcry or electronic trade matching.
- A trade must involve a long, short or spread position which creates an exposure to market risk or closes out a position and thereby removes market risk. It follows that it is improper if it is entered into in conjunction with a separate arrangement with another person which removes the element of market risk.
- Examples of improper trades include prearranged trades not exposed to the market's pricing mechanism, trades entered into in order to indemnify losses, accommodation trades and wash trades.
- Cross trades (trades with yourself) are acceptable if done to fulfil opposing customer orders, or where the firm itself wishes to take a house position opposite to a customer and the cross is consistent with applicable duties of best execution. Crosses may also be used to achieve exchange-for-physical trades and for administrative purposes (eg transfers to other market participants) provided that the rules of the exchange are complied with.

More recently the FSA has also investigated the use of 'historic price carries' and other non-market price transactions in relation to the LME. A historic price carry is a transaction where, at maturity, the transaction is rolled over to the next delivery date without settlement and the price remains as originally agreed. If the difference between the current market price for the new delivery date and the original contract is not paid, credit is being given for the change in market price. A white contract is a transaction which is entered into off the exchange because it is a forward purchase transaction for which the delivery date is so far in the future that it does not yet correspond with any exchange-tradeable contract. After time this bar will be lifted and the contract may be eligible to be brought onto the exchange, though at that time the contractually agreed (and now old) forward price will be some way off the current market price. The FSA has not outlawed these arrangements, but in some cases they can fall foul of conduct of business rules if mirrored in dealings with customers.

5.6.3 Legal and other controls on manipulative behaviour

Before the new code of market conduct, abusive conduct had been controlled primarily by the criminal law and the rules of organised markets. Where there is no formally established exchange, there have been other codes of conduct such as the wholesale market regime under s 43 of the 1986 Financial Services Act, which binds market participants to minimum standards.

Criminal sanctions are imposed for insider dealing (in relation to certain kinds of securities only and only in respect of abusive action by individuals), making false or misleading statements, promises and forecasts to induce people to enter into an investment agreement and creating a false or misleading impression about prices. Criminal prosecutions have fallen into disfavour owing to difficulties in securing convictions. Whether this is attributable to bad prosecution strategy, inadequate evidence or inherent difficulty in the offences is unclear. It is likely that the existence of the offences deters much behaviour in the grey area where the applicability of the criminal law is uncertain, so it is arguable that offences such as this are doing a useful job. The new code of market conduct covers slightly different ground and may have a similar deterrent effect.

The remit of exchanges does not enable them to assert jurisdiction over non-members, though the LME has attempted to obtain information from members about their affiliates' dealings in commodities traded on the exchange. Failure to adhere to exchange rules can lead to disciplinary action and adverse reports to regulators, potentially subjecting a firm to a second round of disciplinary sanctions for infringement of regulatory rules.

The problem with all of this is that it is very difficult to draw a universal line round what is clearly unacceptable—there is a gradual change from what is legitimate position-taking or hedging activity to what is abusive. The subjective element is not really capable of being codified into legal rules any more than 'dishonesty' is. Peer pressure is usually relied on to deter bad behaviour, since markets do not work (and therefore repel business) unless there is a reasonably secure high standard of conduct.

Firms may become the victims of abusive behaviour and will therefore wish to manage the market risk which ensues. One cannot of course control the behaviour of other market participants. But firms can influence the behaviour of the market generally by 'playing the game'—eg participating in disciplinary tribunals when requested—thereby ensuring the maintenance of standards. To some extent it may be possible to vet an exchange's rules and settlement arrangements to see whether there are safeguards against abuse. In off-exchange markets there is likely to be more risk, particularly where the products or behaviour falls outside the scope of the criminal laws. Controlling one's own behaviour also helps, which is a question of operational risk management.

REFERENCES

FSA guidance on proper trades

- Securities and Investments Board *Guidance No 1/93: Proper Trades in Relation to On-Exchange Derivatives* (April 1993).
- FSA *Market Abuse* Consultation Paper 10 (June 1998)

FSA investigation of LME trades

- Securities and Investments Board *A Review of the London Metal Exchange* (December 1996).

FURTHER READING

- The Securities and Investments Board (FSA) *Stock Borrowing and Repo in UK Equities: Market Conduct* (October 1997).

5.7 MARKET CRASHES

5.7.1 Anatomy of crashes

Serious market disruption may not be an everyday phenomenon, but in one market or another something exceptional is likely to be happening all the time. Major worldwide crashes may not happen more than once a decade, but international linkages and speed of information flows mean that shocks transmit very easily from one marketplace to another, increasing the frequency as well as the reach of disruptive events. Firms need to manage exceptional swings in markets as well as more normal market conditions.

Market crashes might reasonably be categorised as operational risks because of the difficulty of taking pre-emptive action to control them. But you can be better prepared to handle a crash if you are affected by one if you have some understanding of their origins and the ways they are tackled by the authorities.

5.7.2 History lesson: the market crash of 1987

Various factors were blamed for the collapse of equity prices worldwide during October 1987. Distinguish two kinds of factor: those causing the crash and those which accelerated and spread it once it had started. Studies of the 1987 crash and the behaviour of markets in similar conditions suggest that there was no single cause of the 1987 crash.

- Possible causes An unsustainable speculative bubble in the booming market which preceded the crash; government policy effects; investor psychology.
- Possible aggravating factors Derivatives; computer-assisted trading; market structure and settlement mechanics; market closure.

Some of these are difficult to verify empirically, but some observations and conclusions emerge from the studies.

Observations

- Not all crashes follow bull runs.
- Downwards movement on prices does not always spread contagiously from one market to another.
- Economists' models of 'efficient markets' and 'non-efficient markets' do not explain the size of the market movement.
- Downward spirals infect markets across borders; local macroeconomic policy cannot be solely to blame for crashes.
- Noise trading is relevant to the spiralling effect. Traders trade more when volatility rises. When the trading floor is noisy, panic pricing prevails; reliable information as to what is 'at the market' is difficult to get. These things increase volatility.

Conclusions

- Crashes start with ordinary market influences, such as government policy changes, increases in interest rates, new economic data.
- Investor and trader psychology plays a major role. The mood of traders can be influenced by the policy of the exchange (not to mention things like the weather: the British hurricane of October 1987 occurred in the week before the crash, causing not only widespread damage but also the closure of the London Stock Exchange for a day). Default backing and willingness to ride out storms helps stabilise markets.

Other features of the market crash of 1987 included:

- **Market closure** The Hong Kong Futures Exchange closed for 10 days. The HKFE closure was needed at the outset because of the huge volume of uncompleted settlements which had built up. The closure did not prevent prices finding their level on reopening.
- **Default backing** The closure period was used by the HKFE to put in place HK$ 4 billion default backing. Thirty four members of the exchange failed to pay margin calls following the day of the crash and there was concern that the default could spread to other exchange participants. An increase to the default fund was needed to restore confidence.
- **Invoicing back** The exchange considered invoking its power to cancel all contracts. The decision was taken not to do so since the effect on those whose positions were hedges would have been severe.

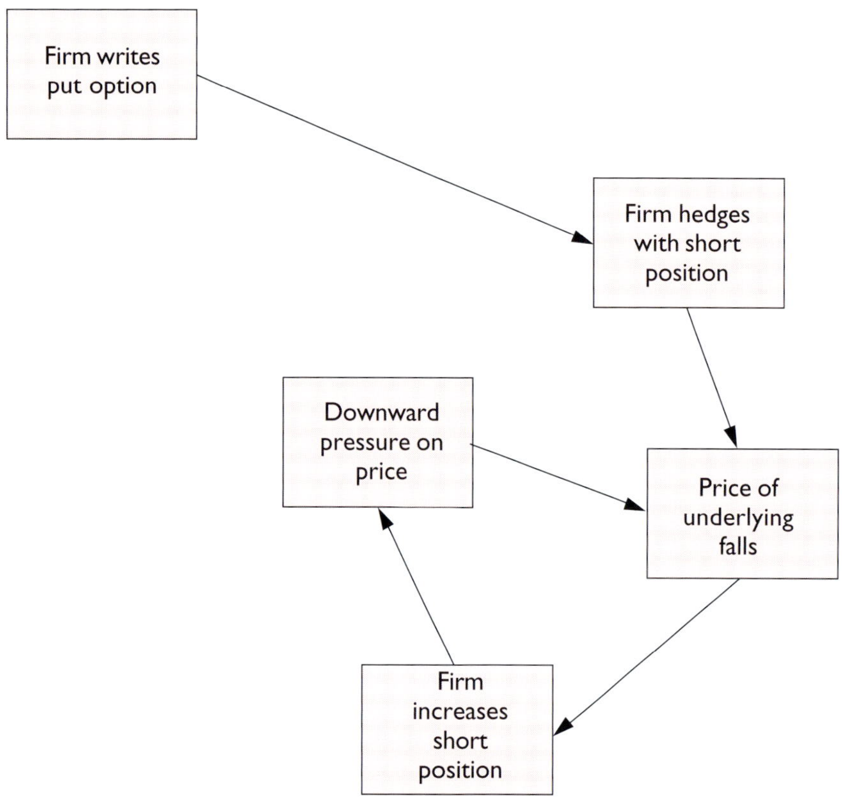

Feedback trading—downward price spiral

Hedging strategy can (according to theorists) lead to a vicious circle accelerating a market crash. If the effect of taking short positions depresses the price of the underlying, it may be necessary with a dynamic hedging strategy to keep shortening the position in order to maintain the hedge.

Circuit breakers

Cooling-off periods have been introduced by various exchanges—cessation of trading for specified periods if prices change by more than a given percentage in a short time. To the extent that crashes are attributable to panic these may be beneficial, but may lead to a backlog of unexecuted orders since investors will continue to relay instructions while trading is suspended. Circuit breakers also deny market participants the opportunity to hedge, impede price discovery and might be self-generating (in periods of high volatility, the market expects a hiatus, traders increase activity to compensate for the foreseen interruption, thereby exacerbating the problem).

5.7.3 Protection against market crashes

Management of extraordinary movements in market prices requires a more qualitative response than everyday market risk. Knowing what to expect depends on the quality of the stress-testing and scenario analysis conducted by the firm—that in turn depends on careful choice of exceptional market risk event situations for analysis. A survey by the Bank of England in 1997–98 indicated that banks improved their stress testing in response to the Asian market shocks of that period, which sounds like a case of the stable door being closed after the horse has escaped. The art of scenario analysis is to consider events which have not happened; stress testing by playing a re-run of a historical market risk event on your computer is only of limited help.

Risk management does not stop there. The firm needs to formulate a policy for managing risks outside the reach of models. Reaction to market shocks is more like crisis management than everyday risk control: if the risk event is outside the firm's own control, whether you emerge unscathed depends on your ability to react effectively. The nature of the risk event is less important than the smooth handling of the problem—see further section 4.4.

Knock-on effects

Counterparties may become vulnerable and may suffer liquidity or solvency problems which mean that their reliability is in question. This may have knock-on effects for the firm's own viability, just as for serious operational or credit risk events. Credit spreads may widen contrary to expectations. The firm may experience large exposures outside the usual limits. The ability to control these may depend on the liquidity of markets. Whether the strategy for management succeeds may depend on having more than one line of defence—contingency planning is vital.

Exchange powers

Understand the default backing of the exchange: know whether you can be 'assessed' for extra cash. Understand whether the exchange operates via a central counterparty or whether there is direct exposure to other market participants. Understand the right of the exchange to demand additional levels of margin and consider whether this could endanger your cash management. Understand the legal powers of the exchange to terminate contractual arrangements. Know whether the exchange can (and whether in practice it will) transfer defaulters' client positions to other exchange members.

Stress testing

Stress-test your positions against extreme price movements and envisage failure by key market participants.

5.8 LIQUIDITY RISK AND ITS MANAGEMENT

5.8.1 Liquidity in markets

This section is about market liquidity risk: the risk that the market has dried up, so you can't close out a loss-making position. Market risk is intricately linked to liquidity risk. My loss may multiply if I cannot close out my position: this worsens a market risk. Models assume certain levels of liquidity; if the assumptions are wrong, the losses may become threatening. In emerging markets liquidity problems may be acute.

All market positions require some assumptions of this type. You cannot close out a short position if you cannot enter into a long position or find a seller willing to part with the underlying asset. You cannot close out a long if you cannot enter into a short or find a buyer for the underlying asset. Even where cash settlement is allowed, some means of fixing the price for cash settlement is needed, which usually requires a basis in the physical market.

Liquidity issues also arise in relation to credit risk: where you have managed credit risk by taking collateral, your protection depends on the liquidity of the market in the collateral. Marking the position to market introduces one assumption about liquidity (the market in the investment); taking collateral another (the market in the collateral). See further section 7.5.5 as to market risk assumptions relating to collateral.

Wherever non-cash property is concerned, you may need to make assumptions as to the rapidity with which you can realise the property in order to manage your own liquidity position. Market liquidity is only a subspecies of this.

5.8.2 Control of liquidity risk

Position limits should be determined by reference to liquidity factors.

Assumptions as to the holding periods for particular instruments should be regularly reviewed in the light of changing market conditions. Where exceptional market conditions are experienced, more conservative parameters should be used.

Standby facilities may be arranged for non-cash assets of which the firm has frequent need, in the same way as standby loans are set up for cashflow needs. Usually a custodian is involved. The custodian will lend or repo out the needed securities or currency in return for the provision of collateral of some description. Repo and stocklending arrangements should be checked for legal effectiveness in the relevant jurisdictions (the considerations are similar to those for taking collateral by the outright transfer technique—see section 7.5.1). Similar arrangements in the commodities markets are less well developed in practice but are theoretically possible.

6

Control of operational risks

6.1 NATURE OF OPERATIONAL RISKS

6.1.1 Introduction

Everybody's definition of operational risk is different. Operational risk is the sweep-up category for everything else: so everybody's list of the most important operational risks vary. Any attempt to cover the subject exhaustively is bound to fail. Instead the approach here is to look at some general control strategies and to select for a more detailed review a few operational risks of common concern.

Dr Kubler-Ross says that there are five stages of dying: denial, anger, bargaining, depression and acceptance. Operational risks are a bit like this: eventually you have to accept that there is something there; it is made rather less painful if you cope with the five steps manfully.

Operational risk events are the cause of almost all recent failures of major financial institutions and almost all near-misses. Firms which do not run significant amounts of credit or market risk (such as fund managers) are susceptible to operational risk, sometimes of astounding magnitude. Yet operational risks are least susceptible to measurement and, for that reason, it is tempting not to have a fully fledged risk management strategy.

The components which can be found in many operational risks include:

- element of human error;
- no forewarning of the risk event.

This gives the clue to control of operational risks. Rather than measurement and setting limits, the emphasis is on identifying the risks and putting in place information systems which alert management to potential risk events. Personnel are of crucial importance. Unlike managing credit and market risks, you have to spend money to save money in operations: operations does not generate the income, so these funds have to be fought for.

Operational danger arises when change occurs. The Basle Committee identifies in particular changes associated with: new operating environments; new personnel; new IT systems; new or rapidly expanding business areas; new technology; new products; corporate reorganisation including mergers; and expanding overseas or acquiring overseas operations. If these are the danger areas, firms will be expected to have policies to meet them. Firms are expected to document their control procedures and produce the document for scrutiny by their regulator.

6.1.2 Black spots for operational risk

Operational risk events which are internally generated are often attributable to lack of controls. Control failures arise when your eye is off the ball—so establish failsafe devices which spring into action when eye and ball are parted. Look for things like new business lines, new geographical expansions, major corporate upheaval (restructuring or merger)—the business equivalents of marriage, birth of children, moving house and death which the psychologists tell us are the things which cause most upheaval in our real lives.

New products: Guidance from the SFA

This guidance relates to credit derivatives, but seems pretty good stuff generally:

'Among the factors which should be considered during the new product process are the following:

- whether the new business falls within the risk appetite of the firm, as established by the Board or equivalent management body;
- an exact description of the type of products to be introduced;
- accounting policies (which firms may wish to discuss with their external auditors);
- valuation methodology, and systems for ensuring that this policy is adhered to;
- authority and level of knowledge of risk managers and/or independent price-checkers;
- format and content of risk reports;
- limits, and systems for measuring and monitoring usage of those limits;
- type of documentation to be used and other legal risks;
- clearing and settlement procedures;
- adequacy of the firm's computer systems for representing the new transaction type(s);
- reliance on key staff;
- risks arising from the remuneration strategy.

Senior management should approve the procedures and controls and management at all levels must understand and enforce them.'

Case study—e-money

Many banks are establishing new ventures based on dematerialised banking—no branches, no people, no cheques, just electrons. The Basle Committee has published a formidable risk management paper warning of the danger areas and helpfully setting out possible risk mitigation strategies. There is a long list which includes guidance on each of these areas:

- unauthorised system access, inadequate customer security practices, employee fraud, security breach, customer privacy unprotected
- counterfeiting of e-money, forgery;
- service provider failure, system deficiencies, e-money issuer default or illiquidity;

- systems obsolescence, dinosaur staff;
- customer repudiation of transaction, borrower default;
- competitor institution suffers problem with similar product, linked Internet site problems;
- legal uncertainty, cross-border regulatory non-compliance, money laundering.

Of course many of these things will be relevant in existing business lines—particularly where the business is highly IT-dependent (see further below at section 6.5).

REFERENCES

Basle guidance on e-money

- Bank for International Settlements *Risk Management for Electronic Banking and Electronic Money Activities* (March 1998).

SFA guidance on new products

- SFA Board Notice 414 *Credit derivatives* (April 1997).

6.1.3 The operational process

Many operational risks arise out of one stage or other of the firm's ordinary business activity. Following the typical transaction through from start to finish and the relationships arising in it identifies various danger areas.

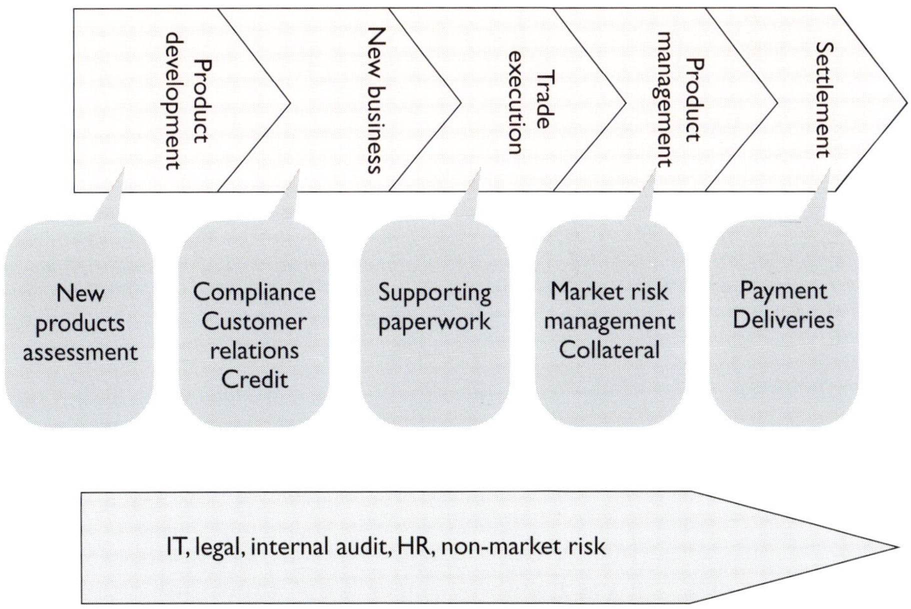

Operational risk from soup to nuts

Operational risks can arise at every step in the business process, from the moment the product is first thought of to the moment the last trade in the product is settled and the profits are banked.

- **Obtaining orders from the customer** Knowing your customer and giving satisfaction seem obvious. But customer dissatisfaction is a potent source of claims and litigation (pensions misselling, Gibsons Greetings) and reputational risk. This type of operational risk is considered at section 6.7.
- **Executing the orders** Keeping records of what was said and what was agreed may be important for error resolution. Trades may have to be matched. Transaction confirmations are of crucial importance. Evidential questions are considered at section 6.4.3.
- **Using the back office** Transactions rarely go straight to the out-basket once the order is placed. Documentation may be needed (see section 6.4.3). There may be margin and collateral to sort out. Settlement arrangements have to be made. The obligations of both parties have to be calculated and reconciled. Reports and statements may be needed. Deadlines may have to be met.
- **Settlement** Settlement risks are regarded by some as operational risks on the ground that the settlement system is outside the firm's control. Settlement risk is a species of credit risk and is therefore considered in section 7.8. However, note that insurers may be reluctant to underwrite the effectiveness of industry infrastructure: it is for the firms participating in settlement systems, as well as regulators, to press for improvements.

6.2 GENERAL STRATEGIES FOR CONTROLLING OPERATIONAL RISK

6.2.1 Control

Operational risks divide into those which the firm can control by effective internal management and staff discipline and those which it cannot. Different approaches may be needed for these two categories, though some risk management techniques (such as insurance) might be available for both. For every perceived operational risk an evaluation of the most effective (which includes the most cost-effective) technique to reduce the risk to an acceptable level.

Internal controls are what will generally be used to mitigate operational risks of internal origin. Even where coupled with some other type of risk management such as insurance, it is likely that the firm's controls will have to be well-developed: not only will the regulators require controls to be in place, but third party sellers of risk protection will also wish to conduct due diligence surveys of controls and their effectiveness.

Controls are considered in more detail in section 6.3.

6.2.2 Insurance

Insurance is one means of managing various types of operational risk, in particular risks of external origin over which the firm may have little control. Some firms shy away from purchasing insurance for risks which are within their control—there is perhaps something disreputable about suggesting that the risk is not fully controlled? Where the risk arises in the course of a business activity which is central to the firm's profitability, this feeling will be particularly strong. But everyone needs to recognise that some risks (in particular, perpetrators of fraud) will find a way round all controls. A second line of defence may be prudence rather than an admission of failure. Where one-off risks are involved, rather than recurrent risks, insurance can smooth the effect on the balance sheet.

On the other hand, insurance may not be the right answer. It may be better risk management to have a contingency plan as well as, or instead of, insurance. Bomb damage recovery is better done with immediate off-site back-up than a fat payout two years after the event. It is not possible to eliminate all business risk through insurance.

Legal considerations

There are peculiar legal issues with insurance policies:

- There is a duty to disclose everything to the insurer which the insurer could regard as relevant to the risk he is assuming. Failure to disclose results in an unenforceable policy. And the insurer will only start mentioning non-disclosures when he investigates a claim. Where group policies are concerned, who is responsible for disclosure and who has the information which ought to be disclosed?
- Unless special arrangements are made, insurers who pay up on liability insurance policies have the right to defend claims brought by third parties. This includes the right to fight or achieve a settlement regardless of the firm's wishes or the reputational cost involved.
- The insured is not saved from the obligation to mitigate losses if a risk event occurs. Only the loss which reasonably flowed from the event will be recoverable, so failure to mitigate will reduce the amount of the claim as well as complicate and delay the payout by the insurer. Insurance policies are not like performance bonds or letters of credit—there is no practice of immediate payment against documents in the insurance market.
- Where there is more than one policy covering the same loss:
  - both policies could be inapplicable, because of a term to that effect in each of them; and
  - if both insurers are liable there will be delay and a dispute as to which should pay.
- Policy wording is sometimes arcane, old-fashioned and inapplicable to the risks which you are trying to manage. Do not stand for any nonsense on this. If your broker says it's non-negotiable, find out why. In some cases there is industry guidance recommending best practice for insurers, which will be difficult to defeat; in other cases it's simply a case of old (and probably bad) legalese which nobody understands and nobody dares to change. You are not managing the risk if you are not sure whether you are covered.

Various common types of insurance policy bought by financial sector firms include the following. Comprehensive policies are becoming available, covering all the above areas and including areas of risk previously not thought readily insurable such as losses due to unauthorised trading.

- **Banker's blanket bonds** Covering losses due to employee dishonesty, loss or damage to tangible property (but not electronically recorded data or cash at another bank), losses due to forgery of documents purporting to be issued by the firm or reliance on forged documents purporting to be issued by someone else, losses due to receipt of counterfeit currency and malicious damage to buildings and contents. For the (in)applicability of this type of policy to rogue traders, see section 6.6.2.
- **D&O cover** Covering losses sustained by directors and officers of the firm in respect of breaches of contract, trust, or other duties. The firm may also be indemnified in respect of taking action against directors and officers.

- **PI cover** Covering losses and liabilities caused by the firm as a result of its negligence. The firm is usually at risk of losing this cover if it makes admission of liability without the consent of the insurer.
- **Computer cover** Covering damage to equipment and loss of data. The policy may go no further (eg breakdowns may be excluded) and may stop short of paying out in respect of consequential losses arising from downtime—such as lost business or third party claims.

Exclusions from policies can cover a wide range of issues but ones to look out for include: losses caused by fraud or malice; personal injury and death; fines; remuneration claims; deliberate breaches of contract by the firm; lost or damaged property; advice; loss in value of investments; and insolvency of the firm or counterparties. Other limitations of scope to be noted are:

- It is now standard practice to exclude from an insurance policy any liability relating to year 2000 problems suffered by the insured. Older policies may not contain current wording and may continue to apply even though the loss does not appear until years later.
- Bespoke policies covering breaches of security, what your employees send to customers over the Internet, downtime and so forth will be more expensive.
- Insurance brokers are rarely lawyers: if your broker tells you you're covered, check with the legal department anyway. You aren't relying on the broker as your insurer even if you can sue him for getting it wrong.

Finally, remember that insurance is credit risk. Investment banks are offering products which perform economically in a similar way to insurance. In those cases there would be no question about assessing the credit status of the counterparty. Insurers should be treated similarly; where a Lloyd's policy is involved, the availability of Lloyd's default backing should be checked. Likewise consider whether any credit risk on the *broker* is involved—to whom are the premiums paid and through whom are claims submitted and paid?

6.2.3 Outsourcing

Where a firm feels a need for greater expertise in an area, or feels that personnel and costs can be better controlled that way, it may be appropriate to have some third party manage that function on the firm's behalf. Outsourcing may bring cost savings too and thus become relevant for functions closer to the core of the firm's business. Outsourcing involves a surrender of control.

Regulatory requirements

The FSA has published guidance on outsourcing which includes the following requirements for banks. These rules apply even where the supplier is another company within the bank's group. The guidance will be of relevance to non-bank firms too.

- The integrity of systems and controls must be maintained.
- The FSA and auditors must have access to information and if the supplier is overseas, there must be no legal impediment to access.
- Notification to the FSA must take place if a bank intends to outsource a task which materially affects its business or impacts on its systems and controls; if the agreement with the supplier includes penalties for termination; or if the bank's internal or external auditors find problems with the supplier.

- The internal audit function may not be outsourced.
- Sub-sub-contracting is rarely acceptable unless the sub-sub-contracted function is not material to the bank's business or its custodianship.
- The supplier should be competent and financially sound and have good relevant knowledge and expertise.
- Contingency planning should cater for failure of the supplier, termination of the agreement with the supplier and non-performance on the part of the supplier.

Where functions are outsourced which would, if carried on by the firm itself, require the responsible employees to become 'approved persons' (see section 2.5.2), it may additionally be necessary for the employees of the supplier to be 'approved'.

Service level agreements

The agreement with the supplier is obviously crucial. Supply and service level contracts require specialist input. The objective is to allocate the risks fairly between the parties. Such agreements are useful to transfer some risks (convert them into credit risk on the supplier) but will rarely be a complete substitute for other forms of risk management such as insurance and internal controls. The FSA's guidance contains additional requirements:

- The bank must oversee the supplier, monitor the supplier's performance against targets and exercise remedies.
- The supplier must adhere to the bank's customer relations policies where the supplier liaises direct with the bank's customers.
- Appointments by the supplier of staff to key positions should be monitored as they may constitute notifiable appointments for the regulatory purposes of the bank.
- The *supplier's* external auditor should be familiar with the supervisory requirements.
- Termination arrangements should be carefully considered: the bank will wish to retain the benefit of work done before termination and other rights which ensure that termination does not disrupt the bank's business. If the supplier is acquired by a competitor of the bank, the bank should have the right to terminate.
- Where the supplier services more than one financial institution, there need to be procedures such as Chinese walls to ensure that there is no leakage of data from one institution to another.

Other issues which a service level agreement might cover include: functionality, responsibility for specifying the requirements against which the system has been built, response times, operational hours, permitted downtime, maintenance provision (including response times), error tolerance, resilience of the system to change such as increases in volumes or disasters, changing the services or the system and consequences of service level breaches or system failure (including restart times). This is not an exhaustive list and specialist legal advice will be appropriate where a major new system is being commissioned. In addition, the obvious matters such as price, ownership, payment, start and end dates and other boilerplate issues will have to be considered.

6.2.4 Automation

Since operational risks are frequently based in human failings, automation can be a solution. Automation is substitution of one type of operational risk (human error) with another (IT systems dependency). Automation can be costly, may require recruitment of additional specialist staff and can make control arrangements and monitoring more opaque. As to IT-related risks generally, see section 6.5.

Software products are becoming available which can assist with more and more functions. Checking and monitoring can be done automatically. Confirmations can be generated automatically. Transaction status reports and settlement failure analysis can be done automatically. But most of these arrangements are bolt-ons to systems which are already managing market and credit risks. And there is no machine which can perform the intelligent senior management double-check which involves intuition and experience which the programmer does not possess.

Fewer products are available to tackle operational risks other than human error. Low-frequency operational risks are virtually impossible to eliminate through automation. However, there are some areas in which software solutions may be of assistance. Systems status can be checked and reported on automatically. Operational risk management is largely front-loaded: once you are aware of the risk, you can decide how to control it. So the art is in knowing where the risks lie. But computerised products are there primarily to answer questions, not to ask them. Intelligent systems which appear to ask questions about operational risks and lead the respondent through a maze of assistance depend on the product designer's understanding of the firm's operations: the questions will have been pre-loaded into the machine. In theory a product designer could have greater experience than the firm in handling operational risks, so could provide expert advice. But often the firm is better placed to understand its own operations than any outsider and these products will add value by stimulating thinking about areas of risk not yet discovered by the firm, rather than supplanting a firm's own imaginative thinking.

Straight-through processing

Cutting out the errors associated with re-keying the same data and the risk of it being doctored deliberately, must be a good thing. Some of the issues will be the same as ordinary ones relating to use of correspondents and agents (think, for example, of customers' use of money-machines belonging to other banks via link arrangements). But:

- Can STP work for the kinds of product you use? Bespoke OTC derivatives will not fit comfortably into a system which is designed for voluminous repeat business (eg securities buys and sells).
- Note the cascade effect of a single keying error: one error affects the whole process and feeds into many other records and systems. Is the mistake irretrievable?
- Cutting out the middle-man cuts out a line of defence: who checks that the trades smell right, where is the segregation of duties?
- Who is the counterparty and who is liable if the data inputted are duff?
- Increasing the dependency on IT systems brings in all the IT-related risks.
- Does STP make someone who was a counterparty into an agent—has he just become a mere piece of pipework?
- Does the STP mean that the contract is entered into at a different time, with compliance (eg sending confirms) and legal (eg interest period) consequences?
- Does an intermediary's altered role mean that your own role is different—for example, you can no longer rely on the intermediary to check the status of the counterparty or to comply with money laundering and other know-your-customer rules, etc (see section 6.7), or

you can no longer rely on dealing through the intermediary to insulate you from local licensing or other regulatory requirements?

- Consider whether other risks are exacerbated: legal risks related to contract formation; agency risks, particularly with regard to allocation of bulk-bought positions (see section 8.3.1); ownership of intellectual property; which jurisdictions are relevant for regulatory and counterparty assessment purposes (see section 2.2.4).

Bear in mind also that exchanges may impose rules relating to STP, where the effect of the proposed arrangements is to give direct access to an organised investment exchange in circumstances where the exchange would expect to have control over the behaviour of all those directly using the market. The Forum of European Securities Commissions (FESCO) has issued, as a consultation draft, standards for regulated markets which address this point: direct-access arrangements should ensure adequate protection to the market, that the allocation of responsibilities between access provider and customer is clear and that there are safeguards to allow detection of abnormal orders and prevention of orders which would breach credit or position limits. Access providers must remain responsible for orders which are entered into the market from the member's computer system.

In this context, also consider:

- whether your firm is exonerated from compliance (or subjected to greater burdens of compliance) where orders are directly placed by customers;
- whether the customer is relying on your firm to check the suitability and accuracy (eg lack of craziness in price) of a directly placed order;
- whether the customer can get your firm into trouble for market abuse (see section 5.6);
- whether indirect access jeopardises your firm's regulatory status;
- whether the arrangements are secure, how instructions can or should be validated and how any encryption arrangements might be implemented;
- what effects computer or transmission line failure have on the contract formation process and who takes responsibility for the consequences (eg failed order-cancellation).

6.2.5 Contingency planning

Some operational risks are not only outside the scope of controls but are unpredictable. Some operational risk events arise despite state-of-the-art controls and reporting systems. Firms need to be prepared to contemplate that something will slip past the defences and cause a serious problem. Risk management becomes a question of restoring the firm to business as usual in the shortest possible time frame with minimum disruption. The general principles applicable to major unforeseen risk events are considered in section 4.4.

REFERENCES

FSA guidance on outsourcing

– FSA *Guide to Banking Supervisory Policy*, Chapter OS.

FESCO guidance on access to markets

– Forum of European Securities Commissions *Consultation Paper on Regulated Markets* (July 1999).

FURTHER READING

- British Bankers Association *Operational Risk—An Industry Discussion Paper* (April 1999).
- International Swaps and Derivatives Association Inc *Derivatives Settlement* (1998).

6.3 INTERNAL CONTROLS

6.3.1 Structure of control systems

Nowadays there are huge manuals devoted to establishment and maintenance of internal controls. The main features of these are summarised at section 4.2 because they are relevant, not just in the sphere of operational risk, but in relation to every species of risk. For operational risks with internal origins, however, these controls form the first line of defence against risk events. If they fail and there is no other risk defence in place, risk management becomes an issue of containment rather than avoidance.

Error reporting is a crucial element. Breaches of limits and discipline are only part of the reason. Minor errors often betray a more fundamental problem. Nick Leeson hid his losses in an unreviewed error account which should have had a zero balance. Customer complaints, if analysed, might reveal a trend showing up operational failings. Valuation disputes may mean a pricing defect or a failing in documentation arrangements. Times and dates can be as important as parties and amounts. And don't forget that positive deviations from expectations (things turning out much better than predicted) may conceal a nasty shock.

Much of the guidance talks about a 'control culture'. This is more than using the right psychospeak—it means practical action. So: actions as well as words, such as factoring in control compliance into remuneration arrangements and promotion; ensuring that reporting and accountability lines are clear; supervising the decision-makers; having smooth information flows; follow up the reports of internal auditors; and ensuring that failsafe management mechanisms are in place. If risk self-assessment is used (see section 3.4) is there a penalty for discovering problems? Some banks penalise problems discovered by internal audit which should have been identified during self-assessment (but watch the dangers of internal audit being categorised as the enemy).

And of course there is a danger of overkill. Having some sort of control for everything may make the system too cumbersome and may create a culture where people fear to innovate or to take any decision because of the bureaucracy that accompanies anything new. At worst, the firm stagnates, becomes risk-averse and unprofitable.

How to control your business

Six steps to being a controls freak

- Know the business.
- Specify staff duties.
- Impose reporting lines.
- Check up on everything (challenge the assertion 'it's done, so it's done right').
- Separate the checkers from the doers.
- Follow up exceptions.

6.3.2 Regulatory guidance on controls

The Basle Committee and IOSCO guidance on internal control systems (see section 4.2.2) mentions that control activities should include the following:

- top level reviews;
- activity restrictions in different divisions of the organisation;
- setting quantitative exposure limits;
- books and records requirements;
- physical controls (eg secure arrangements for cash, title documents, other records etc);
- documentation standards;
- approvals and authorisations procedures;
- monitoring procedures;
- verification, valuation, reconciliation, checking for compliance.

Policies and procedure to implement these activities will typically include:

- designating lines of authority in risk management, including assigning responsibility for compliance;
- ensuring risk management and control staff have appropriate expertise while remaining independent of risk-generating activities;
- having effective internal accounting controls and audit procedures;
- validating models used for measurement of risk, fixing of prices etc, including stress-testing and sensitivity analysis;
- determining contingency plans;
- reviewing new products and business activities;
- verifying data: by audit, but not exclusively; by testing, but not exclusively;
- reporting exceptions and breakdowns of controls;
- rotation of audit personnel;
- reviewing controls periodically to keep pace with developments in business and technology.

Specific guidance for controls in banks (which will be helpful to other types of financial sector firm) has been given in the UK by the FSA in the RATE paper, discussed at section 2.4.1. The paper gives detailed lists of matters to consider under various headings, which include controls, organisation and management.

Controls, organisation and management—the FSA view

The FSA's RATE paper (which sets out risk-based principles for supervision of banks) lists various factors to be considered under these headings:

Controls

- Decision-making framework.
- Risk management framework.
- Limits and standards.
- Information technology.
- Financial and management reporting.
- Staff policies.
- Segregation of responsibilities.
- Audit and compliance functions.
- Money laundering controls.

Organisation

- Legal structure.
- Relationship with other parts of the group.
- Reporting lines.

Management

- Four eyes (ie at least two individuals to be involved in all significant decisions).
- Fitness and propriety.
- Board composition.
- Non-executive directors.
- Cultural attitude.
- Corporate planning and strategy.

6.3.3 Segregation of duties

All the guidance, all the time, gives top priority to one thing: segregation of duties between the trading function and the internal control and risk management function.

Examples of segregations which should take place are:

- front v back office control;
- approval of disbursement v drawing of funds;
- utilisation of customer v proprietary accounts;
- transacting in banking v trading books;
- selling v providing position information to customers;
- reviewing documentation v counterparty credit monitoring.

Senior management are in a difficult position here. As they have to oversee everything they tend to straddle the segregational boundaries. And, worse, because of their seniority, they may be relatively immune from challenge by risk management staff. This leaves a particular risk of imprudent practices (or even fraud) developing among senior staff. Firms should consider how to put in place failsafe structures to enable junior staff with suspicions to voice concerns without fear of jeopardising their positions.

6.3.4 Anatomy of failure

The Basle Committee groups control breakdowns which bank supervisors who participate in the committee have seen into five categories:

- Inadequate management oversight and accountability; failure to develop a strong control culture within the organisation; bad relationship between reporting lines and corporate governance.
- Inadequate assessment of risk of certain activities.
- Inadequate adherence to basic control precepts: segregation of duties, approvals, verifications, reviews of performance.
- Inadequate information flow upwards to senior management.
- Inadequate audit and monitoring.

6.3.5 Physical controls

Physical controls have been around so long that it is obvious that everyone knows how to operate them. But increasing dependency on electronic systems means that this expertise is diminishing. Regulatory guidance provides a useful checklist—this, which relates to IT systems, comes from the SFA:

Physical risks to hardware include fire, flood, theft, electrical storms, sabotage and accidental damage. To minimise these risks:

- Standard fire regulations should be observed.
- Temperature, humidity and dust should be properly controlled.
- Systems should be protected from power surges with an uninterruptable power supply or line filter.
- Doors to computer rooms should be locked or protected by a card swipe/pin system and keys, cards or codes should be given only to authorised persons.
- A burglar alarm should be installed.
- Portable PCs should be locked away at night or secured to desks.
- Confidential data on portable PCs should be encrypted.
- An asset register of all equipment should be kept and should include the make, model and serial number.
- All hardware should be fully insured.
- There should be a disaster recovery plan in place to cope with these eventualities. It should be tested regularly.

REFERENCES

Basle and IOSCO guidance on controls

- Bank for International Settlements *Risk Management Guidelines for Derivatives* (July 1994).
- IOSCO *Risk Management and Control—Guidance for Securities Firms and their Supervisors* (March 1998).

RATE paper

- FSA *Risk Based Approach to Supervision of Banks* (June 1998).

6.4 MANAGEMENT INFORMATION SYSTEMS

6.4.1 Why MIS are important

An essential part of control is knowing what is going on. But information flows need to be rather more extensive than routine reporting. There are three aspects: understanding the business at a strategic level and the sources of operational risk in it, in order to generate the right sort of reports; reporting on the business being conducted; and evaluating the reports, identifying exceptions and taking action. There is a tension between gathering 'interesting' data (which is too bulky to read and interpret) and 'relevant' data (which, because it has been sifted down to the bare minimum, may omit unusual matters which could allow emerging risks to be identified). The data are no use at all if they are not interpreted by someone: file and forget is just a waste of resources.

Identifying novel sources of risk requires a risk culture of the sort the regulators seek to foster. You can't lay down office procedures which require all staff to think up five new sources of risk before breakfast. Imagination plays a key role here; but so does re-examining your previous thinking, challenging the assumptions, double-checking what you know to be incontrovertibly reliable information. Moving staff around, particularly those who are not afraid to ask the questions which are in everybody's mind, is one way of tackling this.

Staffing policy has a major role in a control system. Pitfalls include rewarding risky behaviour, employing temporary staff who may not have the same ties of loyalty as permanent staff, outsourcing key processes where controls ought to be retained in-house and so forth.

Information systems are of two types: human and electronic. Neither can be exclusive of the other. Management needs to understand what is going on and human contact is an important part of that.

6.4.2 Record-keeping—regulatory guidelines

The FSA's guidance on records and internal control systems highlights numerous issues. What follows are some of the headlines.

- Records should:
  - capture the nature of transactions and assets, income and expenditure arising from them;
  - provide details of parties, amounts, dates, locations, rates, fees, security and priority of entitlements;

- allow identification, quantification and management of exposures;
- allow monitoring of assets and performance of the business;
- detail exposure limits;
- state when transactions are entered into on behalf of others (eg agency or fiduciary arrangements).

- Records should include:
  - strategic and financial plans and budget;
  - procedures and controls manuals;
  - correspondence files, internal memos and minutes of meetings;
  - registers of authorised signatories etc;
  - deal tickets, confirms, vouchers, loan files and other transaction documentation;
  - asset registers;
  - suppliers' invoices;
  - tape recordings of dealers' telephone conversations.

- Information should be retrievable from the records in order to:
  - show the health and results of the business;
  - analyse assets and liabilities (including valuation) and off-balance-sheet positions;
  - analyse cash flow;
  - produce a sensitivity analysis relating to changes in (for example) exchange and interest rates, market prices, etc;
  - allow trend analysis.

- Control systems need to control assets coming into the firm, assets leaving the firm, assets held by the firm, entering into obligations by the firm and the continuing liabilities of the firm.

- Control systems are to ensure:
  - the business is prudently planned and carried out;
  - transactions are entered into when authorised;
  - assets are safeguarded and liabilities controlled; losses from irregularities are minimised and identified when they occur;
  - accounting records are complete, accurate and timely;
  - capital adequacy, liquidity, profitability and asset quality can be regularly and timeously monitored;
  - risks of loss can be identified, assessed, quantified, monitored, controlled and provided for;
  - regulatory returns can be produced.

Monitoring procedures, which are crucial where operational risks are concerned, should include:

- regular review of reports showing exposures against limits;
- procedures for identifying, reporting and resolving breaches of controls and limit excesses;

- getting the data in more than one way, carrying out reconciliations and investigating the anomalies;
- procedures for monitoring staff behaviour at critical points in the business process, eg transaction initiation and settlement, data entry into reporting systems, etc;
- regular reviews of risks particularly expected for the type of business: so, for example, banks will be exposed to liquidity risks if depositor behaviour changes and to solvency risks if loans become problematic.

6.4.3 Evidence, lies and audiotape

Evidential rules

In general, hearsay evidence ('well Aunty Gladys said Uncle Eddie did it, so it must be true') used to be inadmissible. Curiously, English court procedure categorises all sorts of things as hearsay, such as documents which suggest that Uncle Eddie did it. But there are now so many exceptions to the hearsay evidence rule that most useful information can be got in front of the court somehow. So, regardless of whether the evidence is a handwritten note, a formal written contract, an order slip, a tape-recording of a phone call, a security videotape of dealing-room behaviour, an e-mail, a computer record on disk, an intranet posting or an electronic scribble on a bulletin-board, it may be valuable and it may be put in evidence. The rules differ between different types of proceeding and the weight given by the court to hearsay evidence may be very low.

Once the material is before the court it must be shown to be authentic. With electronic records proving authenticity can be burdensome. It is probably worth having some procedure for rendering copies of electronic records into paper form and having sensible individuals appointed to oversee the process, so that they can prove authenticity if needed without undue hassle.

For discovery and privilege, see section 6.8.4.

Documentation practices

A report from the Basle Committee on practices in the OTC derivatives markets highlights a number of operational deficiencies relating to documentation. Some of the issues apply equally validly in other business areas. Data capture is an essential part of management information supply and where data capture and documentation practices are linked (as they should be, at least at the level of reconciliation), management may be fed a misleading picture if documentation lags behind.

- Master agreements Failure to agree (and sign, as evidence of agreement including approval at the appropriate level of authority) master agreements may distort the firm's exposure to counterparties, since netting may not be effective without an agreement. Including words such as 'subject to the terms of the ISDA master agreement' in a confirmation gives some legal protection, but not much. Agreeing some, but not all, of the terms may not be good enough: for example, failure to agree the parts of an ISDA schedule which require an election between alternatives to be made may leave the agreement unenforceable under a relevant legal system.
- Confirmations Failure to confirm may, in some legal systems, mean that there is no enforceable agreement. Written confirmations may therefore be of more than evidential value. But evidence is useful even if tedious to compile. Written confirmations and automatic matching systems also help the control process, enabling errors and limit breaches to be detected. Quantitative measures of exposures and risks are no more reliable than the records on which they are based. Disputed confirmations can lead to mis-reporting or even non-reporting.

Other documentation matters to consider are:

- whether a 'perfect' hedge is based on differing documentation, giving different rights—this can be particularly important in relation to credit derivatives, where 'standard' sets of default terms are hard to come by and (even if they exist) may not cater for special default circumstances which are peculiar to the reference entity;
- whether 'old faithful' language is being relied on, notwithstanding that it is obscure, outmoded and probably ill-suited to modern circumstances;
- whether 'legal sign-off' is being relied on as an excuse for not reading the documents—if the lawyers were briefed wrongly, or the documents were produced for a special deal, then the wording probably does not work;
- relying on the documentation team to fill in the missing commercial terms, because the traders did not consider the issues at the time of doing the deal—it is better to involve the legal team up front, rather than reach a half-agreement 'subject to documentation'.

And of course all this assumes that the draftsman gets the legalese right.

Taping

Tapes are no different from papers in that there should be a policy for retention and destruction of records. There are some additional considerations:

- Where recording takes place through a firm's internal switchboard and network, information that recording will occur should generally be given to all parties to the call.
- The EU ISDN Directive may be implemented in such a way as to require consent of participants to listening or storage of communications and even to allow recorded persons to listen to and copy the recording.
- There is FSA guidance on tape retention in the London Code of Conduct which applies to firms trading in the wholesale money markets. Taping is strongly recommended; tapes should be kept for at least two months and preferably longer; if there is a dispute the relevant tape should be retained until the problem has been resolved. Management should ensure that tape storage is free from the risk of tampering. The SFA is less prescriptive but reminds firms that, because tapes are recycled, traditional documentation which is sound and legally enforceable is the primary defence. Defects in documentation can only rarely be cured by reference to tape-recordings.

REFERENCES

FSA guidance on records and control systems

– FSA *Guide to Banking Supervisory Policy* Chapter R2, s 4.2.

Basle guidance on OTC documentation practices

– Bank for International Settlements *OTC Derivatives: Settlement Procedures and Counterparty Risk Management* (September 1998).

FSA guidance on taping

– FSA *London Code of Conduct* paras 48–49.

6.5 IT SYSTEMS RISK

6.5.1 IT risks

IT systems are a critical component of all firms and are a fruitful source of operational risk. Risks include:

- design and acceptance testing error;
- inadequate functionality and compatibility;
- bugs;
- systems and power supply failure;
- communications network downtime;
- abuse and security breaches;
- impermanence of electronic records;
- audit trail deficiencies;
- teleworking and remote access circumventing visual and other human controls.

The risks associated with IT systems can be deeply rooted and recurrent.

- **Technical staff** Only a few staff understand the system, who tend not to be the people responsible for the core business. The technology rescue team may have access to both front- and back-office systems. The technology team are best equipped to identify and exploit flaws in the accounting and control systems and perpetrate frauds. And who carries out the essential double-checking—if it is left to the IT systems staff, will the independence of controls be compromised?
- **Dinosaurs** Senior staff, being older, are threatened by computers, don't have them on their desks, don't understand the issues. But these are the people ultimately responsible for risk management.
- **Dependency** If the system fails, so does the business. But the system is often provided by outside suppliers of hardware and software. The firm is not in control of its own destiny. Even if in-house products are used, how is the firm satisfied that they have been properly tested? Who has the expertise to sign off? What recourse is there if things do go wrong?
- **Internet** Security breaches can be done from afar by hackers; staff can download unsuitable materials at their office terminals; staff can use terminals provided by the institution to carry out fraudulent or improper activities; sacked staff can engage in piracy and wrecking on their way out.

6.5.2 Management of IT risks

Since the array of IT risks is itself so diverse there is no single risk management solution. Human resources strategy and controls will play an important role. Not allowing IT systems to fog up lines of accountability (eg by automating them out of existence) or to abolish monitoring is obviously important.

For new systems, acceptance testing is the first line of defence. Do not rely on legal remedies such as statutory protection given in the Sale of Goods Act. This was first written in 1893 and its provisions are unlikely to give the kind of sophistication needed for modern equipment and software. Make sure that your lawyers understand your IT department's needs and main fears about the new system. Make sure that your tests are designed to fit your firm's requirements, rather than an external consultant's preconceptions. Make sure that the tests provide measurable results which can then be assessed against a benchmark, so you know whether the system is up to scratch. And don't pay the full price (or take some sort of protection) until you are completely satisfied.

Contingency planning has a role. Back-up systems, procedures for managing glitches and downtime and for changeover to new systems (including backcapture of old data) all need to be planned.

Other approaches to risk management, such as insurance, may also be appropriate. Note the points at section 6.2.2 about IT-related insurance cover; and see the Basle Committee guidance on risk management for e-money referred to at section 6.1.2.

6.5.3 Valuation and pricing

Numerous instances have come to light recently of sizeable losses being sustained by institutions because of mis-pricing or mis-valuation. Sometimes the defect is attributable to mis-calibration of models. For more on models, see section 3.2.2.

Evaluation of pricing models should be done by someone independent of the person selling the product. The assumptions underlying the model need to be identified and challenged. Nor is it sufficient to have one mathematician check the work of another. People from a different discipline within the organisation are better placed to bring an objective view, a different perspective which will flush out any false ideas.

Dual authorisation is often advisable. New products usually require sign-off by a team of different disciplines: compliance, legal, credit, finance, etc. Some degree of flexibility is needed though or you will never do any new business. Make the policy on the degree of caution expected of each person involved explicit, so there is no carping along the lines of 'credit are always too keen to stifle new business' or 'legal are too uncommercial'. See further section 4.3.2.

And in case something does go wrong, the transaction can be structured so as to provide early warning of a problem. Collateral arrangements are helpful here because they provide regular opportunities to assess the cost of the transaction: marking the trade to market may reveal the error earlier than otherwise because there will be a dispute over its valuation. Clauses in agreements which allow for early termination without fault on either side may be appropriate where the risks are difficult to assess.

6.5.4 Relationships with other parties

Counterparty relationships are increasingly important in IT. Data and other material come from sources outside the firm. Some of this material is crucial for the firm's operations. Yet the electronic nature of this material means that there is often little documentation constituting an agreement as to who is responsible (a) for the reliability and accuracy of the material and (b) for the material not damaging or contaminating your own systems. The general law is not much help in this area either, since the technology is new and relevant case law often takes decades to build up. Part of the risk manager's job is to see whether these risks cannot be managed by clear agreements with those persons with whom data is exchanged.

6.5.5 Security

Security is a key risk with IT systems. Is your system safe from manipulation? Can your system tell you if data have been manipulated (unlike paper records and inkblots, one electron is pretty much the same as another)? Can the system be put at risk accidentally—for example, by switching unexpectedly from training to trading mode as reportedly happened in one case causing a significant loss? Is the system at risk when disaffected employees leave the firm—theft of data or sabotage may occur—a risk management strategy may have to be built together with the human resources department. Where the system records ownership of property or other entitlements (such as what is owed by the firm), particular security precautions may be appropriate.

Precautions include password protection, virus-elimination software, review of what gets accessed by whom, restricting people's ability to input data without a second person's sign-off, encoding data (particularly when transmitted outside the firm), keeping records of users who obtained access (though note the problems of identification when someone logs on as somebody else). Security consultants are available though (of course) expensive.

6.5.6 Internet risks

The Internet is international, gives instant access to potential customers, has wide spread, is cheap, allows dialogue and can enable downloading of vast amounts of material. But these features, particularly its openness and accessibility, create operational risks. Some are highlighted in this section. Others which are relevant include straight-through processing (see section 6.2.4), regulation (see section 2.2.4), legal risks (see section 9.4.3) and crisis management (see section 4.4). Some (but not all) of the risks can be contained by legal drafting.

Why is the Internet different?

Actually, it isn't. It's the same issues. Some of them are written in larger print. The ones to think about depend on the focus of your business area, but these will usually be relevant in the financial sector:

- Cross-border reach This means the 'which jurisdictions are relevant?' questions become more important than usual; in particular consider which jurisdictions are relevant for:
  - regulatory issues;
  - legally effective contracts and disclaimers;
  - establishment and carrying on business;
  - taxation.
- Distance selling The rules on remote contracting are relevant.
- Telecommunications E-commerce of any description has its special pitfalls.
- Security Everyone knows the Internet is far too insecure—but so is the phone and so is face-to-face dealing; although the way the risks manifest themselves is different, the problems are the same. One area where special rules apply is encryption.
- Contracts When your contract was concluded and strange implied terms can be important and are problematic over the net (see section 9.4.3).

Distance selling

The EU Distance Selling Directive for consumer financial services is likely to lead to legislation to the following ends:

- the consumer needs time for reflection after the deal is closed;
- the consumer needs to be allowed to withdraw from the deal (cooling off);
- the consumer needs to be sent a hard copy of the terms of the deal;
- the consumer needs compensation if the service is unavailable;
- the consumer needs protection from cold-calling.

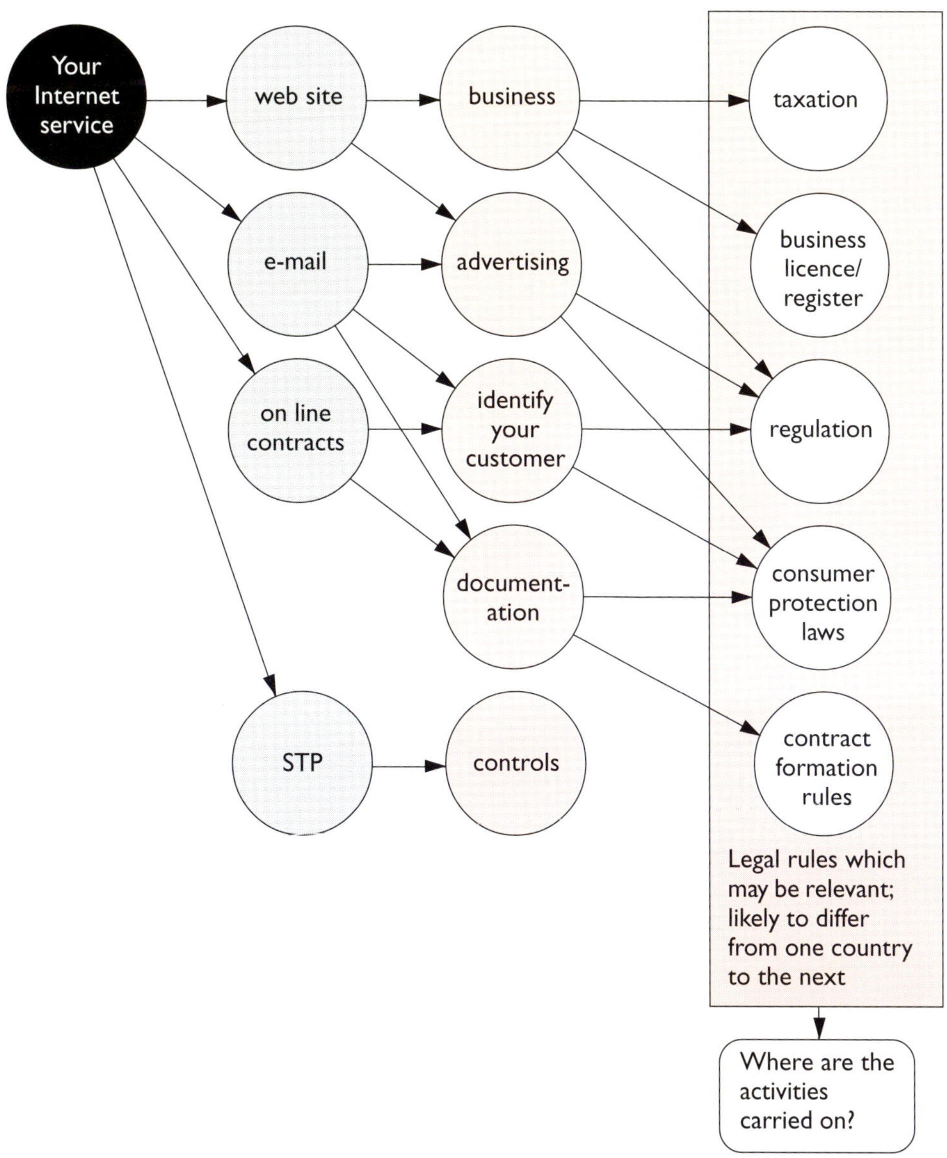

Mysteries of the Internet

If you are offering an Internet service vast numbers of legal rules can potentially apply. These will usually stem from the types of activity which are involved in the service which is proposed. Unfortunately, the legal rules will differ in each jurisdiction, so it is necessary to work out in which countries the activities will take place in order to check up on the legal rules which are relevant.

Hidden Internet risks

Some of the less obvious control and risk issues are listed below:

- **Orderly markets** Buying and selling via a bulletin board is easy but does not imply any level of investor (or market participant) protection. So, there could be no investor compensation; no regulation; no guarantee of contract conformity or proper prices; no minimum level of liquidity, etc, regardless of the apparent respectability of the platform provider. And the platform provider might (in each jurisdiction which regards itself as relevant for these purposes) be acting perfectly properly in providing the facilities it does.
- **Encryption** The law is fiendish in its complexity (and absurdity) because of the overlap with national security (keeping secrets hidden from the enemy). Some secure products may not be used.
- **Email and electronic records** Are they tamper-proof and are paperwork preservation procedures being followed?
- **Distance selling** What special laws apply (provision of information, right of withdrawal, etc) and do they apply to intermediaries as well as contracting parties?
- **Data protection** Are additional data protection registrations needed because data is being gathered?
- **Telecommunications** Do any telecommunications and broadcasting laws apply?
- **Intellectual property** How do copyright rules apply to downloaded materials; can trademarks and other valuable rights be purloined from your website; how can you protect your right to use a website domain name?

Crimes, wrongdoing and other Sunday-afternoon pastimes

Firms can be victims as well as perpetrators of Internet-based wrongs. As to being a victim, Internet risk management is primarily a question of taking steps against foreseen risks. Much of the current emphasis is on Fort Knox style self-protection rather than (as with, say, other risks of fraud) a public policy approach which relies on the law to deter bad behaviour. But security is expensive and complex.

Needless to say, the criminal law is miles behind. The law of theft was brought up to date in 1978—the previous legislation dated principally from 1861. Offences tend to be based on nebulous concepts like fraud and on Victorian values (ie tangible property). The criminal law is still struggling with theft from bank accounts, treating them as if they were bags of gold (try applying the concept of 'property belonging to another' to intangible things like rights against a bank or a bond issuer). There are gaps in the law which mean that things like hacking, spamming, malicious deletion of data and divulging cryptographic secrets might fall outside the scope of the criminal law. Then there is a second order of nasty activities like website tampering and junk email, which might fall short of people's notion of crimes, but might be expected to give rise to civil actions for damages, but may not do so.

Criminal law is territorial in scope. Some countries, like England, require to have some part of the offence (unless it is one of a very few exceptions like murder and piracy) committed *in England* before the courts can assert jurisdiction. Otherwise it is a question of (a) some other country taking jurisdiction and then (b) going through the cumbersome extradition process. On the other hand, some countries can regard criminal jurisdiction as based upon the alleged offender's nationality. So if the victim of the wrongdoing was located (and suffered loss) in country X, which states that nothing offensive took place in country X and the perpetrator was in country Y but a citizen of country Z, then neither X nor Y may be able to deal with it.

Part of this problem is trying to fix a location in which things are happening, when of course they are supranational (see further section 2.2.4, which considers the same issue from the viewpoint of regulatory jurisdiction).

FURTHER READING

- SFA Briefing Updates *Minimising Systems Risks—A Checklist* Update 15 (March 1997).
- IOSCO *Principles for the Oversight of Screen-based Trading Systems* (June 1990).

6.6 FRAUD AND THE ROGUE TRADER

6.6.1 Fraud and internal policing

No organisation is completely free from fraud and dishonesty. Most firms have to contend with low-level petty theft and embezzlement from time to time. The human mind will always find some new loophole to exploit; the fraudster is half a step ahead at all times. The job of the risk manager is to make sure he is only that far away and always within the sights. Failure has a high price: even where the firm can bear the financial cost, there may be serious reputational damage which affects the firm's performance for months or years to come. Major frauds lead to large losses and investigations. See section 6.8 relating to handling of investigations and the aftermath of a major loss.

Lessons learned from the each incident have to be used to formulate new, better controls for the future. Effective, visible policing reduces risk:

- a strong control culture means that potential fraudsters won't try to crack the system;
- knowing there will be an investigation and penalties reduces the likelihood of fraud and collusion;
- segregation of functions, dual authorisations and independent monitoring mean that collusion will be needed to buck the system;
- lowering the tolerance threshold reduces the seriousness of incidents staff know they can get away with (nobody complains if you steal a paperclip/an international phone call/a mobile phone/a million dollars).

6.6.2 Rogue traders

The epidemic of rogue traders in the mid-1990s had a few common symptoms:

- Rogue traders work all hours and turn in spectacularly good performance, or so it seems till it all goes wrong—they are perceived to be stars, unchallengeably good at what they do.
- Rogue traders who have caused huge losses were all inadequately supervised: either controls were non-existent (Barings) or they were disregarded (Morgan Grenfell).
- Rogue traders rarely gain much from their activities. Their motive is generally not personal greed, but covering up of past deficiencies in performance. This means that their activities can fall through a net designed to catch embezzlers.

- Rogues become rogues because of a ghastly mistake—the sort of mistake anyone can (and most of us do) make from time to time. But there was no, or no convenient, mechanism in place for owning up. Road designers confronted with steep downhill slopes build in escape lanes to prevent runaways from getting completely out of control and causing accidents—risk managers need to do the same thing.

The Human Resources function is a useful weapon against the rogue trader. Some will have skeletons which can be uncloseted if references are taken up and registers checked when the employees are recruited. Learn to spot the trainee rogue: never on holiday, never delegates, gets irascible about the wrong things, gives superficially plausible but incomprehensible explanations, makes you feel stupid when you ask questions, has sole-contact relationships with customers and (sometimes) has a lifestyle which doesn't match his earnings. The Human Resources department should file risk management reports along with the other parts of the firm.

Insurance can be bought to recoup some of the loss. Insurance policies have their limitations, however (see section 6.2.2). In particular, bankers' blanket bonds traditionally exclude liability in cases where the fraud is not perpetrated for personal gain.

6.7 MIS-SELLING

Mis-selling risks have come to the fore in two guises: retail mis-sales (personal pensions) and treasury mis-sales (derivatives). Although the customers and products were different the errors and lessons are the same. Derivatives are particularly tricky because the losses suffered by the customer can be so large. Yet the *Dharmala* case in England and equivalent cases in the US confirm that a firm is protected when sued by a customer who has suffered loss, provided that the right precautions are taken. Reputational considerations mean that, in the retail market, a robust defence is less easy to make: it can be better to pay unjustifiably than to fight on safe ground and be portrayed in the media as harsh and unfeeling.

Part of the difficulty in selling a complex product (and complexity is viewed from the customer's angle, not the seller's) is whether the salesman has taken on the role of adviser too. The hidden danger here is that the customer may be able to do more than simply escape from his contractual obligations—he may be able to plead that the firm owed him a duty which was breached and claim damages even where the contract was in-the-money for the firm. Where the knowledge gap is very wide there are legal rules which may *require* the firm to act in the customer's interest in order to overcome the presumption that they have unduly influenced the customer. These rules include:

- a person performing professional or quasi-professional services to someone relying on him assumes a duty to exercise reasonable care and skill in doing so;
- although it's obvious, don't forget that a transaction can be set aside if misleading information ('misrepresentation') about it was given to the customer;
- a person who is in a dominant position, particularly where there is a relationship of trust and reliance, may be exercising 'undue influence' with the consequence that contracts can be set aside;
- there may be a contractual duty to advise, especially if relevant regulatory conduct of business rules or market codes of practice have been imported into the firm's terms of business with the customer;

- exclusion clauses often don't work, especially if they are invoked against consumers or are in standard printed terms.

Management of mis-selling risks is thus not solely a matter of knowing your customer (though this is probably the most important thing). All the regulators have rules about knowing your customer; even in the wholesale markets (transactions between 'core principals') it is a requirement that parties and brokers establish whether either party lacks experience in dealing in the product being discussed. Other precautions include:

- Explain the risks to the customer and keep a record of what was said.
- Document any limits on your responsibility.
- Do not assume that the treasury department of a big corporation is as sophisticated as a financial institution. If you need to treat it that way, tell the customer and keep a written record of this and the reasons why the decision was reached.
- Be sensible: is something as complex as a LIBOR-squared swap really the right product for a greetings card company? If it's obviously not a hedge, is it prudent to warn the customer to get independent advice?
- Consider whether normal credit checks are sufficient to decide whether the customer could absorb any losses.
- Consider if approval of the transaction is being given in the customer's organisation at a level of seniority which matches the risks involved.

In order to preserve a 'buyer beware' approach to customers, consider first whether regulatory rules allow you to shift the burden onto the customer in this way; if they do, then contractual provisions (which may have to be drawn to the customer's attention) can help. For example, state that the firm is not providing advice, does not owe any fiduciary duties, that the firm has offered to answer questions (and has done so where questions were asked) and that oral statements by the firm's staff are superseded by the written agreement which contains all terms.

Retail customers

With retail products the considerations are rather different. The problems with pensions mis-selling are not confined to pensions alone. The features of pensions which make firms vulnerable to attack include the long-term nature of the investment, the difficulty of exit without loss of value, the complexity of choice facing the investor which makes it difficult to rank one product against another without hours of study, and the opacity of charging structures. Short-term products such as a share purchase, a motor insurance policy or a bank deposit are unlikely to have these features. Other long- or medium-term products may well do. The buyer beware principle may not be applied by the courts in such cases, as there may be a legal duty to advise if a product is unsuitable—particularly if there is a regulatory rule or principle which is designed to protect consumers from it.

Retail customers may benefit from a wide variety of legal rules which protect individuals. In particular bear in mind that the provisions of the Unfair Contract Terms Act 1977 may apply, preventing the firm from offering substitutes for what was agreed, or from excluding liability, unless reasonable. Similar (but slightly different) protections are given to consumers under the EU Directive on Unfair Terms in Consumer Contracts which will apply across the entire EU. The Consumer Credit Act 1974 contains requirements as to the appearance of contracts, proper interest rates and cooling-off periods. Non-statutory law may impose unwanted fiduciary responsibilities on firms which come to be relied on by their customers as essential to the customer's decision-making. Management of these risks is largely a matter of knowing your customer and playing the game by the rules.

Where a retail customer is a 'non-status' customer—ie one of low credit standing—guidance for dealings is available from the Office of Fair Trading. This guidance contains various principles which are useful in relation to activities other than lending, for which they were designed. They are, not surprisingly, similar in nature and scope to other more detailed regulatory rules in the financial sector.

- Transparency Full disclosure and explanation of all terms and conditions and fees and charges.
- Pressure High pressure sales tactics should be avoided and the customer given time to reflect before being bound.
- Accuracy Material should not mislead and there should be no cold-calling or canvassing off trade premises.
- Brokers Should reveal their status and in particular whether they are subject to a tie to a particular product provider; they should avoid or manage conflicts of interest (eg volume-related commissions); and they should also be monitored by product providers where there is a tie.
- Terms Should be fair and in plain English.
- Reasonable behaviour Firms should not sell unrealistic products—although the firm may profit from a non-status loan even if it is not repaid, that is no reason to burden a borrower with a loan he will certainly never be able to repay.
- Charges Should be explained and increases should reflect the costs incurred by the firm as a result of the event which triggered the increase.

REFERENCES

Dharmala case

– *Bankers Trust International plc v PT Dharmala Sakti Sejahtera*, 1 December 1995, Mance J.

OFT guidance on non-status borrowers

– Office of Fair Trading *Non-Status Lending: Guidelines for Lenders and Brokers* (July 1997).

6.8 CONTINGENCY PLANNING AND INVESTIGATIONS

6.8.1 When a problem surfaces

Control failures lead to operational risk events. Operational risk events often give rise to matters which have to be proactively reported to regulators. Regulators (and in serious cases, others) may then wish to investigate what has gone wrong. This section deals with some of the issues which crop up when an investigation is possible and when things have gone wrong.

Be aware of the duty not to sweep problems under the carpet. Keeping the regulator at bay is best done by making a clean breast of the failings—all firms have them—and explaining to the regulator how the problem is being dealt with. This will usually involve an investigation phase, where the extent of the problem and the deficiencies which allowed the problem to develop are discovered; and a remedial phase, where processes are established to prevent the problem and problems like it recurring. At all stages the regulator will expect to be kept informed. If the problem is serious, or if the regulator considers that the firm's efforts to investigate and remedy are inadequate, the regulator is likely to step in and conduct its own enquiries.

6.8.2 Varieties of investigation

Some operational risk events are inevitable. Operational risk events have a tendency to be followed by internal or external investigations. Part of contingency planning is being ready to handle these efficiently and at minimum reputational cost. Therefore they need advance planning.

There are many different types of investigation. The fact that one has been initiated does not preclude others from taking place. This of course leads to the risk of double jeopardy where an investigating authority is contemplating disciplinary or other punitive action. There is no overriding legal principle which prevents this, despite a few legal rules which prevent people being tried for the same crime twice or litigating the same issue twice. Common features of the investigatory powers available under statute are the right to compel production of documents, to compel the giving of oral evidence (sometimes on oath), the right to disclose the findings to other authorities or to publish them and sometimes the statute allows entry into premises and gives power of search and seizure. (See section 6.8.4 for more details on disclosure of information gleaned in investigations.)

Counterparties and those not otherwise affected by the operational risk event might be caught up into one of these investigations and may be required to produce evidence.

Statutory and other investigatory powers include:

- **Regulatory investigations** Regulators have statutory powers to appoint persons to investigate and take disciplinary action. Disclosure of information between regulators and other authorities is permitted notwithstanding legal duties of confidentiality. Other regulators, such as professional bodies, may seek to inquire into misconduct on the fringes of operational failure (such as the accountancy bodies' investigations relating to BCCI and Barings). Some bodies, such as the Law Society, have statutory backing for their investigatory activities.
- **Companies Act 1985** At the request of the company, its shareholders or the court the Department of Trade and Industry can appoint inspectors to investigate the affairs of a company. This happened in the case of Barlow Clowes.
- **Insolvency Act 1986** Administrators, liquidators and administrative receivers have powers to investigate the affairs of a company under their control. These investigations are usually informal and are done for the purposes of the insolvency proceedings—ie to locate assets and resolve issues relating to claims. As the assets can include claims against third parties, directors or related companies, these are important investigatory powers and can affect counterparties.
- **Parliamentary and public inquiries** Parliament and the Government have constitutional powers to inquire into things and may compel people to attend and produce documents or give evidence. The limits on disclosure of such materials are unclear, but a safe assumption is that everything disclosed to such an investigation could be put into the public domain and be used against the person providing it.

Timing of multiple investigations is important. Civil and criminal proceedings may be taken; a statutory investigation may occur; there may be a regulatory investigation and disciplinary action. The usual rule is that criminal proceedings go first, because of the risk of prejudice if material findings are made in a regime which operates with a lower standard of proof. But civil litigation and regulatory hearings can sometimes proceed concurrently; the courts have stated that where the issues are the same, not more than one tribunal should hear them concurrently.

6.8.3 Internal investigations

An investigation conducted internally may have advantages, particularly in terms of privacy, scope and speed, over an external investigation. But beware the power of the authorities to compel delivery up of papers produced in an internal investigation; and note that the authorities may launch their own investigation anyway, so the work gets done twice with all that entails in terms of cost and lost business opportunities. One approach is to allow the regulators to share in the results of a private internal investigation and to have some say in its scope and conduct.

External advisers may be able to help. They are impartial and beyond internal office politics. They can conduct interviews with relevant staff objectively. External advisers should have trained staff skilled in extracting information from hostile or defensive witnesses.

6.8.4 Disclosure

Documentary and other evidence may be disclosed to other parties. There are two main gateways for documents and other material to leak out to others.

Privilege (immunity from the obligation to disclose) attaches to the following types of document (which includes things like diagrams, computer records and tapes as well as paper documents):

- **Legal professional privilege** You can tell your lawyer what you like and he can advise you freely without fear of disclosure. Legal advice privilege ought to apply generally, but there have been attempts to cut down its scope.
- **Litigation privilege** You can generate documents for the purpose of helping lawyers advise whether to pursue or defend litigation without fear of disclosure. But the dominant purpose of producing the document must have been to obtain this advice. Litigation privilege is unlikely to apply to damaging material produced before writs were in contemplation. Litigation privilege only works reliably in civil litigation. Statutory and parliamentary investigations and criminal proceedings are subject to different rules.
- **Without prejudice correspondence** You can enter into correspondence with your opponent in a genuine attempt to settle a lawsuit without fear that the judge will see the admissions you make in the correspondence if it is marked 'without prejudice' or forms part of a series of without prejudice correspondence.
- **Other forms of privilege** There are further forms of privilege, including public interest immunity and common interest privilege. Some immunity can be obtained by public and even occasionally private persons if it is in the public interest that the material remain undisclosed. The common interest privilege rules are complex but would cover situations such as where two parties have a common interest in the outcome of litigation (eg co-defendants) and material produced by one comes into the hands of the other.

Incriminating statements and documents can be used in criminal proceedings. Admissions by an accused person are called 'confessions' and, so long as they are 'reliable' (broadly, this means not extorted unfairly), can be relied on as part of the prosecution's case. Avoiding production of incriminating documents or statements is therefore an important defensive tactic. Nevertheless there are specific statutory powers of disclosure among regulators, investigators and prosecutors. There has been a lot of debate over the unfairness of fact-finding investigations with coercive, but not punitive, powers generating such material, which then gets disclosed to prosecuting authorities. The European Court of Human Rights has ruled against the UK in this regard and the legal rules surrounding it should be regarded as unsettled.

Note that privilege does not automatically attach to:

- confidential information;
- documents marked 'confidential', 'privileged', or 'without prejudice';
- board minutes;
- correspondence with or between lawyers;
- statements produced to investigating authorities or insolvency officers.

Privilege can also be inadvertently lost if the privileged information is disclosed to a third party. Care needs to be taken in any dealings with outsiders.

6.8.5 Contingency planning

The firm's contingency plan should, as well as addressing the matters mentioned in section 4.4, consider each of these issues:

- **Securing evidence** This may mean backing-up and ring-fencing computerised records, preserving tapes and data which are routinely erased or destroyed, sealing offices, preventing remote access to computer networks, cancelling smart cards and so forth. The procedure needs to be thought about in advance to make sure no angles are left unexplored in the heat of the moment.
- **Liabilities** Potential criminal and civil liabilities of the firm itself may be implicit in what has gone wrong. For example, book-cooking by employees can cause the firm to be criminally liable for false accounting; mis-selling may have led the firm into a situation where it has to disgorge profits and unwind contracts.
- **Employment issues** Some staff will have to be suspended. Others may have to be dismissed. Fair procedures have to be followed to comply with employment law. Any personnel involved who are company directors (eg directors of subsidiaries) should have their positions reviewed from a corporate law perspective too—typical company articles do not provide for suspension of directors under investigation, so the only options are to leave them in office (with full powers and rights to information) or to remove them completely.
- **Taking recovery action against the perpetrator, or tracing assets into the hands of recipients** Timing of such action, relative to any investigation, is important; recovery actions need to start promptly if they are to have success.
- **Need for separate representation for those under investigation** Dividing lines may have to be drawn between the alleged perpetrators, the allegedly responsible senior management and the firm itself. Who pays if different lawyers are needed?

7

Control of credit risk

7.1 INTRODUCTION

Controlling credit risk is not yet a simple question of trading out of your risk position. Trade in credit is relatively illiquid; buyers of credit risk are relatively few. This is presumably because taking credit risk has historically been the business of banks and credit risk assessments have been based on internal scoring arrangements in which secret information about the borrower and subjective criteria, have played important roles.

Sellers of credit protection, on the other hand, are relatively numerous. Nowadays there is a growing market in tradeable credit risk outside the bond markets. Trade and novel instruments make hedging possible along the lines of market risk management. Yet these techniques are not the primary method of addressing unwanted credit risk. Netting and collateral, despite their relative complexity in terms of creating legal, operational and market risk issues, seem to be the favoured approaches.

Know your counterparty

Perhaps the most obvious point, which almost goes without saying, is that credit risk management starts with basic checks on the counterparty. Understand the counterparty's ability to pay. Basic credit controls include:

- check the counterparty's public and other financial information, including off-balance sheet positions if possible;
- check the strategic objectives of the counterparty and understand its overall risk profile;
- check the management quality of the counterparty;
- check the counterparty's profitability;
- check the counterparty's standing among its creditors;
- check the size of the counterparty's positions compared with other market users of similar profile.

Obviously these things are counterparty issues. Counterparty and credit risk are different ways of looking at the same problem. So it is rather artificial to split them up; but there are some things which are more likely to end up in the legal department's in-tray than on the credit committee's conference table. Hence, in this book, 'counterparty' risk has been put in a different chapter.

7.2 TRADING OUT

If there is a market in the credit risk which you are trying to manage, you can manage it in the same way as market risk. Bonds and other forms of transferable credit obligations will lend themselves to being handled in this way. Credit risk management then becomes an issue of diversification, efficient measurement of one's risk position, response to market changes and liquidity in the market when action needs to be taken. (Which sounds simple until you get down to it.)

But much credit risk taken on by financial institutions does not originate in this way. The principles for management ought to be the same: diversification, keeping an eye on things and closing out a bad position all make sense regardless of the type of debt. The problem is that many credit obligations are far less readily transferable than commercial paper: for example, bank loans, credit card obligations, settlement obligations, future exposure on derivatives and so forth. These are not designed to be traded. While there may be no theoretical bar to selling such exposures, the legal complexities and illiquidity of the market may pose formidable obstacles to trading out. Nevertheless there are solutions in some cases:

- **Syndication and loan transfer** Loan documentation may envisage transfer of slices of loans among banks. This is usual only with large commercial loans; though no two loans of this type are very alike and a truly fluid market does not really exist. The crucial point is that it is very hard for a bank to dispose of its exposure at a price seen as sensible: it may be overvalued just before default and undervalued afterwards.
- **Subparticipation** Where a loan transfer is not available, a bank with exposure may offer to pass on interest and principal which it receives from the borrower to a bank willing to acquire exposure. Often such an arrangement involves the new bank taking credit risk on the old bank—like a credit derivative.
- **Securitisation** Loans and other obligations can be transferred to a vehicle which issues freely tradeable debt. This will allow the party with the exposure to credit risk to sell the risk.
- **Diversification** Accept that you are going to suffer some loss due to credit risk events. So long as your credit risk exposure is not too concentrated, you should be able to price your willingness to give credit so as to absorb and be rewarded for taking, this risk.
- **Transferability** Treating credit as marketable allows firms with unwanted credits to trade out of their positions. Traditionally loans (and other credit risk) have not been freely transferable, locking banks into intensive-care procedures with counterparties they no longer trust. Selling the credit can help everybody; this needs flexibility in the documents, or use of synthetic arrangements such as credit derivatives (see section 7.7) to achieve a similar result.

But if none of these is going to work, or if there are doubts about the liquidity of the market in a particular credit, then a credit support solution may be needed.

7.3 CREDIT SUPPORT

Credit risk is no more an on-off switch than market risk: if you can price the graduation between good and bad credits, you can ensure that there is a profitable return on all business. Some transactions may require you to do business with an ill-capitalised or novice entity which has no credit record, or with an entity which is known to fail your credit tests. Other means of managing the credit and counterparty risk, in the form of credit support, need to be found. Credit support issues are often bewildering.

Adequate credit management policy

General

- Decisions on granting of credit should be independent of trading areas.
- Credit policy should be integrated with the firm's general business strategy.
- Credit policy should consider non-counterparty factors such as country and sector.

Counterparty and customer assessment

- Assess legal capacity, suitability of transactions, legality of proposed transactions under counterparty's home state laws, money-laundering, knowledge of counterparty and business factors which may affect counterparty's fortunes.
- Data from rating agencies, credit reference agencies, or net worth as per audited or management accounts is of only limited use.
- Regulated entities are not necessarily a safe bet—capital 'adequacy' is a very crude cushion for counterparty protection.
- Watch the special risks with fund managers acting for multiple funds.
- Assess intra-group transactions prudently.

Risk reduction

- Ensure the front office is constantly aware of limits and their utilisation, especially in global firms.
- Different strategies may be chosen for issuer and counterparty risk; but issuer risk is more like credit than market risk if the transaction has a long lifespan.
- Credit exposure may be reduced in some cases by trading on a DvP basis or by imposing similar timing constraints.
- Guarantees may be mere 'comfort letters', there may be other exposure to the guarantor causing a limit to be exceeded, there may be group-insolvency issues so that there is no real credit enhancement etc.
- Consider use of netting, credit derivatives, collateral, break clauses and resets—and their respective dangers.

Monitoring of exposure

- Should be done on a daily basis.
- Aggregation of exposures to a group of related counterparties should be considered.
- Beware of information overload: fish out the news from the white noise.
- Systems which allow the data to be re-examined from another angle are useful.
- Carry out 'what-if' simulations.

Reviews

- Frequency of reviews: if the purpose of the review is to reassess the strength of the credit, lengthening the review period for strong credits makes no sense.
- Unutilised lines need particular care: they may be called on just because the counterparty is experiencing a credit squeeze from other creditors.
- Check the reward, as well as the risk, side of the equation.

Potential credit risk events

- Watch the signals (slow payment, spurious disputes, accepting bad prices and risky deals, failure to produce accounts, inquiries from other creditors, etc).
- Cut the line or renegotiate it if committed.
- Reduce exposure: by only entering into offsetting trades, or by taking collateral.
- Don't do nothing if a credit event occurs (see further section 8.5).

Only limited guidance has been given by regulators on management of credit risk. Lower capital adequacy requirements apply to firms regulated by the SFA if they have an 'adequate credit management policy' approved by the SFA. But this stops short of explaining the complex issues which arise when using netting, collateral and other credit risk management techniques. ISDA has published useful guidance on collateral which goes a long way towards addressing the issues which arise when this risk management tool is being used.

Common methods of credit enhancement and credit risk management are:

Direct credit support

- **Covenants** A covenant to maintain a financial ratio, or other financial covenants, can be a means of addressing credit risk. But note: an unpoliced, unenforced covenant is a mere promise and does not get you paid if things go wrong. To make it work, you have to have powers of inspection, to carry out double-checks, to complain when limits are approached and to be willing to appear tough and uncompromising.
- **Netting** (see section 7.4).
- **Collateral** (see section 7.5).

Indirect (third party) credit support

- **Guarantees** (see section 7.6).
- **Credit derivatives** (see section 7.7).
- **Insurance** Insurers offer credit insurance. Note, however, that insurance is usually offered on a portfolio basis; and that an insolvency event is usually required before an insurer will pay out. Many of the comments made about guarantees and credit derivatives also apply in relation to protection bought from insurers.

Typically, the most effective way of reducing credit exposure is to net it down and collateralise the net amount—so long as there are genuine two-way dealings and effective systems in place.

REFERENCES

Adequate credit management policy
– SFA Rulebook, Appendix 56

7.4 NETTING

7.4.1 What is netting? Is it the same as set-off?

If you owe me 10 but I owe you 4, we ought to be able to set the amounts off so that you only have to pay me 6. If this works legally, I should not be able to sue you for 4 (or 10) if you have paid me 6. Where payments are due in opposite directions on the same day, we can 'net' them down. Transactions which involve more complex obligations than mere payments and transactions which have different maturity dates, may all be capable of being given values and being netted in this way if circumstances require.

Which type of netting?

Netting by novation

This establishes a running account between the parties. Every time they enter into a new obligation which is to be netted alongside existing obligations to be performed on the same date in the same currency, the value of the obligation is added to (or deducted from) the account. Only the balance on the account is payable. But obligations with different maturity dates cannot be netted against each other, nor can different types of obligation (eg different currencies or different non-cash deliveries).

Close-out netting

This leaves obligations to be performed at their maturity dates but, if one party defaults, all outstanding transactions are terminated and valued. The values are then entered into an account and the only obligation which remains is to pay the net amount on the account. The technique relies on the ability to terminate contracts on insolvency and effectiveness against laws which disallow insolvency set-off. What it does not do is cater for defaults on the settlement date itself, because once the settlement process has started it is too late to close out (terminate) the transaction.

Payment (settlement) netting

This is designed to reduce settlement risk. If each party has to pay in gross on settlement day there is a risk that one might pay but not receive. If these sums can be netted the risk can be reduced.

Multilateral netting

If A owes 10 to B and B owes 10 to C and C owes 5 to A, how much should they pay? With any of the above techniques there would still be three payments to be made because there are no countervailing cash flows to net. A multilateral netting system interposes a central counterparty (the clearing house) which enables each participant to pay only the overall net amount due across all other participants (or, as the case may be, receive the overall net amount). So, A pays 5 to the clearing house; B pays nothing; C receives 5. A multilateral netting system (central counterparty) does not remove credit risk, but replaces the variable credit risk of different market counterparties with the single concentrated credit risk of the central counterparty. See further section 7.8 for some of the risks with multilateral netting systems.

Various different netting techniques exist which have different legal consequences (see 'Which type of netting?' opposite). All share one feature: in the event of default by the counterparty, it should not be possible for the non-defaulting party to be ordered to pay (or perform) its own obligations without a deduction for the obligations of the defaulting party being taken into account, so that the non-defaulting party's exposure is net. This does all depend on the netting working legally in all relevant jurisdictions. While many countries have adopted special laws to support netting, there is by no means universal acceptance of its effectiveness. Due diligence checks are also required by regulators if exposures are to be reported net.

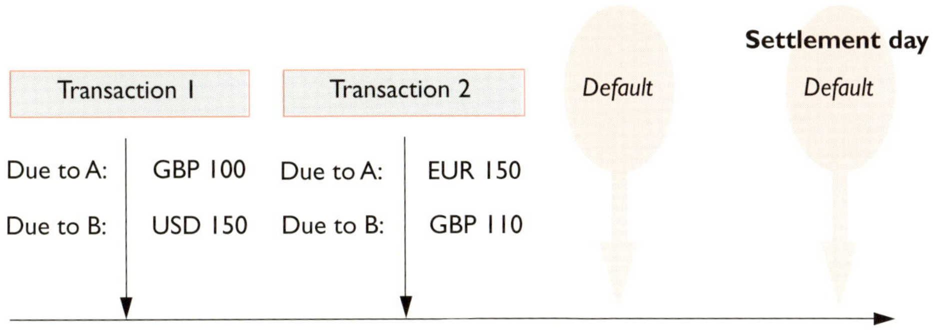

NETTING BY NOVATION	Due to A: Due to B:	EUR 150 USD 150, GBP 10	EUR 150 USD 150, GBP 10
SETTLEMENT NETTING	Due to A: Due to B:	GBP 100, EUR 150 USD 150, GBP 110	EUR 150 USD 150, GBP 10
CLOSE-OUT NETTING	Due to A: Due to B:	Net value of both transactions, (eg about USD 3 due to A)	GBP 100, EUR 150 USD 150, GBP 110

Which type of netting?

This diagram envisages a couple of FX transactions between A and its counterparty B. Two scenarios are presented where B defaults, either (first blob and set of figures) before the intended value (settlement) date, or (second blob and set of figures) on the value date itself. Depending on which netting technique A has used, the outcomes are different.

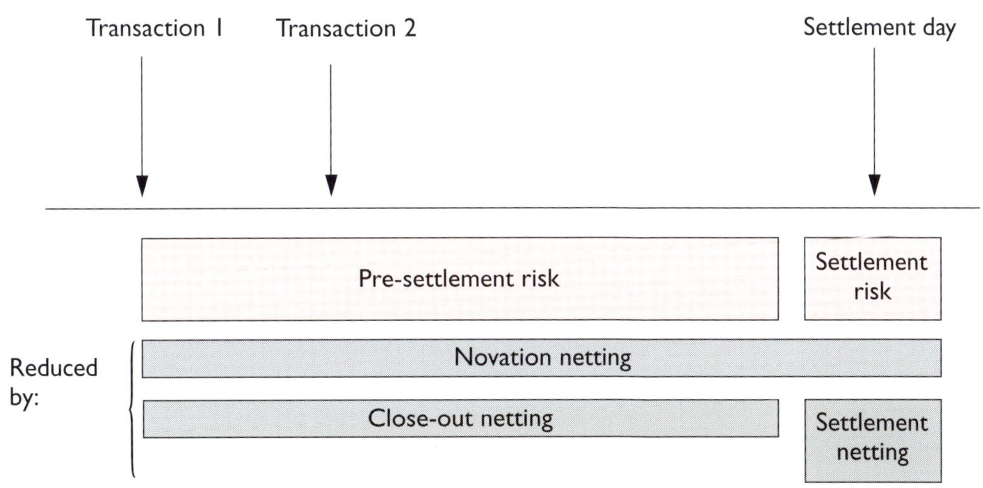

Settlement and pre-settlement risk

Settlement risk, which involves loss of principal (A pays up in full but B defaults and fails to pay) can only realistically occur if B goes into default after failing to make a payment on the value date. By the value date it is too late for A to close out the trade, since he has already taken steps to pay B. Close-out netting is no help in this situation. But payment (settlement) netting and netting-by-novation can both help by pre-arranging a reduction in the expected cash flows on the value date.

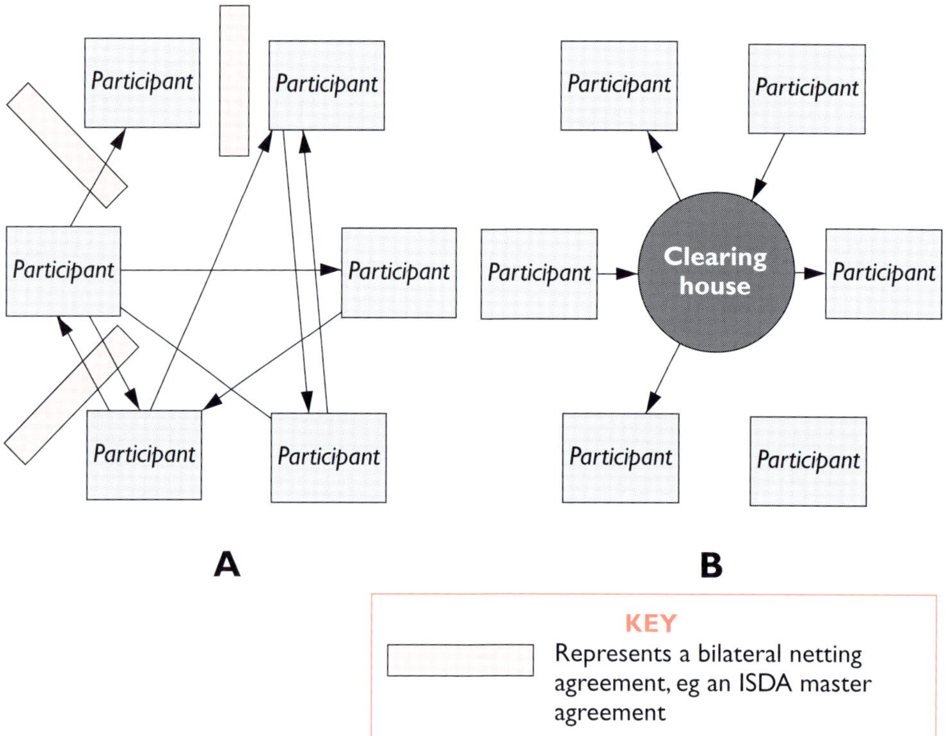

Multilateral netting systems

The two parts of the picture show the same market participants who have done the same trades and compares the situation (A) where some of them have entered into bilateral netting agreements with (B) where they have all joined a multilateral netting system. The cash flows between the parties are reduced and in place of multiple and differing counterparty and credit risks they assume a single credit risk against a single counterparty, the clearing house, which allows accounts payable to one participant to be netted against accounts receivable from another.

Set-off is very similar to all this, but technically:

- set-off is simply a defence to legal proceedings to recover a debt;
- set-off depends on the notion that there are debts due in both directions, so that the countervailing debt is used as a defence (ie a valid excuse for non-payment);

whereas netting envisages that only a single, net, payment is due one way or the other and that this is all that can be sued for.

Set-off after the counterparty goes bankrupt is a valuable right: if I can set off our mutual debts, I get at least a 40 per cent return on my claim (hoping for a dividend on the balance of six which you owe me); if I can't, I must pay four and get a mere dividend on the 10 which you owe me.

7.4.2 How might netting be attacked? Which jurisdictions are relevant?

If netting does not work, the defaulting party (presumably acting by its liquidator) would seek to recover the gross sums allegedly due from the non-defaulting party without giving

Transactions

B claims in gross:
A owes B on bottom transaction

Claims are netted:
B owes A on net claim

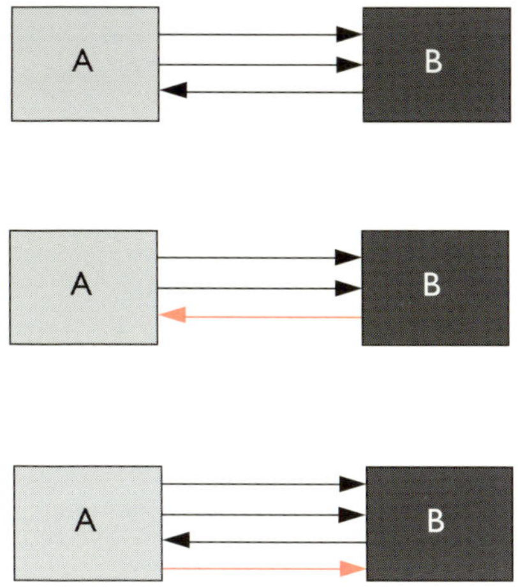

Arrows show claims (A is in the money where B is at the head of the arrow)

Netting: how an attack is made

A and B have done three trades with each other. A is in the money on two of them, so A would (if they are immediately due for cash-settlement) have claims arising from them against B. This diagram shows *claims*, not cash flows, because B is about to default and cash tends not to flow in default situations. If B defaults, his liquidator will want to recover on the one trade which was in-the-money for B (the bottom one of the three trades). A will want the liquidator to amalgamate the in- and out-of-the money trades, and reach a net sum, since on the net basis B owes A rather than vice versa. So an attack on netting is made by *defaulter asserting a claim against non-defaulter.*

credit for what the defaulting party owes. To determine whether netting works, then, you need to know:

- where a liquidator might be appointed (assuming that, in general, liquidators will assume powers given under the laws of the places where they are appointed);
- whether the liquidator would recognise an express choice of law in the netting agreement (which really means whether there are local policy rules which mean that netting is considered bad);
- which transactions the liquidator would select in order to pursue the non-defaulting party (since some liquidations will be limited in territorial extent);
- where the liquidator would take proceedings or otherwise pursue the non-defaulting party (the liquidator may have to step out of his lair since, even if he can sue in his home state, a judgment is no use unless he can enforce it).

Where transactions are entered into in all sorts of jurisdictions, liquidators could be appointed in any number of jurisdictions and cross-border attacks could be launched almost anywhere. One way of reducing the encyclopaedia of potentially relevant jurisdictions is to assume that liquidators are only likely to be interested in upsetting netting if they are appointed in a jurisdiction where the defaulting party has a branch from which a transaction was done. Regulators have concluded that a prudent approach to which jurisdictions are relevant is to be sure that netting is effective:

- under the governing law of the netting agreement and (if different) of each transaction;
- under the law of the places where the parties are incorporated or organised;
- under the law of the places where any branches involved are located.

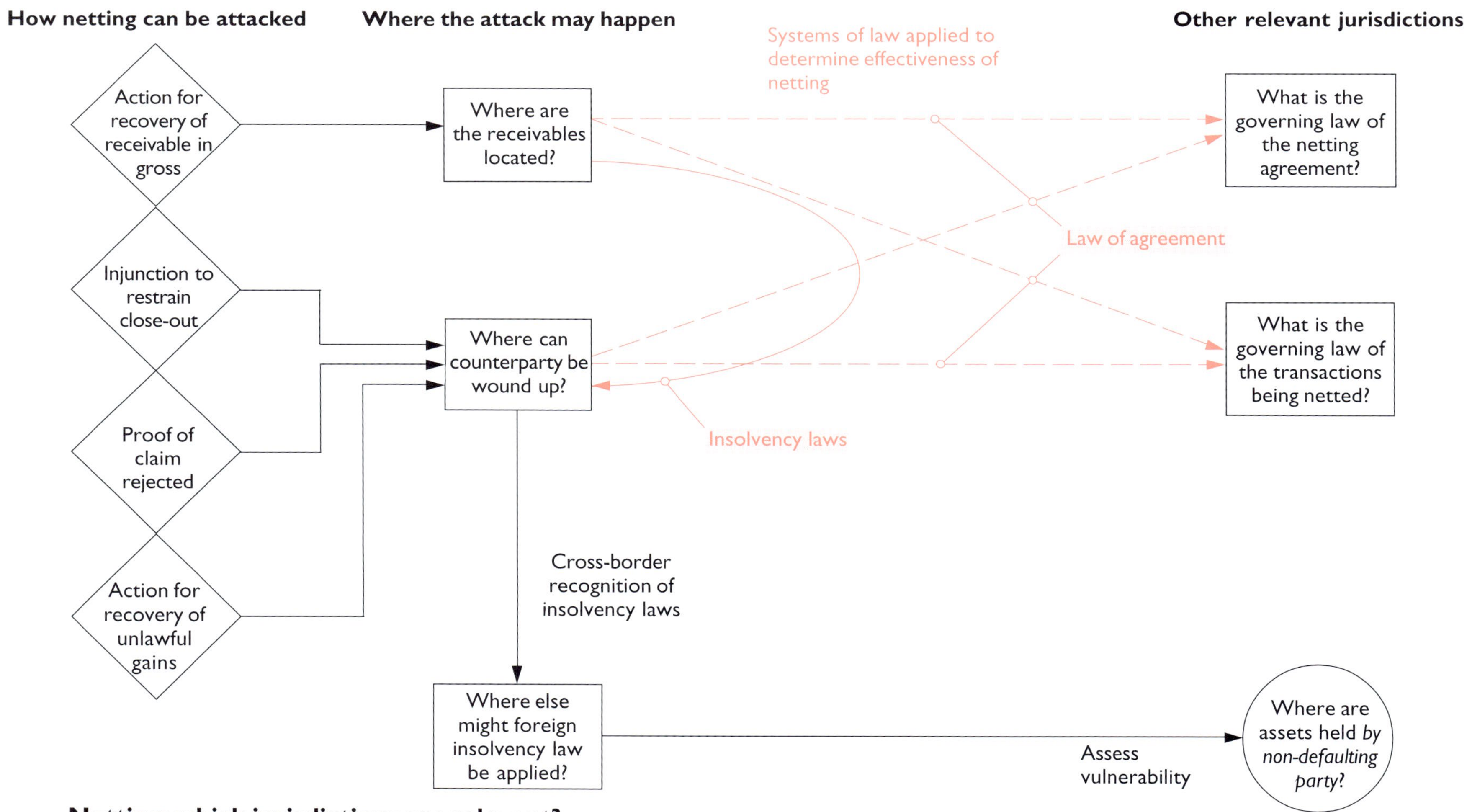

Netting: which jurisdictions are relevant?

To work out which jurisdictions are relevant, remember that netting is a self-help remedy. You will have done the netting in the privacy of your own office; the risk is that the defaulting party can attack you afterwards. So the question is where you can be attacked. To answer this, look at the types of attack. They are broadly claims for money due on transactions (which you have closed out and netted, and therefore not performed) and insolvency attacks. Even when the places where these things can happen have been identified, you need to check the systems of law which can be applied by the courts there to determine the parties' rights. The courts may refer back to the laws governing the documentation and applicable insolvency laws. Although a huge number of jurisdictions is potentially relevant, the ones of immediate concern are those where the non-defaulting party has assets which can be seized or other hostile action taken.

7.4.3 Things to watch out for with netting agreements

Netting agreements need to contain only three terms: a provision for events of default, which trigger the operation of the netting; a provision which terminates the transactions and converts them into a form enabling their values to be netted against each other; and a provision stating that only the net sum is payable in a base currency. But to cater for the risk of cross-border attack and the different types of transaction which are involved, attention should be paid to each of these clauses:

- **Events of default** The events of default should be chosen to reflect the circumstances of the defaulting party. If the defaulting party is a bank which might be subject to regulatory intervention suspending payments, you will wish to treat that as a default; including this event of default is more important than long negotiations about grace periods on payment failures.

- **Termination** The main question here is whether termination should be automatic on the occurrence of insolvency-related events of default. Automatic termination is essential under some legal systems to ensure that the operation of the netting provisions kicks in before bankruptcy rules take effect and dictate that set-offs, or arrangements which achieve a similar result, are disallowed. See further below as to on-balance sheet transactions, in relation to which termination might not be the best way of ensuring netting.

- **Valuation** The issues are practical: who is to do the valuation and are there price sources available? For example, is it appropriate for the *defaulting* party to value its positions? The liquidator of an insolvent counterparty will rarely be inclined to assist and there may be no remedies available to force him to do so at a time which is convenient to you.

- **Set-off** Some sort of provision allowing for aggregation of the values arrived at is needed. ISDA master agreements use set-off. The Futures and Options Association's master netting agreement uses an accounting device whereby the values are aggregated and only a single debt is created. There may be legal preferences in some jurisdictions for one approach over the other.

- **Unpaid amounts** Other sums than those which come from the terminated transactions might be due between the parties. Examples include transactions for which the settlement date had occurred before the event of default but one party has not met its settlement obligations, or cash margin. These sums can usefully be set off against the net sum emerging from the netting calculation. But an extra clause will be needed to achieve this.

- **Transactions covered** Most firms still work on product lines and expect each master agreement to cover only one product, or group of products. But firms are becoming more ambitious and may want their netting agreement to be comprehensive and cover all nettable transactions between the parties. This makes sense in terms of counterparty and credit risk reduction, but beware the legal rules of some jurisdictions which suggest that including non-nettable transactions might undermine the whole netting agreement. See below for further comments on cross-product netting.

- **Designated offices** Some jurisdictions still do not have laws which protect netting or protect it only in very restricted situations. The risk of including a transaction done (or deemed to be located) in a 'dirty' jurisdiction is that the netting is undermined. The purpose of designating offices in a master agreement is to ensure that only branches in 'clean' jurisdictions are included within the scope of the agreement. Confusion sometimes arises as to whether a separate entity, such as a subsidiary, can be regarded as a 'designated office' and thereby brought within the scope of the netting agreement. As to this, see three-party netting below. Sometimes a subsidiary will act as an agent for the main office and should be regarded as a designated office in case the counterparty's liquidator takes the view that transactions entered into through the subsidiary are located in the subsidiary's jurisdiction.

- **Base currency** The master agreement will usually ask the parties to choose a 'base' currency for performing the calculations. Bankruptcy laws usually impose restrictions on the currency in which the net sum can be claimed from the bankrupt party but (note the distinction) it is rare (though not unheard of) for restrictions to be imposed on the currency for doing the calculations.

- **NY law** Sometimes it is advantageous to choose New York (or other US) law to govern the agreement. This is because special protective legislation in the US is available if the netting agreement meets the requirements of the Federal Deposit Insurance Corporation Improvement Act of 1991 (FDICIA). One such requirement is that the agreement is governed by the laws of the US or one of the United States; another is that the transactions and the parties are of specified descriptions. Some master agreement proformas suggest that the parties make 'FDICIA representations' which are intended to assure the other party that the protections under FDICIA will be available.

Other things to watch out for include:

- **Cross-product netting** Some countries which have netting laws which only allow netting of particular products also have rules which restrict effective netting to each allowable product type; so while you can net repos and FX transactions, you cannot set off the net amounts against each other. Apart from such restrictions, cross-product netting is simply a matter of getting the drafting right (though see below for on- and off-balance sheet products). Note also that regulators may not recognise the effectiveness of cross-product netting for capital adequacy or other purposes.

- **Three-party netting** This is more tricky, since there is a mutuality problem. For legal robustness, debts to be set off or netted must often be 'mutual', ie owed between the same persons acting in the same capacity. There are various legal techniques which allow sums owed by a non-defaulting party to a defaulting party to be satisfied out of sums owed by a third person. Essentially these techniques rely on guarantees or collateral arrangements, ie a combination of the credit support techniques mentioned here.

- **On-balance sheet versus off-balance sheet** On-balance sheet obligations, ie things like loans, deposits and receivables, do not need to be 'terminated' on an event of default: the issue here is that they might not yet be payable at that time, so the need is to 'accelerate' them. By contrast, derivatives transactions probably need to be terminated and the mark-to-market loss or gain on the value of the *transaction* calculated. Some transactions, like repos and FX, can have *each* of the parties' obligations accelerated, so that (using the repo example) the redelivery obligation in respect of the securities and the payment obligation of the other party in respect of the repurchase price are both accelerated. The essential thing here is not to muddle up those things that are being accelerated with those which are being terminated, because the valuation methods will differ: where termination happens, the whole transaction is valued (eg by reference to the cost (or benefit) of taking a replacement position in the market as at the termination date); with acceleration, the obligation is clear and its monetary value should be easily ascertainable (eg, in the case of the securities leg of the repo, the termination date market value of the securities) without complicated valuation mechanics, though there may be a need to give credit for early payment. Note also that the regulators may not recognise the effectiveness of netting of on against off-balance sheet obligations for capital adequacy or other purposes.

- **Master agreements** There is no reason why net sums which emerge from master agreements should not be set off against each other (provided of course that set-off works under all relevant jurisdictions). The issues are more likely to be practical than legal ones: for example, if agreement A terminates all transactions subject to its terms on Friday and agreement B does not terminate its transactions till Tuesday, can I be forced to pay up a net sum due from me under agreement A on Monday?

7.5 COLLATERAL

7.5.1 Collateral techniques

The objective of taking collateral is to convert credit risk (right to receive money) into market risk (right to sell property). The techniques available for effective rights over collateral depend on the asset. The terminology is totally confusing. The following list is based on English law rights:

- **Charge or mortgage** (in the US, called a lien; in Europe, called a pledge) This is a security interest: the property still belongs to the collateral provider and must, if no right of enforcement arises, be returned. A mortgage involves a transfer of title (ownership) to the collateral taker and so is likely to be visible to outsiders. Charges can be 'floating charges' over a class of assets—the essential characteristic of a floating charge which distinguishes it from a fixed charge is that the collateral provider is permitted to deal with the collateral. The collateral taker cannot keep the collateral after an enforcement event but must sell it to satisfy his claim.
- **Lien** Liens generally arise by operation of law, not by contract, and usually do little more than allow the lien taker to retain possession of the collateral. Liens do not without special drafting confer a right of sale; if they do, they are better described as 'charges'.
- **Pledge** This is confined to chattels (tangible non-land property). Possession of the chattels must be taken (actually or symbolically) in circumstances where it is clear that a security interest was to be granted. The collateral taker cannot keep the collateral after an enforcement event but must sell it to satisfy his claim.
- **Outright transfer and set-off** Ownership of the collateral, complete and utter, is transferred to the collateral taker. All the collateral provider is left with is a contractual right to have some equivalent property reconveyed to him at a later date. If he defaults, the value of that entitlement is calculated and set off against the amount he owes. It works like a repo, except that no sale price or repurchase price is actually paid. The collateral taker can keep the collateral after an enforcement event, or, if preferred, can sell it to satisfy his claim; but as it belongs to him, he may have sold (or stock-lent) it already.

For many financial institutions, where securities collateral is concerned, there will be a choice between charge (security interest) and outright transfer. As to which technique to use, see the table below. Often one of the factors will be decisive: for example, if set-off is legally ineffective in a relevant jurisdiction, that rules out the outright transfer technique. In other situations, either because the nature of the collateral is too complex to provide this choice, or because the party whose credit is in doubt would not feel familiar or comfortable with any other approach, a charge will be the only commercially feasible option.

Issues for collateral taker	Charge (C)	Outright transfer (ORT)	Verdict
Rehypothecation/repo/ reuse of collateral allowed	Not usually. A security interest taken under art 8 of the Uniform Commercial Code in US states which have adopted it (eg New York) is a notable exception	No problem	ORT
Registration requirement	Often	No	ORT
Requirement for legally effective set-off in jurisdictions where collateral is located/ collateral provider is based	No	Yes	c
Taxes payable	Not usually	Frequently taxes can be payable by the collateral taker in respect of (a) transfers of the collateral to and from the collateral provider and, (b) income received on the collateral which is accounted for to the collateral provider	C
Standard documentation available	Yes	Yes, where used in conjunction with OTC derivatives transactions. Otherwise, no	No preference
Effective against moratorium/stay on enforcement of security in collateral provider's default or insolvency	Not usually	Yes	ORT
Recharacterisation risk	Not usually, though sometimes a fixed charge can be recharacterised as a floating charge	Still a significant risk in some jurisdictions	C

Issues for collateral taker	Charge (C)	Outright transfer (ORT)	Verdict
Enforcement procedure cumbersome	Not usually. Sale at a fair price is usually all that is required. Some jurisdictions may impose special rules (eg sale by auction or through the court)	No. The collateral taker owns the collateral so he can realise it when he likes.	ort
Retain gains in value of collateral on/before enforcement	No. Excess proceeds of sale after enforcement must be handed back to the collateral provider even if the collateral provider still owes other debts to the collateral taker	Yes	ORT
Insider dealing	No	Under some countries' insider dealing laws, acquisition of securities could be a 'dealing' which, if done by a person with inside knowledge, is unlawful	c
Ownership restrictions/ notification requirements as to holdings in collateral securities applicable	No	Potentially—the collateral taker could become obliged to notify the issuer of the securities of changes in its holding if its holdings aggregate are large	C
Substitution of collateral allowed	Sometimes	No problem	ORT
Negative pledge breached	Probably	Not usually	ORT
Credit risk on collateral taker	No	Yes	C
Voting and income rights retained	Yes, but it is common for the collateral taker to include rights to income within the collateral package	Special provisions are needed, but these are in the market standard documentation	No preference

Other relevant concepts

- **Fixed and floating** A floating charge is one where the charge applies to a changing pool of collateral, which the collateral provider can change when he wishes. A floating charge may give the collateral taker weaker security (he ranks behind certain classes of creditor if the collateral provider goes into insolvency), may allow additional challenges to be made under insolvency laws and may require registration. A fixed charge is one where the collateral provider has no right to withdraw the collateral from the pool unless the collateral taker consents.
- **Recharacterisation** If a court were to regard an outright transfer arrangement as a disguised attempt to create a charge it would be said to have 'recharacterised' the arrangement. Likewise a fixed charge could be recharacterised as floating if the collateral provider is given too much control over the collateral. The downside of recharacterisation is that some additional requirement (such as registration) is required if the arrangement is recharacterised and failure to satisfy the requirement invalidates the arrangement completely.
- **Rehypothecation** Where the collateral taker wishes to re-use the collateral provided to him, eg to pass it on to a third party as security for his own obligations, or to repo it out. This is generally not permitted under a charge, with the notable exception of some security arrangements under New York law.
- **Substitution** Where the collateral provider wishes to replace the collateral with other collateral. The principal danger here is that substitution may cause a 'fixed' charge to be recharacterised as a 'floating' charge. Substitution involves releasing collateral—reversing the steps taken to create the interest and creating an interest in different collateral—potentially requiring the steps to be taken all over again.
- **Enforcement** The ability of the collateral taker to 'enforce' its rights over collateral is central to the effectiveness of the collateral arrangement. The collateral taker needs to be able to convert the collateral into cash in the event of a default by the collateral provider. The usual means of doing so is by sale and retention of the proceeds. This is different from the usual meaning of 'enforcement' in connection with legal rights, which connotes court applications and so forth. Enforcement of collateral arrangements may not require the intervention of the court. (In the US, this process is called 'foreclosure'; under English law foreclosure is a rarely used remedy which involves cancellation of the debtor's indebtedness and requires a court application.)
- **Haircut** The value of collateral may go down instead of up. The collateral taker will usually reflect the market risk inherent in its interest in collateral provided by discounting its present market value by a percentage (the haircut) agreed with the collateral provider. Note that the haircut size has nothing to do with the credit standing of the counterparty (contrary to what some counterparties try to argue in negotiations).
- **Negative pledge** The collateral provider may have promised its lender (or other persons) not to provide any security to any other person—in order to protect that lender's priority entitlement to the collateral provider's assets. There is no such thing as a 'standard' negative pledge—some are so widely drafted that they prohibit creation of outright transfer style collateral.

Cash collateral

There are three methods of taking cash as collateral:

- **Set-off** If the collateral provider deposits cash with the collateral taker, the collateral taker owes a debt to the collateral provider: it's no different from an ordinary depositor–banker relationship. When the collateral provider's obligation to the collateral taker becomes due and payable, instead of getting the collateral provider to pay up and ask for his deposit back, the collateral taker can set off the two opposite debts.
- **Charge** If the cash is already deposited with a third party bank, and it is not sensible to break that arrangement, the deposit could be charged to the collateral taker. This arrangement is just like any other charge over receivables, so enforcement is by sale or awaiting maturity and receipt. Charges can be used even where the deposit is placed with the chargee, as the statement in the famous *Charge Card* case which suggested otherwise has now been overruled. Enforcement in the latter scenario is probably by way of set-off.
- **Flawed asset** The ability of the collateral provider to recover his deposit is modified. One variant is that the deposit is repayable only if the obligations owed to the collateral taker have been discharged in full (a 'conditional repayment' flawed asset). No need for enforcement arises, since the collateral taker never needs to repay if the collateral provider defaults. The other is to provide for the deposit to mature only as, and to the extent that, the obligations owed to the collateral taker themselves mature. Enforcement in the latter scenario is by way of set-off.

Regulatory preferences are for combinations of these, in particular where a flawed asset is used.

Where a set-off arrangement is used, cross-border analysis (which jurisdictions are relevant) raises similar questions to netting arrangements: where can the liquidator seek to recover the deposit notwithstanding the collateral arrangement?

In jurisdictions where set-off in bankruptcy is uncertain, charge-based arrangements may be more effective; in which case the cross-border analysis for non-cash collateral is more likely to assist.

7.5.2 Advantages of collateral

Collateral is increasingly used as the preferred credit enhancement technique. So what are the advantages?

- **Doing business with credit-unworthy customers and counterparties** There are lines of business you just wouldn't do with poor credits: in particular derivatives transactions where the exposures are highly leveraged and volatile. Provided that collateral flows can be managed with sufficient flexibility to even out these features, the credit risk may be reduced to a tolerable level.
- **Regulatory capital advantages may follow if collateral of particular types is used** The FSA regards Zone A OECD Government debt and cash as risk-reducing. Other types of collateral, though, may not reduce counterparty risk weighting—collateral exchanges one asset (counterparty risk often weighted at 100 per cent) with another (where debt

securities are concerned, issuer risk which may also be weighted at 100 per cent). Because the risk-weighting categories are very crudely drawn, do not be surprised that regulatory recognition of collateral is stingy.

But as ISDA says: 'collateralization will have no effect on your counterparty's default probability, will not improve the counterparty's credit rating and may or may not reduce the credit exposure risk interval or maturity when calculating credit exposure. The major benefit of collateralization should be viewed as an improved recovery rate in the event of default of the counterparty.'

And don't forget: collateral is *entity specific*: there is no point in having tons of collateral from X International Limited if your exposures are to X Securities (Cayman) Limited, unless you have tied the cross-collateralisation down properly in the documentation.

7.5.3 Potential attacks on collateral

One of the reasons that verification of collateral is so complicated is that there are numerous grounds for attack. The more grounds, the more risk that some additional jurisdiction is relevant and the more checks that have to be done.

- **Underlying debt unenforceable risk** If the secured indebtedness is unenforceable, nothing is owed to the non-defaulting party and the collateral will have to be returned even if all precautions had been taken.
- **Capacity, authority risk** As for any other transaction, a party's capacity, corporate procedures and requisite licences to enter into a collateral arrangement should be checked. Where the collateral provider is a different person from the credit risk counterparty, there may be additional concerns (see guarantees, section 7.6).
- **Contract and recharacterisation risk** The collateral technique chosen must be embodied in a binding contract. There may be a risk that the contract fails to comply with special rules about contracts (does it need to be a deed? must it be in a particular language? does it need to include specific clauses?). There may also be a risk that the contract is interpreted as having a different effect from that intended: ie becomes 'recharacterised' as a different transaction.
- **No proprietary interest risk** Without a proprietary interest, the contract to provide collateral is only a contract and merely creates additional performance (credit risk) obligations. The contract alone may not be enough to create the proprietary interest. For example, it may be necessary to transfer the collateral into the collateral taker's name.
- **Perfection risk** To retain priority over other creditors in all circumstances, yet more steps may be required. Typical examples are registration of charges and giving notices to debtors. (Unregistered charges which require registration are not completely ineffective. They are only void against liquidators and administrators. Unfortunately it tends to be in liquidation or administration that you need to rely on them.)
- **Insolvency attack risk** This is the hardening period problem. Insolvency office-holders can attack pre-insolvency transactions on a variety of grounds (see table at section 8.5.2).
- **Sub-custodian risk** Many securities are held through an international clearance system; the system (Euroclear or Cedel Bank, for example) keeps the securities with sub-custodians. If the sub-custodian cannot deliver up the securities to the order of the clearance system (eg because they have been seized by order of a local court), the security may be less valuable than assumed.

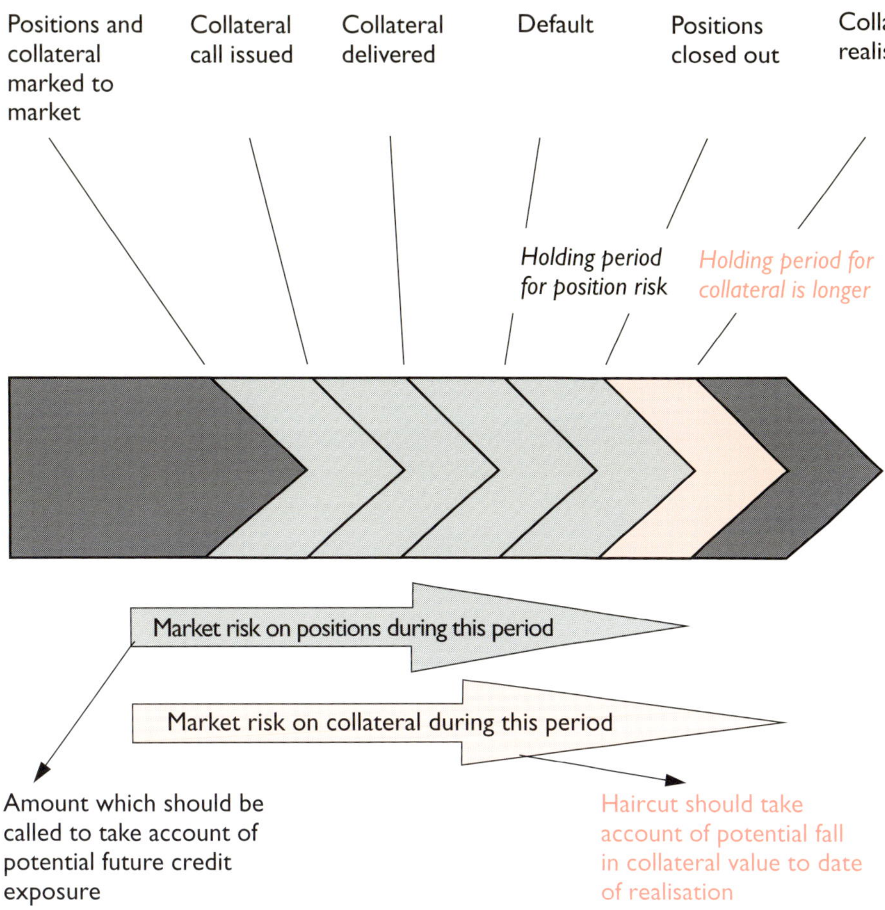

How much collateral do we need?

The collateral management team will know that from time to time the value of positions and collateral already held are to be calculated and a collateral call should be issued in respect of any shortfall. The size of the call is likely to be determined by the collateral documentation, which may not reflect the risks involved. There will be a time lag before the collateral arrives. If there is a default, there will be further time lags before the firm can close out the position and before the firm can realise the collateral. If the collateral is illiquid the last of these may be substantial. Market risk projections need to be done not just on the positions but also on the collateral.

7.5.4 Which jurisdictions are relevant?

The starting-point is where you want to enforce your rights over the collateral in a default scenario. If your arrangements do not work in a default situation, they are worthless. The first question to ask, therefore, is how you propose to enforce: usually it will be by sale, but where cash is concerned, sale is not usually necessary. Cash will be produced where the collateral's worth is in payments that it generates: bank deposits, book debts and bonds are the most common examples (but also consider income flow under securities, rental payments, royalties and other sources of cash).

If you wish to enforce by means of sale:

- Where is the sale to take place (where the collateral is located)?
- Is the collateral arrangement effective there?
- Could the local court apply foreign law? (In practice, there is a good chance that the local court will apply (a) the governing law of the documents to ascertain their effect and (b) the bankruptcy law of the defaulting party.)

- Where foreign law is applied, is the collateral arrangement effective under these laws? (Where foreign law is relevant, it may determine more than one of the issues listed above.)

Where are securities located?

Legal systems are not very good at answering this question. Securities are intangible and therefore have to be given an artificial location. Where securities are held through a chain of custodians, clearance systems and so forth in different countries the location question becomes very complex indeed—but it is important because you need to know the location in order to perfect your collateral.

Article 9(2) of the EU Settlement Finality Directive tries to cast light in this murky area by fixing definitively the place where securities held through a chain of intermediaries are located. Following the line taken in the New York Uniform Commercial Code, the Directive looks at the 'entitlement' which the holder of the securities has—namely, his right (however lawyers may characterise it) to demand that the custodian, settlement system, or whatever which has a record of the entitlement hand over the securities which are *recorded in his name*: that is, the intermediary next in the chain (the proximate intermediary). This is, after all, what most people rely on commercially—if my securities are held 'in Euroclear' that means that to sell them I would generally transfer them to another Euroclear account-holder and the transfer is evidenced simply by book entries made by the Euroclear operator. The location of the book entries showing *this* entitlement is deemed to be the location of the securities to the exclusion of others, such as the books of the issuer of the securities (which may be blissfully unaware of the existence of the ultimate investor).

While article 9(2) sounds like a brilliant panacea for a problem from which only lawyers currently benefit, it has a few snags:

- It has been criticised in some jurisdictions for potentially altering substantive legal rights to securities, since under some legal systems the rights in the securities are different from the rights represented by the 'entitlement' against the proximate intermediary.
- This means that some countries are deeply resistant to changing their laws in this area and wish to implement article 9(2) in as narrowly focused a way as possible.
- Article 9(2) strictly applies only to securities collateral provided via a designated payment or securities settlement system (it is for EU member states to 'designate' systems, primarily to protect participants in the system against settlement finality risk—see section 7.8.2 for more on finality) in order to secure liabilities which arise in connection with the system—so securities collateral provided by A to B to secure liabilities which arise on (say) OTC derivatives transactions which have nothing to do with the system are not covered.
- So securities which are Ruritanian Government bonds held in Euroclear could be deemed to be located in Belgium if given as collateral to the Euroclear operator to secure an overdraft on a cash account in Euroclear, but in Ruritania if given to another Euroclear account-holder to secure other liabilities.
- Different EU countries perceive the problem differently and so some states will implement article 9(2) so as to avoid the 'two places at once' problem just described, whereas others will not.
- There are situations where the proximate intermediary looks like the wrong choice—for example where the proximate intermediary is a mere custodian holding on a bare trust rather than a central securities depository.

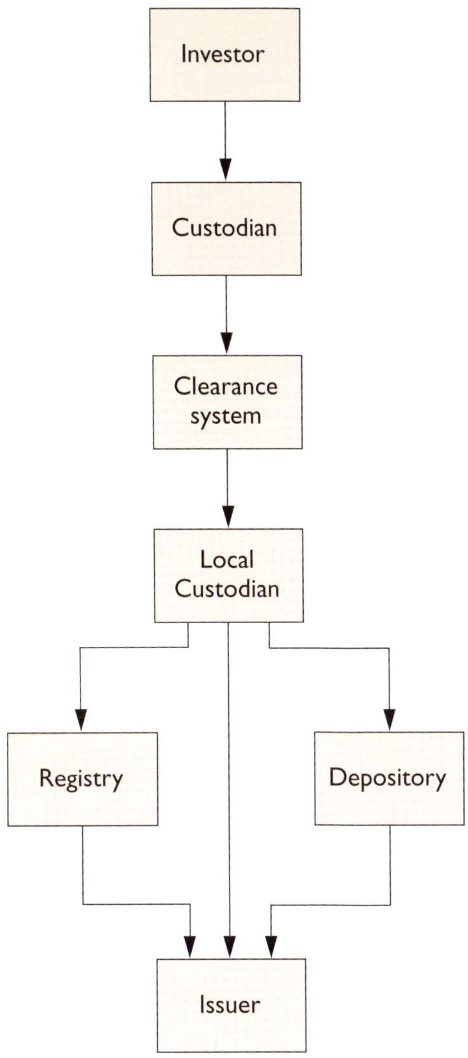

Where is securities collateral located?

The Issuer has issued securities. These are not dematerialised: the certificates are held with a Depository. In this example, ownership of the securities does not depend on possession of the certificates (they are not "bearer instruments"), but on entries in a register maintained by the Registry. The records at the Registry show that the securities are all held in the name of a Local Custodian. Some of the securities are being traded through an international Clearance system such as Euroclear; so the Local Custodian records the Clearance system as holding a tranche of the securities. Participation in the Clearance system is limited to certain entities only. One is the Custodian who holds blocks of securities for his customers, which include an Investor, to enable them to trade in the securities.

In this example any of the countries in which Issuer, Depository, Registry, Local Custodian, Clearance system or Custodian are located could be relevant to the question how a security interest created by Investor should be perfected.

Different countries solve the conundrum in different ways. The two most common are:

- *The proximate intermediary approach*: the Investor regards his interest as located (enforceable) where his own interest is recorded, ie on the books of the Custodian. The Custodian regards his as located where his interest is recorded, ie on the books of the Clearance system, and so forth.
- *The look-through approach:* The Investor regards himself as having securities, not some rather vague rights against an intermediary, on the assumption that at each step in the diagram beneficial entitlement to the securities is being held on trust (or subject to equivalent fiduciary obligations which do not allow the securities to be seized by creditors if the intermediary goes bankrupt)—so he regards them as located where the Issuer is (or possibly where the Registry is, if different).

There is a growing movement in many countries towards the proximate intermediary approach as this is often more pragmatic.

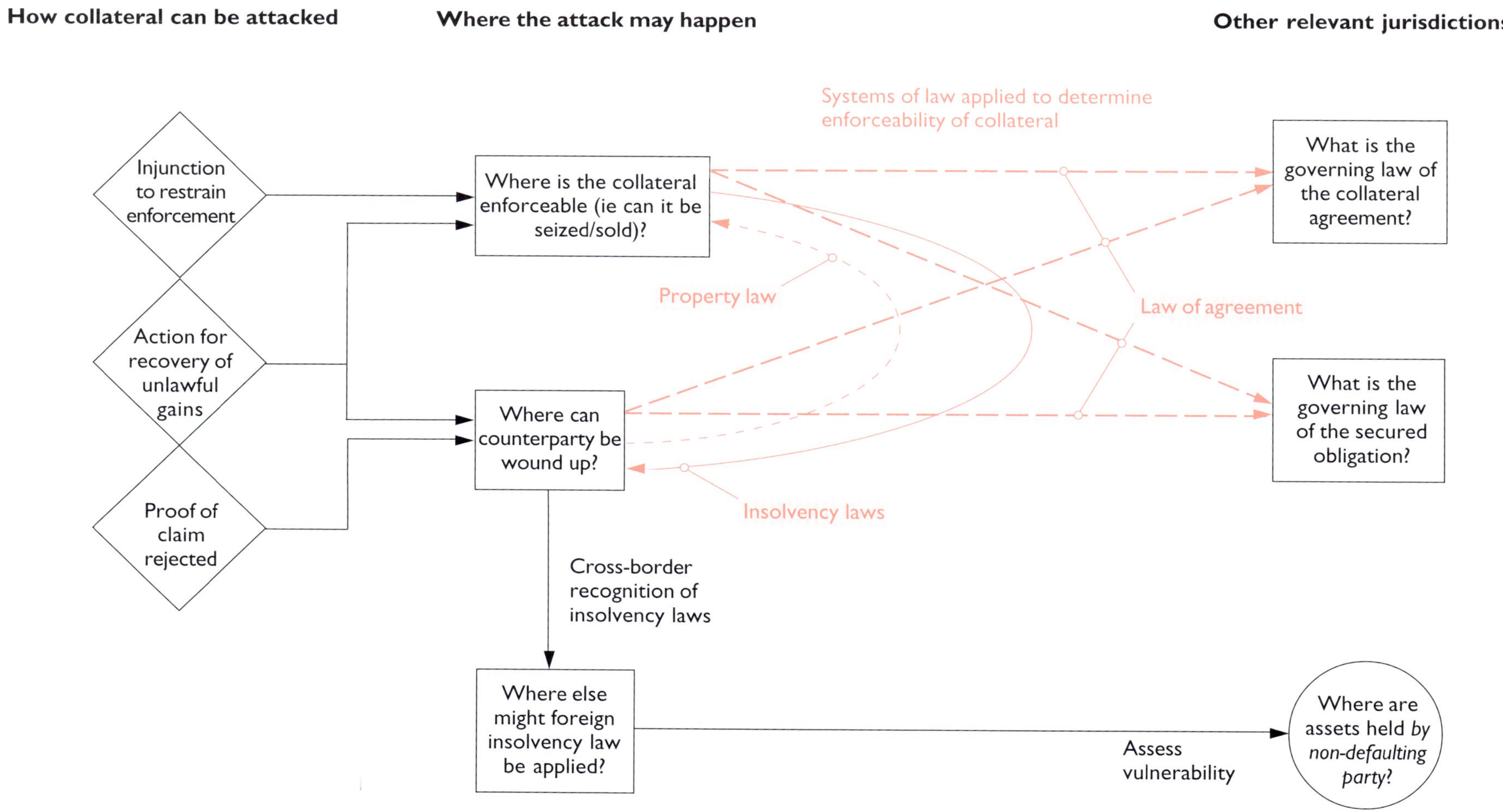

Collateral: which jurisdictions are relevant?

The issues here are similar to those involved in netting (but of course they are a bit more complicated). Again the principles are self-help, so look where you can be attacked, look at the types of attack possible—as usual these include contractual and insolvency legal issues, work out where you are vulnerable so as to focus defensive effort where it is best used. Collateral adds in the extra factor of using *property* that might be claimed bac re the property (the collateral) is located; as to where collateral is located, the best place to start thinking is the place where you want to enforce your rights (ie sell the collateral).

7.5.5 Drawbacks of collateral for credit risk management

- Volatility of the collateral needs to be managed as well as volatility of the underlying exposure. Closing out the credit exposure becomes only half the problem of credit risk management: realising the collateral so as to turn it into cash becomes another one. The holding period in respect of the collateral position may be different from the credit exposure, especially if the market in the collateral is subject to different dynamics. Haircut methodology is frequently crude—of necessity where the collateral provider does not possess sophisticated modelling capability—leaving the collateral taker with market risk on the collateral and a potentially uncovered credit position. When the value of Russian debt securities fell by 80 per cent in 1998 nobody's haircut was sufficient to leave them covered after the drop. Complex collateral management systems are needed to tie up all the price movements which are involved.

- Correlation risk needs to be considered. If the collateral deteriorates in value while the credit exposure being managed increases, the risk management is deficient. So, as ISDA advise, avoid strong correlation to the exposure and avoid strong correlation to the counterparty.

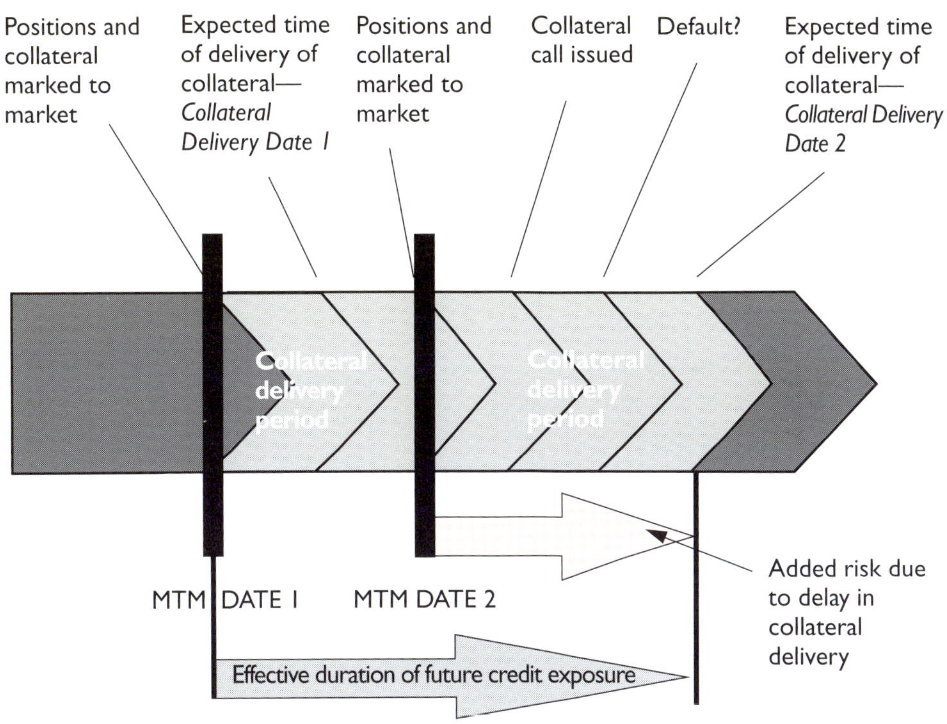

What is the duration of the market risk?

This diagram looks in more detail at what might happen if there were a default shortly after a mark-to-market date. If the default happens during the period while you are still waiting for collateral to be delivered, it is not much help to you. So, your valuation of *positions* at MTM Date 1 needs to take account of the delay in receiving collateral after MTM Date 2, since only collateral received following MTM date 1 can help manage the credit exposure arising before Collateral Delivery Date 2.

- Timing issues relating to collateral are complex. Collateral is provided at intervals. Market prices change daily. You measure your exposure as x; you estimate that your exposure may increase to $x + \sqrt{t}(x)$ by the next measurement day; you therefore call for that much collateral (taking into account applicable haircuts); the collateral is provided in due course. But how simple is this? With cross-product collateralisation can you harmonise the mark-to-market timings? Taking into account delays in settlement, is there unmanaged credit exposure during the period between measurement and delivery of collateral? If you are the collateral provider, rather than the collateral taker, is there unacceptable delay before collateral is returned? Do the timing mismatches have an impact on your dynamic hedging strategy?

- Documentation issues are also complex. Different systems of law will apply if the collateral is situated in more than one place; it may be necessary to use more than one document. Where collateral provider, exposure and collateral are in different places and collateral consists of part cash and part securities, there are zillions of issues to consider. Collateral is no use if documentation is not up to scratch—as with all credit risk management techniques you will be dealing with an insolvency practitioner, not your normal relationship person, if things go wrong and *his job is to attack defective collateral arrangements*.

- Settlement issues need to be considered. Where settlement delays could be a problem or settlement failures would be unacceptable a collateral agent may have to be used. This adds a further layer of counterparty or custodial risk into the picture, increasing the cost of collateralisation.

- Valuation of collateral is complex but vital. Its volatility determines the appropriate haircut. But counterparties may dislike your models and resist calls for excessive amounts of collateral. How are these disputes to be resolved? Is it more efficient to have something rough-and-ready but to manage the residual credit risk in some other way?

- Liquidity of the collateral is essential to enable speedy realisation. With long-term counterparty relationships, have you built in machinery to preclude once eligible collateral from being provided to you if its liquidity falls?

- There are 1001 tax issues to consider. ISDA has produced a checklist, which includes capital gains taxes (crystallised on transfers of collateral or foreign currency conversions); transfer taxes (such as stamp duty); income taxes (particularly in relation to manufactured income provisions in outright transfer scenarios); and other duties and levies (eg in relation to cross-border property or currency transfers). It may also be worth investigating sales taxes though in practice these rarely seem to cause problems.

- Foreign exchange risk may have to be taken into account where collateral realisation will occur in a different currency from that in which the exposure is crystallised.

- Collateral allows business to be done with weaker credit counterparties. Weaker credit means higher risk of default, which means greater exposure to the volatility of the collateral. And an agreement to provide collateral is no use at all if it is not performed, so defaults in provision of collateral have to be treated as seriously as non-payments.

- Collateral arrangements among financial institutions are increasingly reciprocal—ie you give as well as receive collateral according as the position is out of or in the money. Where you give collateral on the outright transfer basis, or under other circumstances which allow the collateral taker to rehypothecate the collateral, you create an exposure *to* the counterparty—namely the obligation to return the collateral to you—if the position is over-collateralised.

- Availability of acceptable collateral in sufficient quantities has become a problem in recent years as more and more institutions have begun relying on collateral as a means of managing credit risk. This means that OECD government securities and cash are in relatively short supply and relatively expensive for counterparties of weaker credit standing to provide. Other types of collateral, which may be more volatile and therefore more risky, may have to be used.

- One source of hassle is disputes. As well as valuations, the common sources of argument include: timing of valuations (whether historic prices are acceptable and whether in fast markets London or New York close-of-business timing is intended); trade matching (whether a transaction is within the collateralised portfolio); waivers (where a party has historically not relied on the strict legal rights in documentation but in times of stress decides that it wishes to do so).

Checklist of risks: ISDA

ISDA's 1999 collateral review draws attention to these risks:

- **Legal risk** that the collateral rights were not properly created or perfected, or can be attacked on other legal grounds
- **Operational risk** that monitoring, operations (failure to make calls, errors in calculations, missing transactions, rehypothecation and substitution errors, delays, custody problems) and settlements fail
- **Issuer risk** that the securities which are used as collateral are issued by an issuer which itself defaults (a risk which is only a problem if the counterparty defaults at the same time; but look for correlations)
- **Concentration risk** that collateral of the same type is demanded from a number of counterparties, placing dependence on a particular issuer
- **Correlation risk** that counterparty and collateral-issuer default simultaneously so that the collateral is worthless to protect against the credit exposure to the counterparty
- **Liquidity risk** that the collateral cannot be sold on the counterparty's default in good enough time without adversely moving the price of the collateral.

7.5.6 ISDA's recommendations

In its 1999 collateral review, ISDA has issued 22 recommendations in a number of different areas, the more significant of which are:

Credit analysis

- Collateral is a complement to, not a substitute for, credit analysis.

Risk management

- Composition of collateralised portfolios should be reviewed regularly for risks introduced by collateralisation.
- Rigorous controls and automation to minimise operational risk in the collateral function should be imposed.
- Collateral, payments and settlements functions should be co-ordinated.
- Understaffing and inadequate calibre staff in the collateral function should be avoided.
- Quality data should be supplied to the collateral function to enable appropriate and timely decision-making.

Dispute resolution

- Detailed and where appropriate, automated reconciliation procedures should be implemented.
- Terms of agreements should be applied consistently to ensure predictability.

Shortening the collateral cycle to reduce exposure

- Credit support documents should be revised to enable shorter cycles for valuation, delivery and liquidation of collateral.
- Firms should consider adding to their agreements a term stating that, on a failure to deliver collateral which cannot be corrected immediately, cash will be delivered instead.

Types of collateral

- A wider range of collateral assets should be considered.
- Haircut methodology should be reassessed.

Initial margin

- Policies should be developed for determining whether and how much 'initial margin' (an increase in the exposure which the collateral must cover, typically calculated by estimating the delay between the last marking-to-market and the time at which the portfolio and collateral can be liquidated) should be called.

Legal and documentation

- Collateral agreements should address the risk of shifts in relative credit quality between the parties.

Cross-product netting and collateralisation.

- Firms should identify systems, documentation and operational enhancements necessary to implement broader cross-product netting and collateralisation.

Substitutions and liquidity

- The substitution mechanism in credit support documents should provide for minimal time-lag in execution of the two transfers involved in a substitution.

REFERENCES

FSA capital rules on collateral

– FSA *Guide to Banking Supervisory Policy* Chapter NE, section 4.

ISDA collateral recommendations

– ISDA *Guidelines for Collateral Practitioners* (1998).
– ISDA *1999 Collateral Review* (March 1999).

7.6 GUARANTEES

Guarantees raise a number of peculiar legal issues:

- Corporate benefit What do I get out of it if I guarantee your debts? Companies have to show some sort of corporate (commercial) benefit from entering into transactions. Where a guarantee is provided by a sister company or a subsidiary, the benefit is not obvious and if it is absent there may be grounds to set aside the transaction later.
- Statute of Frauds Guarantee arrangements must be evidenced in writing signed by the guarantor. This is not usually a problem except where informal third-party collateral arrangements are used. Third-party collateral involves the collateral provider answering (to the extent of his property, if no further) for the liabilities of someone else and this falls within the requirement for writing in the Statute.
- Special defences Guarantors are given a range of special defences against creditors. Some of them are sensible (if the underlying debt is discharged, so is the guarantee) but others are very arcane (if the debtor is given time to pay, the guarantor is let off completely). These peculiar rules can be eliminated by good drafting.
- Right of indemnity and contribution Guarantors can claim to be reimbursed by the debtor and co-guarantors. This can interfere with the creditor's right to pursue his primary claim in full against the debtor unless excluded by good drafting. On the other hand, if you are the credit support provider, beware the rule against double proof: you will be denied the right to claim your reimbursement in the primary debtor's bankruptcy until the creditor has been paid off in full.
- Partial guarantees Guarantee of part of a debt is discharged when the part is paid. So it is less use to have a guarantee of the first £100 owed than a guarantee of the whole debt, limited to £100. The principle is easy to state; and the drafting is easy to get wrong.
- Guarantee-like instruments LCs, performance bonds, credit derivatives and options may all behave like guarantees and need equivalent provisions in their documentation. Some are subject to special rules which apply over and above the principles which apply to guarantees. Some of these instruments are newly developed and the extent to which guarantee rules apply remains to be decided by the courts.

7.7 CREDIT DERIVATIVES

7.7.1 The terminology

Credit derivatives have been around long enough to develop their own jargon. Sometimes the seller of a credit derivative is not selling protection against credit risk but exposure to it. Knowing which kind of derivative is involved is central to understanding this. First, though, the basic terminology:

- the *reference credit* is the bond (or other debt) of the party which might default, whose credit risk you are trying to manage; so the *reference entity* is the party concerned;
- the *recovery value* of a reference credit is the value of the reference credit after a credit risk event has occurred: this will rarely be zero; it may be determined by a poll of dealers or in some other way.

7.7.2 The species

- **Credit default swap (or option)** The issuer makes only a payment upon the default of the reference credit; the buyer pays a periodic fixed payment. This helps the buyer (who may, for example, be trying to reduce credit risk to the reference entity) by eliminating the effects of the reference entity's default. Baskets of reference credits may be used with this and with other credit derivative products.

- **Total (rate of) return swap** One party undertakes to pay, upon the occurrence of a credit event, the amounts due from the reference entity as and when they become payable, but the other party must undertake to pay to the first whatever is received from the reference entity. Plus the first party must pay any appreciation in capital value of the reference credit (and the second must pay any loss of value). It's a bit like fixed and floating payments on an interest-rate swap (risky ≈ floating ≈ whatever is received). (Ssshh: it's like credit insurance: see section 7.3.)

- **Credit spread option** With a put option, the issuer bets that the credit (eg as measured by the difference between the reference credit and some 'fixed' point like a government bond) will not exceed *n* basis points; if it does, issuer must (if buyer so chooses) buy the reference credit at an agreed strike price or make a cash payment. Call options would also be possible.

- **Credit linked note** Issuer undertakes to pay a defined sum on the occurrence of a credit event. A CLN is on-balance sheet. (It's also like credit insurance.)

How the derivative behaves on a credit risk event is important. A seller of protection may pay a cash sum equal to the difference between the net present value of the obligations of the reference credit (if it had been fully performing) and the actual recovery value. This is typical with credit default options. Sometimes the seller simply delivers the reference credit: this is typical with credit linked notes. A third possibility is to do nothing: because cash flows going one way are the actual cash flows being paid under the reference credit, then all that changes is the net sum paid on each payment date (though there may also be machinery to close out the cash flows by reference to the recovery value of the reference credit). This would be typical with total return swaps. If a basket of reference credits is used, the consequences to follow from a credit risk event will have to be carefully thought through.

7.7.3 Things to watch

- **Double credit risk** If you buy a credit derivative, you don't just buy exposure to the reference entity. Sure, if the reference entity suffers a credit risk event, the consequences will follow (eg cessation of payment flows or settlement procedure activated). But if the seller suffers a credit risk event you are in a pickle too. In some countries this dual credit risk may bring regulatory capital disadvantages.

- **Insurance and gaming risk** These are legal risks which, like Scylla and Charybdis, are twin dangers which come and grab you from opposite sides. Steer too close to Scylla and you will find that a credit derivative is void because it is deemed to be an insurance policy; and in many countries only authorised insurers can do insurance. Steer the other way, for example by having no 'insurable interest' (ie, broadly, economic interest in the risk which is being hedged by writing the credit derivative) and it risks being characterised as a 'gaming' (gambling) contract, which may also be illegal. Under some regulatory regimes there may be no middle course.

- **Credit risk events** Getting the events of default right is difficult. Don't forget that what is important differs according to the reference entity (government v corporate paper: governments don't usually go into liquidation, either might do a rescheduling of sorts, corporates don't usually declare interest holidays). The reasons why you are writing a credit derivative can also be important: how sensitive should the trigger be? If a basket of reference credits is used, the credit risk event will have to be carefully thought through.
- **Confidentiality and insider dealing** The provider of credit protection may wish to hedge his risk by (for example) taking a position in the reference credit. Closing out the position at the time of a credit risk event may involve questions of insider dealing: how does the protection provider know when to act to his best advantage? Is it because the reference entity is obliged to give information about its circumstances to the protection provider? Would action by the provider worsen the reference entity's position?
- **Mismatches** If you are buying credit protection, it may look sensible to cover your credit position for seven of the 10-year lifespan of your exposure. But what happens at the end of the seven-year period—will it be possible to replace the hedge? At what cost—particularly if the quality of the credit has deteriorated? Other mismatching issues to watch include the events of default in the reference credit (or the circumstances which you regard as a credit risk event) and the circumstances in which the protection seller pays out. Regulators may also be sniffy about unmatched hedges.
- **Correlation risk** If the seller of credit protection has too much correlation with the reference credit, the dual credit risk is heightened: for example, it may make superficial sense to buy a credit derivative referenced to a Thai electricity company engaged on a new hydroelectric project in Thailand from a Thai bank with close understanding of the reference entity. But not if the Thai economy is just about to head south fast.
- **Unwind risk** Credit derivatives enhance a bank's ability to treat credit risk like market risk. And to develop dynamic hedging programmes to manage a portfolio. But this might require the bank to be able to cancel a derivative transaction in circumstances where the counterparty is unwilling to do so (at least at a tolerable price).

7.8 SETTLEMENT RISK

7.8.1 The nature of settlement risk

Credit risks become acute on settlement day: unless there is delivery-versus-payment (DvP) or payment-versus-payment (PvP), the risk of default is transformed from a risk of having to replace the transaction (the credit risk is the replacement cost, factoring in liquidity and market risk for the holding period) into a risk of paying (or performing) in full and receiving nothing (the credit risk is the full principal amount of the transaction). Although the period of exposure should be short, the delays in the settlement process between irrevocably committing oneself to making payment or delivering performance and irreversibly receiving delivery or payment can be several days, depending on the market.

Controlling settlement risk can be difficult, since the settlement systems will rarely be completely within the firm's control. NB: cash-settled transactions (those where a single payment flows, which satisfies both parties' obligations, on settlement day) involve no settlement risk.

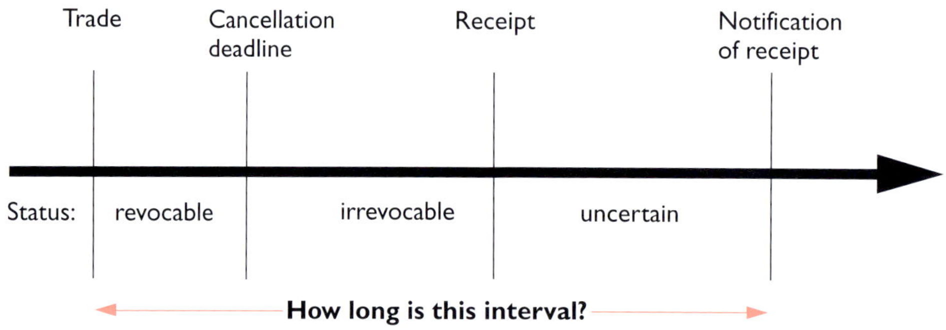

The problem of settlement risk

This diagram originates from the Foreign Exchange Committee which operates under the auspices of the Federal Reserve in the US. Traditionally FX settlement risk had not been measured as a credit risk exposure, but the truth is that you pay your own currency away long before you know, for certain, that you have received the currency receivable with finality. The diagram divides up the settlement risk period into stages when you can revoke your own payment, when you can't, and when the money is credited to your account (eg at the central bank) but either you don't know that or (if you do) there is a question as to the finality of receipt.

7.8.2 What is finality?

Whether a payment or a securities transfer is involved, the central question in relation to settlement risk is whether the transfer has happened with finality. But different people mean different things by this word and that makes a nice recipe for confusion and bad risk management. Here are some candidates for the best way of defining finality:

- **A transfer is final when it is unconditional** This definition is unsatisfactory: what conditions are we talking about? Confusion is likely to arise because of the temptation to think about the conditions on which the transfer *obligation* depends. If these are satisfied, nobody could argue that a transfer is not due, but equally it does not mean that a transfer has been made, let alone made with finality.
- **A transfer is final when the obligation to pay is discharged** This formula focuses on the right concept: the performance of the transfer obligation. Unfortunately it does not help much, since the obligation to transfer is probably discharged when a transfer is made with finality. If something can happen which means that the transfer is illusory then the chances are that the obligation has not been satisfied. Closer analysis of the settlement process is needed.
- **A transfer is final when the payer can no longer revoke it** This looks more attractive, since it focuses on the mechanics of transfer. The settlement process can be stopped by the person obliged to pay or transfer securities. If he is no longer entitled to do so then the transferee has a reasonable degree of comfort that the cash or securities have been received with finality. Or does he? Revocation is only one of a number of possible threats to finality. What if the system allows for the reversal of transfers if something goes wrong, which may have had nothing to do with the payer? An example of this is an unwind in a net settlement system (see section 7.8.3).
- **A transfer is final when the rules of the system will no longer allow reversal** This formula turns attention away from the payer towards other potential risks, but does not lose sight of the importance of revocation by the transferor. The difficulty here is that the rules of most settlement systems are contractual and may not withstand an attack under

insolvency laws. For example, if a transfer is made via a normal correspondent banking relationship, it is a question of contract terms whether a credit entry in the correspondent's books has to be reversed or not. These may be vulnerable to attack by a liquidator under zero-hour laws, or as preferences, or under other insolvency laws: see further below. Most legal notions of finality have carve-outs for fraud and insolvency.

- **A payment is final when there are no legal grounds to reverse the settlement** This formulation should capture all the insolvency and fraud risks which will affect the system operator. By focusing on the system, there is still some room to attack *the transferee* outside the system, and achieve justice for the victims of fraud or for creditors. The other users of the system should be unaffected. To illustrate the distinction: A steals B's securities and transfers them to C through the system. Under the relevant legal rules C must give them back to B. This is not a finality problem, since the reversal of the transfer occurs outside the settlement system. Contrast the situation where X transfers securities to Y then changes his mind (or goes bankrupt and his liquidator changes it for him) and the system operator is legally required to treat X's transfer instructions as void. This is a problem for the system and is therefore a finality issue.

Threats to finality divide into the following main classes:

- **Revocation risk** This is the risk that the payer might legitimately cancel the transfer instruction at a time when the transferee had been led to believe that the payment or securities had been received. So long as the settlement system does not advise the payee of receipt until after the transfer instruction is irrevocable, this risk should be negligible—provided, of course, that the users of the system understand the way the system works. If this risk can arise, it suggests that the rules of the system could be improved.
- **Illegality risk** This is the risk that to make the transfer might become illegal under general legal principles, notwithstanding that the rules of the system allow the transfer to be made. The parties could find that, despite the wishes of either of them, the transfer is unwound. Examples of laws which could have this outcome are sanctions and money-laundering legislation. The only practical solution to this difficulty is to make sure that the parties know what the possible legal risks are and put in place monitoring arrangements to ensure that they are not taken by surprise.
- **Attachments and tracing risk** This is the risk that the money or securities which is the subject matter of the transfer did not belong to the payer, because of some superior claim by another person, such as a person who has attached a bank account, or a person from whom the money or securities were fraudulently extracted. The means of dealing with this risk are again related to knowledge—in many legal systems it is hard to penalise either party if ignorant of the circumstances.
- **Preference risk** This is an insolvency-related risk. Most legal systems give a liquidator or other bankruptcy official a power to attack some pre-bankruptcy transactions as detrimental to the general body of creditors. Typically, a payment of pre-existing indebtedness, made by a company which cannot afford it, gives a ground for such an attack. Usually, however, there is a requirement for the liquidator to show that the payee knew that the payer was insolvent at the time or (which is much the same thing) that the payment would prejudice other creditors. Knowledge of the facts will, in these cases, enable the payee to form some judgment as to the reliability of the payment. Similar attacks can also be made on transfers of property other than cash in some jurisdictions.
- **Zero-hour and void disposition risks** These are also insolvency-related risks. Under some legal systems payments and other property disposals are disallowed after a certain point in a company's descent into insolvency (ie 'dispositions' are void). If and when,

subsequently, a bankruptcy order is made, any payment or disposal made after that point can be reclaimed by the liquidator for the benefit of creditors generally. The feature of these insolvency laws is that they do *not* generally require the liquidator to establish that the payee or recipient of property knew about the payer's insolvency. Zero-hour laws are a particular species of void disposition law which invalidate payments and other property disposals after midnight (zero hour) at the start of the day on which a bankruptcy order is made—in other words, if a payment is made at 10 am and a bankruptcy order is made in the afternoon, the payment is void *even though at the time nobody could possibly know for some hours that bankruptcy was even contemplated*. Worse, some void disposition laws allow for the risk period, within which transfers can be attacked retrospectively, to stretch back to the date on which the bankruptcy petition was presented, which can be as long as several weeks.

The EU Settlement Finality Directive is intended to eliminate most if not all of these threats in relation to participants in payment and securities settlement systems which are situated in the EU and have been designated by member states as being of importance, eg with regard to systemic risk.

7.8.3 DNS and RTGS system

There are two fundamental types of settlement system: real time gross settlement (RTGS) and daily net settlement (DNS). The risks inherent in the settlement process depend crucially on the type of system. Daily net settlement is the arrangement which has historically been in use, largely because it is operationally easier for the system operator.

Real Time Gross Settlement and Daily Net Settlement

(These arrangements are typical rather than universal; the rules of any particular system should be consulted in order to ascertain what variations exist)

Real time gross settlement

Principle: each settlement is separately and immediately processed and participants make or receive a separate payment into or from the system for each settlement

- Where payee funds/borrowing limits permit, payment instruction is processed
- Payee is notified when processing is completed
- Payers must pay in or borrow in order to fund each payment; if payer has no funds in the system at the time of the payment, payer may borrow (subject to provision of collateral) or the payment will fail
- System makes funds available to each payee immediately upon processing each payment

Daily net settlement

Principle: settlements are aggregated and netted and participants make or receive a net balancing payment into or from the system at the end of the day

- Where risk limits permit, payment instruction is processed in real time
- Payee is notified in real time, even though payment is not yet final, when processing is completed
- Net payers make net inward transfers of funds before end of day in order to cover any net short position which would otherwise result
- System makes net outward transfers of funds to net payees at end of day

DNS Systems have the following drawbacks:

- in the event of a payment default by a participant, it may be necessary for all the settlements in the system to be unwound, unless one participant can be prevailed upon to provide the missing funds;
- to minimise the risk of an unwind, the system may require participants to make available liquidity to plug a non-payment by a defaulter and, to minimise the risk to participants, may impose strict position limits;
- the legal robustness of multilateral netting cannot be relied on in all jurisdictions, giving rise to the possibility that a liquidator of a failed participant (whether or not a net payer) seeks to unwind settlements.

7.8.4 Settlement risk in payment systems

Settlement risk in payment systems arises largely in the foreign exchange market, where participants are exchanging one currency (paid via one system) for another (paid elsewhere). Market initiatives include:

- **Netting** Settlement netting and novation netting can reduce the size of the payments which are due to be made on settlement day. (But not, unless supplemented with additional language, close-out netting. It is too late to close out once the settlement process has begun. ISDA terms provide for both close-out and settlement netting.) Multilateral netting through a central counterparty can reduce the risk still further—according to one source up to 80 per cent compared with bilateral netting and up to 95 per cent compared with settling gross. But netting cannot eliminate settlement risk. The problem is that you cannot net apples against pears and there is still an interval between making an irrevocable payment and receiving an incoming payment with finality.
- **Contracts for differences** A variant on netting which is designed to eliminate foreign exchange settlement exposures is to offset a currency payment obligation shortly before settlement day by entering into a tom-next swap. When settlement day arrives, the original payment obligation and the payment obligation under the swap cancel each other out. The system relies on a never-never perpetual postponement of the moment when an actual payment needs to be made, though other risks such as market and operational risks are put in the place of settlement risk. Where the bulk of foreign exchange transactions are done for speculation or hedging purposes, rather than requiring actual delivery, contracts for differences represent effective risk reduction.
- **Fed Report Practice Recommendations** The Federal Reserve Board has made a number of practice recommendations relating to FX settlement risks, which can reduce the period and size of settlement risk. These include overhaul of correspondent banking arrangements, monitoring of non-receipts and prompt follow-up, establishment of netting arrangements, effective credit risk control and fire-drills for crisis management.
- **The CLS Bank project** A full PvP solution to foreign exchange settlement risk called Continuous Linked Settlement is being built which is intended to achieve settlement between counterparties to a transaction in different currencies by book transfers in the counterparties' accounts held at a single multicurrency bank.
- **RTGS** Real-time gross settlement ensures that you get your money immediately, rather than waiting for a computer system to do end-of-cycle calculations—by which time one

of the participants in the system may have failed, thereby giving rise to a risk of unwind (see further section 7.8.3 on types of settlement system).

7.8.5 Settlement risk in securities settlement systems

Securities settlement systems come in all sorts of guises. This makes the risks they entail very difficult to evaluate. The Basle Committee has categorised their ability to deliver DvP into three groups, which have different degrees of risk. The basic ideas (daily net settlement v real time gross settlement) are the same as for payment systems; the key difference is that securities are not cash.

Model 1	Model 2	Model 3
Securities transfers settled gross in real time	Securities transfers settled gross in real time	Securities transfers settled net at end of cycle (typically daily)
Payments settled gross in real time	Payments settled net at end of cycle (typically daily)	Payments settled net at end of cycle (typically daily)
Risk of high settlement failure rate owing to need for participants to have high liquidity in securities and cash at all times	Finality of securities transfer precedes finality of payments	Failure to deliver the net amount of securities or cash could cause an unwind
Credit risks arise because need for liquidity encourages making of credit advances to participants	Banks involved in settlement process are typically required to guarantee the payments (thereby exposing themselves to credit risk in the event of an unwind) to overcome the timing mismatch	The system operator may require participants to provide standby cash- or stock-lending facilities to reduce unwind risk in the event of failure of a participant to deliver or pay his net obligation

Securities are not cash

What is cash? Cash is not hundred dollar bills stuffed under the mattress. When you get your salary you don't get paid in dollar bills in a brown envelope. Cash is a payment obligation owed by a bank. If you are yourself a bank, cash could be a payment obligation owed by a central bank. The point is, however you look at it, cash is something owed, not something you can touch and own. Securities are different . . . or are they?

The law does not yet think of securities accounts in the same way as bank accounts. If securities are credited to my account with a custodian or broker I assume that means that I *own* them—if he goes bust then I can still retrieve them from the wreck. (Not so with cash, even if I do talk about 'my money'.) Of course securities may be dematerialised, so that 'ownership' means having one's name registered as the owner in the definitive electronic record; and where an intermediary such as a custodian is registered instead of me, 'ownership' probably means having unchallengeable rights to have one's name substituted for that of the intermediary's. Chains of intermediaries complicate things, which is why taking securities as collateral is so involved.

How does this affect securities settlement systems? Because the system may not be able to transfer 'ownership' unless it has access to the definitive register of owners. DvP is not really DvP if you part with your cash and do not get final and irreversible transfer of title in return. So in any securities settlement system it is worth looking at what rights the system does give you when it is holding the securities to your account. Technically it is very hard to line up irreversible payments with irreversible transfers of ownership of securities, because it is rare for a bank to be the holder of the definitive register of ownership and thus to be able to guarantee simultaneity of transfer.

Things to watch in securities settlement systems

- Liquidity (both for cash and securities) needs to be available; with RTGS systems, in significant volumes.
- Fail rates will be higher for RTGS systems because DNS systems eradicate timing problems. RTGS operators' liquidity arrangements need additional scrutiny.
- Overdrawn securities accounts indicate a system which is not transferring true 'ownership' of securities—you cannot own something negative—what is going on here (like cash accounts) is that the securities account represents the operator's promise to deliver the relevant number of securities.
- Guarantees of finality may be offered by a DNS system operator to reduce the impact of fails: either the operator or a third party will guarantee that the cash or securities recorded as credited to a participant's account cannot be taken away if at the end of the processing cycle a participant has not put in the net amount of cash or securities due from him.

7.8.6 Reducing settlement fails

Settlement failures may be because of insolvency, or because of failure to obtain securities or cash in the right currency in time. The problem is that you may not know the reason for the failure: the second type may be a symptom of the first, but the second type may give no more difficulty than a liquidity or funding cost which can be reclaimed later from the other party to the failed settlement. With international trades in securities, there is a particular risk of failures where settlement is dependent on receipt of securities across borders; transactions get stuck when they encounter DNS systems with only one processing cycle a day. Dependency on Victorian plumbing can lead to an assumption that the system, rather than the participants in it, is to blame when things go wrong.

Oiling the machine

Various processing techniques allow the system operator to deliver a more efficient service:

- Queuing and order or processing A must deliver 100 to B; B must deliver 150 to C; B puts 50 into the system knowing that 100 is due to reach his account shortly. The system has to decide in what order to process these transactions in relation to the other few thousand demanding its attention. It is inefficient to keep submitting a transaction for attempted settlement if it is repeatedly going to be rejected because the parties do not have the requisite number of securities in their accounts. The B-C transaction cannot settle until the A-B transaction does. If the system can spot that settling the A-B transaction also unblocks the B-C transaction it should go to the head of the queue.

- **Partial settlement** A must deliver 100 to B; B must deliver 50 to C; A has only 60 in the system but expects the balance of 40 later in the day. If a partial settlement of the A-B transaction is allowable, the B-C transaction can also settle.
- **Overdrafts and cross-collateralisation** A must deliver 100 securities of type 1 to B; A has 200 securities of type 2 in the system but none of type 1. Type 2 securities are worth more than type 1. If the system operator can treat the type 2 securities as collateral and allow A an overdraft on his type 1 securities account, the A-B transaction may settle (but note that B does not get ownership of type 1 securities, simply a promise by the system operator that 100 type 1 securities will be delivered to him or to his order).
- **Circles processing** A must deliver 100 to B; B has to deliver 120 to C; C must deliver 45 to A. Each of A, B and C reckons that if C, A or B respectively delivers securities first, the number of securities which he himself has to deliver will be reduced. This tends to encourage all three to put their securities in at the last possible moment and probably means that all three transfers will fail. Circles processing operates a net settlement system in miniature for these transactions, thereby breaking the deadlock.

For more on clearing and settlement systems, see sections 8.2.3 (discussion of counterparty relationships which can arise) and 10.5.3 (description of regulatory requirements applicable to multilateral netting systems).

REFERENCES

Federal Reserve Board practice recommendations on settlement risk

- New York Foreign Exchange Committee *Reducing Foreign Exchange Settlement Risk* (October 1994).

Basle categorisation of DvP systems

- Bank for International Settlements *Delivery versus payment in Securities Settlement Systems* (September 1992).

FURTHER READING

Basle Committee guidance on FX Settlement risk

- Bank for International Settlements *Settlement Risk in Foreign Exchange Transactions* (March 1996),
- Bank for International Settlements *Reducing Foreign Exchange Settlement Risk – A Progress Report* (July 1998).

7.9 INSOLVENCY-PROOFING

7.9.1 Protecting against insolvency attacks

Credit risk events can change whether and when you get paid. In part this is because insolvency officers have special powers. Managing credit risk effectively includes protecting against adverse consequences of credit risk events. For more on insolvency officers' powers, see section 8.5.2. The main causes of concern are:

- **Preference, undervalue** Arm's-length transactions are unlikely to be vulnerable. If the company is solvent at the time of the transaction, it is unlikely to be vulnerable. If there is doubt about the counterparty's solvency and there could be doubt about the transaction (for example, if the parties are part of the same group), check the board minutes of the counterparty to ensure that the counterparty's objectives were proper. And don't forget the obvious: granting security definitely does put the solvent party in a better position and may be a preference.
- **Void dispositions** Dispositions which are void can be validated by the court. Validation is unlikely if the party affected cannot show that it was unaware of the winding-up petition. However, if reasonable steps are taken to check for petitions, there is a good chance of validation. So, if collateral is being posted, carry out a telephone search. (Be aware of the limitations on searches: insolvency proceedings may be initiated in courts outside London which are not linked up in real-time to the register searchable by telephone.)
- **Disclaimer** A liquidator's job is not to cause difficulty for counterparties. His duty is to maximise the estate for creditors. He will not disclaim property or transactions unless there is some benefit to the estate. Disclaiming property is rarely likely to benefit the estate, since the non-defaulting party is allowed to prove in the liquidation for the losses suffered as a result of the disclaimer. Disclaimer is usually a live issue only with leasehold property and rarely causes difficulty in other circumstances. If a liquidator wants to avoid performing a transaction he can just refuse to do so, which is no different from any other defaulting party, except that damages will not be forthcoming because of the insolvency.
- **Moratorium** Administration prevents enforcement of security and taking of legal proceedings. However, other collateral techniques avoid the stay on enforcement; termination clauses (and other self-help contractual remedies, such as set-off and netting) work against administrators; and it is generally unnecessary to sue companies in administration except to preserve rights under the Limitation Acts (in which case the administrator or the court may grant leave to initiate proceedings protectively).

7.9.2 Priority leapfrog

The other means of dealing with the risk of insolvency are to ensure that one is first in the queue to be paid out of the limited assets which will remain when insolvency proceedings start. Jockeying for priority is a special art; aiming for first place is a doomed exercise unless you are an insolvency officer, whose expenses will nearly always rank first.

Cases in which it is possible to get paid ahead of ordinary unsecured creditors include:

- proprietary claims, including claims for recovery of property held by the insolvent person (but which does not belong to the insolvent person). These include entitlement to collateral as well as recovery of assets held in custody. UK client money protection falls into this category (see section 2.7).

- privileged (preferential debt) claims. In the UK few creditors can claim to be privileged and therefore to be paid in full before unsecured creditors. In other countries customers of insolvent regulated financial sector corporations may be entitled to this status.

Other creditors may be playing the same game. Hence the importance of covenants (negative pledges) which require the counterparty not to create security or other rights which allow other creditors to queue-barge. And the risks which go with being a subordinated lender.

7.10 PROPRIETARY CLAIMS

7.10.1 Objectives of proprietary claims

Credit risk can be controlled by obtaining a property right. Collateral techniques, for example, depend on obtaining a proprietary interest in the counterparty's property. The advantage of a property claim is that you can recover the property *as your own* in the event of the other party's insolvency. You can demand that the liquidator hand it back to you without using it to satisfy creditors' claims. In other words, having a property claim converts credit risk into market risk on the property; having cash may be safer even though it means (for those of us not fortunate enough to have accounts at the central bank) credit risk on another institution.

Where the counterparty has gone bust, having a proprietary claim is highly advantageous. Sometimes the law will allow you to claim a proprietary right when you might not expect it; and sometimes it will deny you a proprietary right when you thought you had one. Cases where property rights can arise against unsuspecting third parties include:

- tracing claims where you can follow your own property into the hands of an innocent recipient; where the property is intangible, the rules for tracing are extremely complex and should not be relied on as a means of risk management;
- constructive trust claims where property has been dishonestly dealt with (misappropriated in knowledge that it is trust property; or where a person has dishonestly assisted a breach of trust) the relationship of trustee-beneficiary may be imposed by the court, giving rise to proprietary as well as personal (money) claims.

The table shows some of the cases where you might not get a property right when you thought you might have one. Other situations where a property right can be taken away arise in the context of global custody are considered in section 7.10.3.

The area to watch is where property claims migrate into personal (credit risk) claims. The greatest dangers arise in custodianship and securities clearance systems, where often the answer to this question is far from clear.

Legal situation	Nature of claim
• I have a right to receive certain property held by the counterparty	• Could be either proprietary or personal (personal claims no good in counterparty's insolvency)
• I have a right to demand that the counterparty deliver up certain property to me	• Could be either proprietary or personal—the counterparty could simply be under a contractual duty to buy in some of the property in order to comply with its obligation—eg it has simply taken a short position
• I have a right to demand that the counterparty guard the property and does not deal with it in any way	• Probably proprietary
• The counterparty can substitute different property notwithstanding my rights	• Depends on the nature of the property—if it is 'fungible' (any two securities are alike, so it is irrelevant if I get back the precise one that I gave) then this is consistent with a property claim, but if the property is not fungible it is not

7.10.2 Typical proprietary situations

Firms may have proprietary claims in the following situations:

- Collateral See section 7.5.
- Client money See section 2.7.1.
- Custody See section 7.10.3.
- The bullion market Are the rights really proprietary? Where the securities or other property is unallocated, the rights against the custodian will be mere delivery rights — ie contractual rights only. A promise or undertaking to allocate does not achieve more (see further section 9.5.2).
- Securities held by brokers raise similar issues Shortfalls in client assets raise awkward conundrums if detected when insolvency strikes and it does not follow that clients will receive a pari passu division of what is there (though there is a judicial trend that way).
- Warehouse warrants Possession of warrants is traditionally regarded as equivalent to ownership of the underlying commodity stored in the warehouse and transfer of the warrants is treated as transferring title to the commodity. For more on warehouse warrants, see section 5.5.5.

As to customers' entitlements to compensation in cases where the system fails, see section 8.4.

7.10.3 Custody risk

Assets deposited with a custodian for safe-keeping raise a number of issues:

- will they be isolated from the claims of the custodian's creditors in the event of the custodian's insolvency?

- will the custodian manage the assets effectively, give notice of events (such as investors' meetings) which are important to enjoy the property fully, pass on income and so forth?
- will the custodian operate effective systems, so that time and expense is not incurred in depositing and withdrawing assets from custody?

Of these the most important in the credit risk context is the first: non-compliance with this principle converts my apparent proprietary claim back into credit risk. How could this happen? The following are the primary dangers under English law; if the custodian is situated elsewhere, the risks may be different:

- **Failure to segregate customers' from custodian's assets** If the custodian has failed to segregate his customers' property from his own, the requisites necessary to create a trust may be defeated. So even if there are in theory enough assets to go around, the claimants' claims may be personal (rights which rank alongside those of ordinary creditors) only.
- **Failure to maintain good records** If the custodian has failed to keep records of which customers are entitled to what, the custodian's liquidator will be hard pressed to verify any claimant's assertion that his claim is proprietary rather than personal.
- **Shortfalls in the assets held in custody** If the custodian holds only 10 securities when his books indicate that customers' claims to those securities (which are all acknowledged by the custodian to be property claims) total 100 securities and the custodian is insolvent so cannot buy in securities to make up the shortfall, some of the claimants' claims to property will fail. There are obscure rules in the case-law which can require assets to be distributed on the basis of first-in, first-out, or own-funds-used-first; sometimes a pari passu distribution (equal loss-sharing policy) is adopted. The rules are full of exceptions and are very costly and complex to implement.

To manage these risks, strong covenants, good reputation and effective policing are required. See also section 2.7.2 as to SFA's rules on safe custody.

8

Control of counterparty risk

8.1 CONTROL OF COUNTERPARTY RISK

8.1.1 Why investigate counterparty status?

Perhaps the most important part of counterparty risk is credit. If the counterparty can pay, we shouldn't have a problem. The purpose of this chapter is to challenge that statement. Counterparty issues add seasoning to the basic meat-and-veg of everyday credit risk management.

Counterparty-related risks may be every bit as important in controlling credit risk by ensuring that firms are aware of the risks in their relationships with others. The issues tend to be filed under 'legal' or 'too hard' (which is probably the same thing); this means that important distinctions between counterparty types, which can radically alter the risk that a counterparty or customer might fail to perform, may be overlooked.

The risk profiles of two identical transactions will differ if the transactions are with different counterparties. Two reasons underlie this: the parties will have different creditworthiness and they will have different constitutions. Credit can perhaps be ascertained from accounting records and one's understanding of how the counterparty controls operational risks. Constitutional and other factors which contribute the non-credit aspects of counterparty risk are predominantly legal in origin and need a different approach to control from credit.

Good risk management involves thorough knowledge of your counterparty or customer. Insufficient control can expose a firm to attack or criticism on any of the following lines:

- **Credit risk** If you think you are dealing with X, but your legal counterparty is Y, you need to know about Y's credit. This seems obvious, but it is surprising how in some markets there is confusion about who the true counterparty is.
- **Money laundering** You need to know your customer to demonstrate compliance with the rules in this area.
- **Conduct of business rules** The rules of financial services regulators impose differing requirements according to whether a counterparty is a private customer, a sophisticated investor or a wholesale market player.
- **Capital charges** Regulatory capital requirements differ according to the type of counterparty: for example banks (and, if proposed Basle Committee rules are adopted,

securities firms) are in some cases accorded a 20 per cent risk weighting for counterparty risk purposes, whereas ordinary corporate entities attract a 100 per cent risk weighting.

- Netting In many countries the effectiveness of netting is dependent on 'mutuality' of obligations between the parties. For example, a party contracting as trustee cannot set off liabilities incurred in his personal capacity against sums owed to the trust fund. If the relationship between them has been incorrectly analysed, there is a danger that mutuality may be broken.
- Collateral If collateral is provided by a person other than the person to whom the exposure is incurred, it will be 'third-party security', putting the collateral provider in a legal position equivalent to that of a guarantor. This will mean that additional precautions may need to be taken to ensure that the collateral is effective and enforceable in the default of the primary counterparty.
- Legal capacity, authority and licensing requirements It is elementary knowledge that one should check out a counterparty's capacity to enter into transactions, particularly derivatives transactions. Extra limitations on capacity and authority may come into operation when a counterparty is dealing as trustee, agent or partner.

8.1.2 Counterparty risk is more than credit risk

Non-credit counterparty risks include:

Legal risks

- lack of legal power (capacity) to enter into the transaction;
- failure to follow requisite corporate or other procedures;
- special exemption from legal process (eg statutory or sovereign immunity).

These issues are considered in section 8.1.4.

Structural risks

- wearing the wrong hat (counterparty is acting as trustee, agent, receiver, etc);
- counterparty's identity has not been revealed (eg where trading via a broker);
- counterparty is not who you think it is (where there is an undisclosed agency);
- pattern of trading is not well-understood (eg exchange-traded products);
- woolly thinking (trading with a company within a group does not ensure that the parent will support the subsidiary; taking a parent company guarantee does not ensure that the parent will be able to pay; providing collateral is splendid but whose obligations does it support, etc).

8.1.3 Control of counterparty risk

Possible techniques of counterparty risk control include:

- Due diligence Know your counterparty before you trade. There may be regulatory requirements to ask questions for money-laundering and conduct-of-business reasons.

But it is also good practice. Full due diligence may also involve scrutiny of constitutional documentation which the counterparty is reluctant to produce; press the issue and you may lose the business. What is the alternative?

- **Warranties and representations** Honest counterparties will be reluctant to give warranties on matters they know not to be true. Note that a warranty that somebody has capacity does not make it so: I am not Napoleon because I told you I was. Breach of warranty only gives you a right to sue for damages. If you are relying on a warranty to support your credit risk analysis, think again.
- **Third-party credit support** If X has dubious status, Y may be easier to analyse. But here again there may be dangers: will Y's obligation be dependent on the validity of the transaction with X? It may be necessary to make Y independently liable.
- **Find some other way of doing the trade** Eg take a transfer of property rather than rely on credit exposure.

8.1.4 Dealing with registered companies

Dealing with registered companies is an everyday business so counterparty risk management is a well-trodden path. Things which are commonly checked include:

- **Legal capacity** Can the counterparty do the deal? With companies incorporated and registered in the UK, you can generally *assume* that the answer is yes, because s 35 of the Companies Act 1985 means that limitations on capacity imposed by the company's memorandum of association (the document setting out the company's mission statement) do not apply to dealings with outsiders.

  Potential pitfalls:

  — *Is* the counterparty a registered company? Building societies, companies incorporated by royal charter or private Act of Parliament, local authorities, unincorporated associations, anything without 'Limited' or 'PLC' (or their variants) at the end of its name and anything which is not incorporated in the UK are not registered companies.

  — Section 35 only helps if the transaction was the 'act of the company' so you have to check whether the proper corporate procedures were followed—see below.

  — Look out for statutes and other things which have the same effect as incapacity—transactions rendered void and so forth—when you are told the company has capacity, you are still some way from a legal, valid and binding transaction.

- **Due corporate process** Has the counterparty taken the internal steps necessary to bind itself to the deal? With registered UK companies, again you can *assume* most of the bureaucratic steps have been followed, because s 35A of the Companies Act 1985 says that limitations on directors' powers to bind the company do not apply in dealings with outsiders.

  Potential pitfalls:

  — Registered companies again.

  — Section 35A only works if there has been a transaction decided on by the directors. To get the benefit of the section you need a board meeting. Case law says you can avoid looking into whether the board meeting was properly called, quorate and so forth if there is a board minute and nothing suggests that things are amiss. Lawyers will usually check from all available public information (eg registered names of current directors) that everything appears to be in order.

— The rule only applies to people dealing in good faith. So, no turning a blind eye to oddities which have come to your attention. But you don't have to investigate things in other circumstances.

— Everyday deals aren't done by directors. So does this mean that everyday deals aren't binding? Directors can delegate their authority to enter into transactions. But you need to be sure that the directors have duly done so in relation to the types of transaction you have in mind. This may mean (depending on the type of transaction) getting a list of authorised traders from the counterparty, or checking the scope of any power of attorney being relied on.

- Documents Are they binding? Even if the deal is properly authorised then the person who signs the document, or affixes the company seal (or whatever the appropriate means of executing the document is) needs to be duly authorised to do so. Again there are protective laws: s 36A of the Companies Act 1985 says that a document signed by two directors, or a director and a company secretary and expressed to be executed by the company, is duly executed; so is a document which is sealed 'in the presence of and attested by its clerk, secretary or other permanent officer or his deputy and a member of the board of directors' and you can rely on the document if these things purport to be so, under s 74 of the Law of Property Act 1925.

  Potential pitfalls

  — Distinguish authority to enter into the transaction from authority to execute documents—in some cases these are split, though in markets where deals are concluded orally the two are (or should be) joined.

  — You need to be sure that the people who signed as directors or secretary are indeed directors or a secretary in order to rely on s 36A; if you have a board minute giving signing authority to the tea-lady you do not need to worry about this.

REFERENCES

Reliance on capacity etc without checking

– Companies Act 1985, ss 35, 35A and 36A; Law of Property Act 1925, s 74.

8.2 UNDERSTANDING COUNTERPARTY RELATIONSHIPS

8.2.1 Checklist for a new counterparty relationship

- Who is the counterparty—which legal entity is involved; are different entities fulfilling different roles in different parts of the transaction; have each of the entities been assessed for the role they are to fulfil?

- Legal type of counterparty (registered company, building society, company incorporated by royal charter, industrial and provident society, individual, housing association, local authority, etc).

- If it's none of these, is it because it's a fund/it's a trust/it's a partnership—see inset box at section 8.3.
- Constitutional or statutory oddities applicable despite status as registered company (special laws relating to banks, insurance companies, investment firms, etc).
- Trading on own account or in some special role (trustee, agent, receiver, etc).

8.2.2 Exchange-traded products

Identifying the counterparty is less straightforward than it might seem where exchange-traded products are concerned. In the futures markets, exchanges such as LIFFE and LME, which are cleared through LCH, require market participants to deal on a principal-to-principal basis. Other markets, such as MEFF and OM, recognise brokers' customers as direct counterparties of the clearing house/exchange and envisage the broker acting as the customer's agent. The picture is confused, however, because:

- MATIF operates on a third basis: although the market is a principal-to-principal market, the exchange will step in in the event of a broker's default and transfer the customer's positions to a solvent broker;
- on some exchanges where the customer is acknowledged as a counterparty of the exchange, the broker is obliged to underwrite the customer's positions;
- in the US and even in the UK, a broker may act in a dual capacity: as principal for the purposes of duties owed to customers, but as agent for the purposes of regulation, eg if dealing as principal in futures contracts would normally require regulatory authorisation; so
- economically, the broker is regarded by his customer as acting upon his orders—this appears to describe an agency relationship.

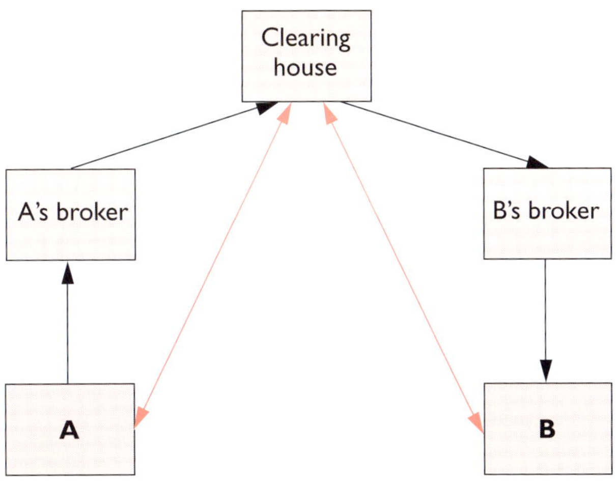

Do indirect participants have a counterparty relationship with the exchange or its clearing house?

A clearing house will often require to deal with its members as principals, ie it will not recognise any of its members' customers as having any rights or obligations vis-à-vis the clearing house. In some cases this model is varied—the clearing house agrees to owe obligations direct to the members' customers, so that the members' solvency ceases to be a concern for customers. The quid pro quo is that customers must agree to meet margin calls and other obligations on the contracts (though the primary responsibility for this will remain with the members).

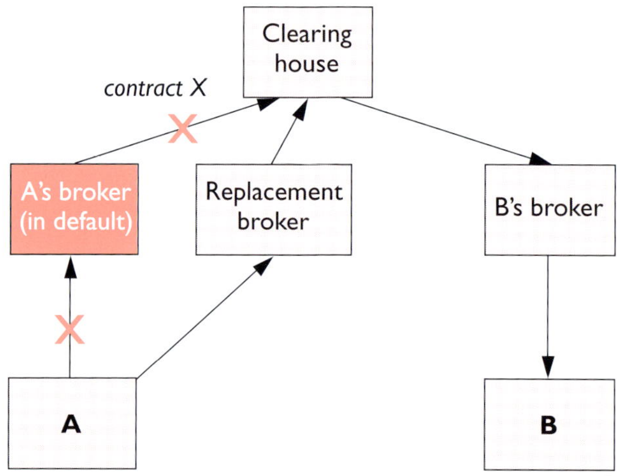

Can indirect participants benefit from a transfer of defaulter's contracts?

Some exchanges and clearing houses undertake to transfer customer positions held through a defaulting member in order to insulate the customers from the default. Where this happens, difficult questions arise as to whether the replacement broker may require the customer to provide him with margin in respect of the transferred positions, even though the customer may already have provided margin to the defaulting broker—the margin may have disappeared and the process of extricating margin from the defaulter may be difficult if the customer and clearing house have to deal with a liquidator. Where the members of the clearing house must deal as principal, there are also legal questions about the old positions held through the defaulter: must any loss on *contract X* be offset against margin held by the clearing house and must the customer share the benefit of any gains on *contract X* with other creditors of the defaulter?

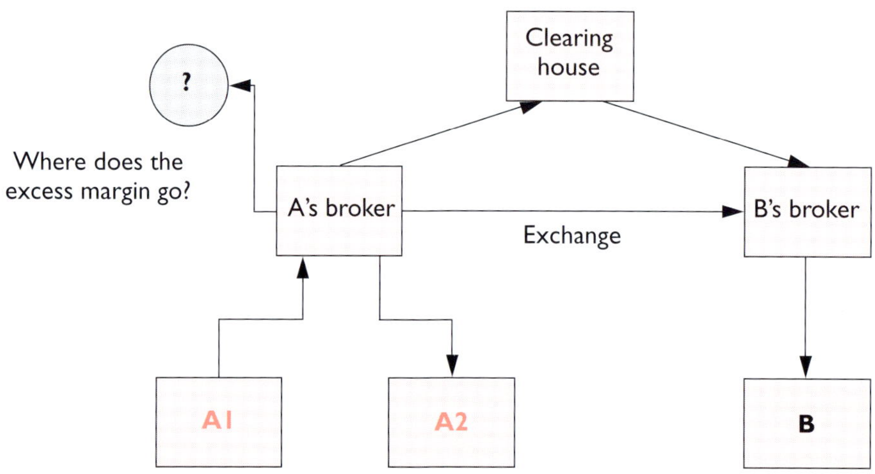

Net margining

If the clearing house operates a net margining system, it will allow a broker to offset countervailing positions even if they have been taken on behalf of different clients. This means that the broker's margin requirement vis-à-vis the clearing house will be reduced by comparison with a gross margining system. If the broker acts as principal, though, the broker needs to ensure that he is supplied with adequate margin to cover him in case his client defaults. So the client will often put up margin to the broker which the broker does not need to pass on to the clearing house. Where does the excess go? If it is cash margin it may be retained by the broker and used in his business; or if client money rules apply, it may be segregated from the broker's own assets.

Margin: cash passed up the chain to a broker is not beneficially owned by the customer. Cash is only a debt (except in rare instances overseas)—a credit risk. But credit risk on whom? It may be difficult to ascertain who the counterparty is in relation to the credit risk involved with margin. The counterparty could be the broker; but client money rules may subject the money in his hands to a trust in favour of the customer. 'Money' in such circumstances means the claim the broker has against his bank or upstream broker or counterparty. So the customer may be taking credit risk against an unknown broker or bank.

The picture is further complicated because the customer may not know whether the broker has offsetting positions reducing the upstream margin requirement which cause the customer's margin to be deposited at the bank rather than passed on to the next broker up the chain.

8.2.3 Securities clearance and settlement systems

Participation in clearance and settlement systems is difficult to analyse. There is a fundamental question: are the securities which I hold in the system 'mine' or do I simply have a contractual right to have the securities delivered to me? If I have only got a contractual right, I am exposed to credit (performance) risk on the person who owes me this obligation; if not, I am not concerned if he goes bankrupt (see further section 7.10).

Issues to watch out for include:

- Am I dealing through a correspondent? If I am not a direct participant in the system, does this mean that I am taking credit risk from the moment when I part with my securities to a person who is a direct participant?
- Is my interest as a client recorded on the system's books?
- Has my correspondent excluded liability for losses or fails?
- Does the system give me (or my correspondent) a property right in the underlying securities, or does participation in the system necessarily mean that I am dependent on the system operator's ability to perform?
- At what moment does transfer of property occur? If the system does not offer DvP, what is the nature of my interest at each point in the settlement process?
- Does the system offer a guarantee of performance or payment and if so who is the guarantor?
- Where are the securities located if they are held through a clearance system? If intermediation changes the place where they are located, it may change the rules about how property is transferred (see further section 7.5.4).

Many of these questions are explored further at section 7.8.5.

Note the confusion in terminology: some people use 'clearing house' and 'clearing system' interchangeably; but some distinctions between clearing and settlement remain. Clearing houses in the derivatives markets act as a central counterparty to all trades, providing a multilateral netting service whereby member A's long position entered into with member B can be netted off against member A's short position entered into with member C. What the clearing house does is net the *obligations* of the parties. Settlement systems achieve the settlement of those obligations. Some settlement systems work by means of multilateral netting DNS systems—see section 7.8.3—so can be called 'clearing systems'.

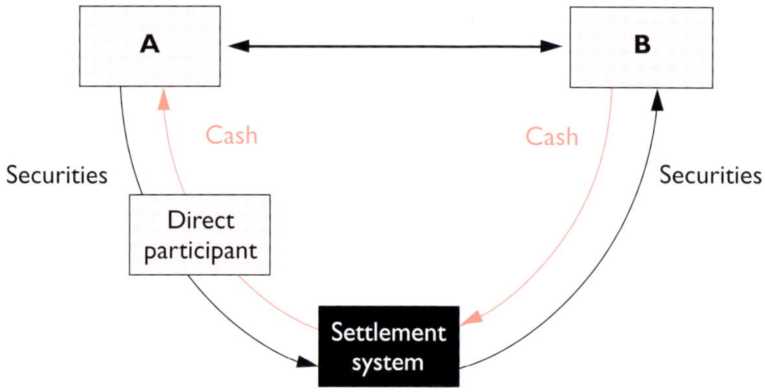

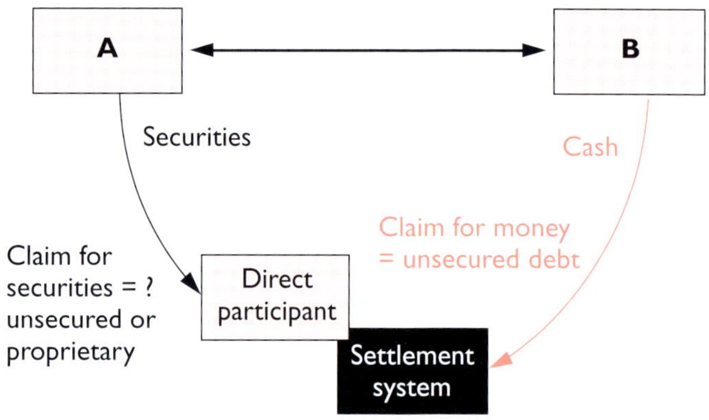

Participation in a securities settlement system

A has agreed to sell securities to B. B is a participant in the applicable securities settlement system (eg CREST). A is not. (On some exchanges, B is described as a 'clearing member' of the exchange. This does not necessarily mean that the exchange is served by a clearing house in the sense that derivatives exchanges have clearing houses.) A has to pass the securities to B; B has to pass cash to A.

In order to settle with B, A has to pass his securities to a person who is a direct participant in the settlement system. At this point A may lose his proprietary right in (ownership of) the securities and be left with a mere personal (unsecured debt) claim against the direct participant. Then there is the cash leg. Unless the settlement system does not offer DvP, the system must debit the cash accounts of a participant at the same time as it credits its securities account (or vice versa). So what does a 'credit' on a cash account mean? Presumably, that one is taking credit risk on the system operator, or in a system such as CREST, the settlement banks which stand behind it.

The Lamfalussy standards for multilateral netting systems are a limited yardstick for DNS systems' risk management (see section 10.5.3). In particular, the standards propose that participants' involvement should be subject to credit limits. Applying the Lamfalussy tests to securities settlement systems is not easy and it is brave to assume that such a system which is Lamfalussy compliant is a completely robust system.

For more on clearing and settlement systems, see sections 10.5.3 (description of regulatory requirements applicable to multilateral netting systems) and 7.8.3 (discussion of settlement risk).

8.2.4 Clearing services

Counterparties may offer a 'clearing' facility. This can mean:

- Either directly or through intermediaries, the counterparty participates in one or more clearing houses which 'guarantee' the performance of the transaction. This type of clearing facility is typical in futures markets where the customer's objective is to centralise and route margin calls and settlements through a single point of access to the markets.

- The counterparty participates in the settlement system for the market concerned and will use its right of access to enable customers' trades to be settled where customers themselves do not have such access. This type of clearing facility is typical in cash securities markets where direct participation in the settlement system is limited to a few robust market members. In the UK the rules of the London Stock Exchange provide two 'models' of clearing facility of this type: Model A clearers act as agent for another member of the exchange in reporting and arranging settlement; Model B clearers assume liability for the transactions as well as reporting and arranging settlement.

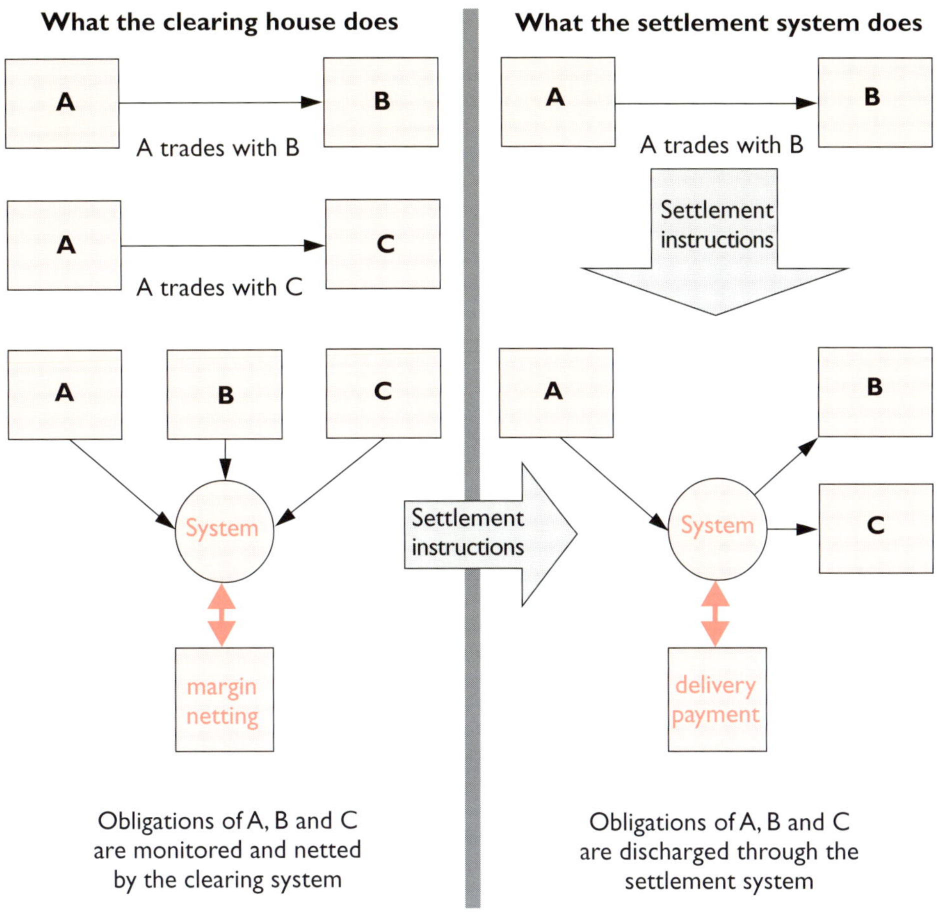

Clearing house and settlement system

A and B have entered into a trade which involves, at some stage, delivery of securities to settle the trade. If the trade was done on a 'cleared' market, the trade done by A may be offset against an opposite trade done between A and C, since the clearing house may allow this if the two trades are due to settle on the same day. On settlement day, A, B and C will have to settle up with the clearing house rather than each other. On the other hand, if the trade was done over-the-counter or on an exchange which does not have a clearing house, then A and B will have to arrange settlement with each other direct, eg by passing securities through the settlement system.

There is awful confusion as to what is a 'clearing house'. On a derivatives exchange a clearing house will typically act as counterparty to each trade thereby insulating members of the exchange from counterparty risk on other members. But the expression can also mean a settlement system: settlement systems which operate on a DNS basis (see section 7.8.3) have to tot up the delivery-in obligations of their participants and offset them against the delivery-out entitlements, which is a process very similar to that done by a derivatives clearing house. Clearing houses which operate as a central counterparty also guarantee settlement because they substitute themselves for each participant's original counterparty. But they may depend on other settlement systems to discharge their own and their members' obligations, because they do not operate the book-entry system which transfers title to the assets which were the subject matter of the transactions. So, London Clearing House is an example of a 'clearing system' in this diagram; Euroclear and CREST examples of 'settlement systems'.

REFERENCES

Model A vs Model B clearing

– Rules of the London Stock Exchange, rules 10.13 and 10.14.

8.3 SPECIAL COUNTERPARTY TYPES

Funds	Trusts	Partnerships
• A fund needs some sort of legal shell within which the assets are owned—the shell will be the counterparty • Typically the shell is a trust or a corporate entity (pension funds and unit trusts are usually trusts and investment 'trusts' and OIECs are companies) • Funds which are companies—normal corporate precautions should be taken • Funds which are trusts—trustee precautions should be taken • The fund manager is likely to be the agent of the company or the trustees, so agency precautions should be taken • See further dealing with agents, section 8.3.1	• Trusts are not legal entities in English law • Trust funds are legally owned by the trustees who have to hold the fund, on the terms of the trust, for the beneficiaries • The trustees are the persons entitled to deal with the fund—it is their powers which are relevant, so if the trustees are individuals their own personal capacity should be unlimited • There may also be constitutional limitations in the trust deed which counterparties should check • See further dealing with trustees, section 8.3.2	• Partnerships are only legal entities for some purposes, eg they can own property • Partners have, in general, authority to dispose of the partnership property, but there may be limitations in the partnership deed • In a limited liability partnership, some partners will have only limited personal liability for the firm's debts and usually the 'general partner' (with unlimited liability) has greater powers to deal with the partnership property • See further dealing with partnerships, section 8.3.3

8.3.1 Dealing with agents

Particular issues which arise with agents include:

- undisclosed agency;
- lack of mutuality for netting purposes;
- ineffectiveness of credit and counterparty checks where identity of principal is unknown.

Undisclosed agency should not pose any particular risks to firms which believe that the agent is their true counterparty. The main oddity of undisclosed agency is that the real principal can pop up, declare that he is the true counterparty and sue the firm on the transaction in the place of the agent. However, the firm which has been surprised in this way still has a choice whether to sue the agent or the principal. Credit checks should remain valid therefore. More difficulty arises in cases where the firm believes that their counterparty or customer is acting as intermediary and is uncertain as to whether the counterparty or customer is agent or principal; or where the customer acknowledges that it is a mere agent but is unwilling to disclose the identity of his principals.

Netting one principal's positions against another, or netting a principal's positions against the agent's house positions, will not be effective in an insolvent default because of the rule requiring mutuality. It is immaterial that the non-defaulting party was unaware of the facts. The only solutions are to investigate the position thoroughly or to rely on credit enhancement techniques other than netting.

Checking the identity of the true contracting party is essential to effective risk management. The agent may be willing to carry out counterparty and credit checks and to guarantee the accuracy of the responses. However, if no answers are forthcoming and no adequate credit support is given, the firm may have little choice but to decline the business. In other cases all these details may be forthcoming, but you may be relying on the agent to do other things. Check the 'indirect customer' rules of your regulator—are you relying on the agent to ascertain the proper classification of the customer and, if so, what conduct of business rules apply (risk disclosures, client money rules, cooling off periods and so forth).

Undisclosed principals

Fund managers and others may place orders on behalf of customers whose identity is not known. Sometimes it is unclear whether the broker or manager is trading on his own account or on behalf of a client.

Dealing with fund managers: FSA Guidance on Dealing with Undisclosed Principals

The FSA's guidance to banks on dealing with fund managers acting for unidentified principals (funds) includes the following:

- The primary concern is large exposures: procedures to monitor large exposures should be implemented, particularly with regard to accurate measurement of exposures, compliance with limits, aggregation of positions, and pre- and post-notification requirements.
- Attention should be paid to other controls within the bank, eg monitoring credit limits.
- Banks may only deal on an undisclosed basis via fund managers which are regulated in the UK or under a 'CAD equivalent' regime.
- Documentation should be drawn up in accordance with the FLP guidelines (see section 8.3.2) and address:
  - whether the fund manager acts as principal;
  - whether the underlying client has capacity to enter into the transaction and authorise the fund manager to commit the client on its behalf and has actually done so (the fund manager should at least warrant that this is so);
  - responsibility for settlements;
  - money laundering obligations;
  - disclosure of the underlying client's default by the fund manager;
  - fund manager to hold sufficient funds;
  - allocation of trades;

  and, more obscurely:
  - 'legal/operational risk—this should cover, for example, different legal jurisdictions;
  - types of products;
  - agreed approach to credit-lines, unacceptable names, monitoring etc.
- Credit monitoring should cover the fund manager as well as the underlying customer, for example, covering the status and size of funds, quality and nature of customer base, the fund manager's due diligence process and controls.
- Risks are reduced if transactions are settled via a DVP settlement system within standard market settlement periods (see section 7.8.5).

There is regulatory guidance from the FSA (tucked away surreptitiously in banking supervisory policy on large exposures) and from the SFA (split between credit management policy and a board notice following the FSA's lead on large exposures). SFA recommendations in their credit management policy guidance include: seeking full disclosure of identity; seeking disclosure to persons stationed behind a Chinese wall erected for the purpose of disclosure; and seeking assurances from the agent, including due diligence on the agent's procedures for carrying out the checks.

Some thoughts on dealing with agents:

- take a representation or warranty as to capacity from the person with whom you are dealing;
- if the counterparty claims to be agent for unidentified principals, investigate whether the agent has conducted anti-money-laundering checks;
- check out the credit of the person with whom you are dealing: is he good enough for the loss you may suffer or are you relying on someone to stand behind him?
- if the credit is inadequate, consider enhancing it with collateral or a guarantee from the principal;
- consider whether industry standard documentation can help manage the risks (eg the Gilt Repo agency annex to the Global Master Repurchase Agreement, the Financial Law Panel's suggested wording for dealing with fund managers);
- ensure that the documents reflect the agent's role in checking the type of customer, which risk disclosures are made and the duties being taken on by the firm;
- ensure that you have documented the *discharge* of obligations: if you pay the agent, does that discharge your obligation to the principal; if the principal pays the agent, does that discharge his obligation to you; and think about obligations other than payment obligations, including the boring ones like giving notices and correcting errors.

8.3.2 Dealing with trustees

Particular issues in dealing with trustees include:

- exposure to trustees;
- lack of legal protection against defects in capacity and authority;
- limitations on investment powers;
- replacement of trustees;
- netting.

Trustees are often men of straw. It would be dangerous to incur large exposures to trustees for this reason. Although trustees are responsible for administration of funds which may be sizeable, it does not follow that persons doing business 'with the trust' have direct access to the trust fund to meet their liabilities. Under English law, the contracting party is the trustee and the trustee's counterparty can sue only the trustee for any failures on the trustee's part. The trustee, in turn, can seek an indemnity out of the trust fund, but:

- counterparties of the trustee's have no right of recourse to the trustee's indemnity;
- even where the courts do allow a counterparty to have recourse to the trust fund via the indemnity, the right may be postponed to other interests;
- the trustee can lose his right of indemnity, eg on account of misfeasance or breach of duty to his beneficiaries.

When dealing with a company registered under the Companies Acts, various protections are available to counterparties: they can generally assume that the company is free from impediments in its constitution as to the kind of business it can do and as to the proper corporate procedure to be followed, provided that the transaction in question has been authorised by the board of directors of the company (see section 8.1.4). Unfortunately the law of trusts is not so protective of counterparties and no assumptions of this type can be made in the vast majority of cases; an important exception is where the trust is a pension fund. The only solution is to carry out due diligence on the trustees' powers under the trust deed and the procedure which the trust deed requires the trustees to follow in order to approve a transaction.

Furthermore, there are statutory limitations on the types of investment activity which trustees can enter into. These limitations can be disapplied by appropriate language in the trust deed, but without checking the deed (or taking representations and warranties instead) it is impossible to know. Trust deeds do not commonly deal explicitly with derivatives transactions; where a trustee warrants that he is duly authorised to enter into the transaction this does not guarantee that the trustee will have recourse to the trust fund under his indemnity if he is mistaken.

Trustees may lack authority to deal with the trust fund because they have left office. The right to displace trustees is in some cases (in particular pension funds and charities) given to a third party. There is a possibility in these cases that a counterparty to a trust may continue to deal with a trustee who has lost his authority; there is only limited protection for outsiders under the relevant statutes. Another difficulty with trustee replacement is that incoming trustees are not obliged to take over the obligations of outgoing trustees, though it is commercial practice to do so. Where an outgoing trustee has committed defalcations such a practice may be unreliable as a guide to future conduct. Counterparties can only protect against these risks by due diligence or by ensuring that changes of trustees are monitored and that all incoming and replacement trustees expressly adopt the acts of their predecessors.

There has been doubt as to the effectiveness of netting with a counterparty or customer who is a trustee. Case law indicates that there is no mutuality between sums owed by a trustee in his personal capacity and sums owed to the trust fund; in the absence of mutuality netting may not work if one of the parties is insolvent. However, there is no such thing as an insolvent trust fund: a fund has no liabilities (only a list of claimants, ranked in priority, to what fund may or may not be there). The liabilities of the 'trust' are in law the liabilities of the trustee, though and of course there is such a thing as an insolvent trustee. But the insolvent trustee's insolvency office-holder should not be able to unwind a netting agreement and the fears about mutuality should in most cases be able to be overcome. Guidance issued by the Financial Law Panel in 1997 has helped clarify the law in this area.

Financial Law Panel Guidance on dealing with Trustees and Funds

There are two helpful FLP papers which are potentially relevant when dealing with trustees and funds:

- Financial Dealings with Trustees—Preliminary Discussion Paper (October 1997).
- Fund Management and Market Transactions—Practice Recommendation (September 1995).

The recommendations include:

- Do remember that the trustee is the counterparty.
- Do not expect to have direct access to the trust property.
- Do due diligence to obtain information on the trustee's powers.
- Do use a netting agreement.
- Do take security over trust assets.

The FLP also calls to mind that in the financial markets trustees often deal with their counterparties through a fund manager, so agency issues arise too. The principal issues are:

- documentation which fails to acknowledge the existence of the agency relationship;
- potential lack of legal capacity in the fund manager's underlying clients;
- trades carried out by fund managers prior to allocation to a particular fund and the question of which fund/client is responsible in a case of partial satisfaction of an order.

The FLP recommends draft clauses to deal with the following matters:

- when the fund manager enters into transactions for his own account and when as agent;
- whether the fund manager accepts responsibility for investigating the underlying client's capacity to enter into transactions and whether trading has been duly authorised in accordance with the appropriate process within the client's organisation; and if so, the degree of responsibility shouldered by the fund manager;
- whether, and when, the fund manager (as opposed to its client(s)) is liable as counterparty in respect of unallocated trades.

Some thoughts on mitigating the dangers of dealing with trustees:

- review the trust deed for capacity and authorisation procedures;
- request certified copies of all documentation authorising transactions and effecting changes to the board of trustees;
- enter into a netting agreement;
- take a charge over the trust fund;
- take a representation from the trustees as to their powers under the trust deed and as to their previous diligence and a warranty as to their continuing diligence;
- consider whether industry standard documentation can help manage the risks (eg the Futures and Options Association's trustee annex to the Master Netting Agreement, (and again) the Financial Law Panel's suggested wording for dealing with fund managers);

- check for the removal of trustees; if the trust is an occupational pension scheme, check that the employer has not gone into any form of insolvency procedure, since if this happens removal of trustees may be mandated under the Pension Schemes Act 1993;
- obtain an undertaking from trustees to notify each change of trustees and to obtain from incoming trustees an explicit adoption of previous contracts entered into with you by the trust.

8.3.3 Dealing with partnerships

Some of the issues when dealing with partnerships are:

- capacity of the partnership;
- authority of one partner to bind the firm;
- dissolution;
- special insolvency procedures;
- collateral and netting;
- changes of partners.

Partnerships have no legal personality: they are just a collection of people or organisations acting in common. This gives the clue to some of the complications. Some of the rights and obligations of partnerships have been modified to help partnerships do business and (in a few cases) to help outsiders. For example, a partnership can hold its own property and be sued as a single unit.

Partnerships' capacity may be limited in the same way as trusts. Fortunately the partners' capacity can be assumed in the case of individuals and checked (or the statutory protections relied on) in the case of registered companies. If, however, the partnership's constitution precludes certain activities, there is no statutory or other protection which can be invoked by outsiders to validate the transaction. The transaction will probably remain effective but only as against the particular partner or partners with whom it was agreed. This may of course change the credit or counterparty risk analysis.

A person who is held out to be a partner has ostensible authority to bind the firm. Counterparties dealing with such a person should in theory be able to deal with him in confidence that the firm will be bound even if in fact that person's authority was circumscribed in some way. In practice there may be evidential disputes as to a partner's authority and additional due diligence may be advisable.

Partnerships may be dissolved by operation of law. Dissolution may be automatic on the occurrence of certain events unless the partnership deed provides otherwise—for example, the retirement of a partner. Dissolution requires the partnership estate to be split up among the partners and removes the authority of partners to bind the firm. Clearly dissolution plays havoc with counterparty risk assessment and should be catered for explicitly in documentation.

The treatment on insolvency of a partnership is arcane in the extreme notwithstanding various recent reforms of English insolvency law of partnerships. There is a plethora of different insolvency procedures. It is important to remember that the property of the partnership is a separate estate in insolvency from the estates of the partners. While the partners remain liable (under English law there must, even in a limited partnership, remain one partner with unlimited liability) to top up the partnership estate if there would be a shortfall in payments to creditors, this liability is only as good as the solvency of the partners. If the partners themselves are insolvent, there are highly complex rules about the rights of the partners' personal creditors to participate in the partnership estate and vice versa. It should not be assumed that the partners' personal wealth will be unconditionally available to the partnership creditors.

Partnership creditors can seek to improve their position by taking collateral. Unpaid debts can be pursued through the courts in the ordinary way and a judgment can be enforced either against partnership property or against personal assets of the partners.

Sometimes it is said that partnerships cannot create floating charges. Technically this is untrue. Practically speaking, though, there is a difficulty here: for each of the partners who is an individual, the only limited machinery for registration of a floating charge created by the partnership is the cumbersome procedure under the Bills of Sale Acts, which would have to be followed each time the property over which the charge is to have effect is changed. The consequence of non-registration against a partner will be that the charge will be void against his trustee in bankruptcy. Taking collateral, other than by means of fixed charge, will be difficult.

Netting and cash collateral should be possible, however, since there seems to be no impediment to effective netting and set-off with a partnership, provided that the countervailing claims are all partnership claims and do not relate to the personal affairs of any particular partner.

Where partners change, the rules are similar to changes of trustees: outgoing partners are not liable for debts incurred after they left and incoming partners are not liable for debts incurred before they joined; but in commercial practice these rules are often modified for reputational reasons, so that incoming partners will ensure all old debts are paid and outgoing partners are indemnified in respect of liabilities incurred before their departure so as to give them a clean break. Outsiders can regard outgoing partners as still on the hook until notice is given or an advertisement is placed in the *London Gazette*.

Thoughts on dealing with partnerships:

- obtain a warranty as to capacity and authority;
- get more than one partner to sign;
- take cash collateral or fixed security;
- enter into a netting agreement;
- provide for termination of contracts upon dissolution;
- take warranties as to changes of partners;
- devise a default management strategy in case the partnership, or any of the partners becomes insolvent: which assets are to be targeted, which insolvency procedure is favoured.

8.3.4 Dealing with receivers, liquidators and administrators

Some of the issues when dealing with insolvency office-holders are:

- special powers to upset prior contractual arrangements;
- unusual basis for transacting new business.

Concern is often expressed about liquidators' and other office-holders' powers to interfere with pre-insolvency transactions. These powers differ according to the type of insolvency procedure (see section 8.5.2). Once insolvency has struck, it is generally too late to rearrange an existing transaction so as to immunise it from these powers. But it is worth structuring the transaction properly in the first place and it is worth putting in place a default management (contingency) plan (see section 8.5.3).

Office-holders also deal with counterparties on new, post-insolvency transactions. Usually this is because they are trying to realise the assets of the insolvent company, though in rehabilitative insolvency procedures they may have other objectives. Office-holders step into the shoes of the management of the insolvent company and are thus constrained by any limitations on capacity which the company had. But, if they are administrators, administrative receivers or liquidators, they are given a range of additional powers by statute. These are set out in Sch 1 to the Insolvency Act 1986 and cover most of the things one would expect office-holders to do. A receiver may not be an administrative receiver—it depends chiefly on how much of the company's property is under his control and even if the receiver was appointed 'as administrative receiver' he will not have the statutory powers unless the facts support his claim to this status. As there may be some pitfalls, it is worth asking specialist outside counsel to investigate whether the office-holder has been duly appointed. Once this has been established, usually there is no concern as to whether the office-holder has power and authority to enter into transactions; the issues arise on the terms of the transaction which will usually be quite different from a transaction with a solvent party.

The office-holder will usually be unwilling to give warranties. Taking warranties from the insolvent company would in any event be pointless. The office-holder will not wish to assume personal liability either and will usually exclude this explicitly. He will expect the counterparty to take all the risk that (for example) the insolvent company has no title to the assets being sold or that the credit of borrowers in a portfolio of loans is rock-bottom. Different techniques for managing such major transaction risks have to be found: usually there will be a discounted price to reflect the uncertainties. It may be possible to have an escrow arrangement relating to the price paid, with the funds held safely in a creditworthy bank for a period.

Some thoughts on dealing with insolvency office-holders on new transactions:

- investigate whether the office-holder has been duly appointed;
- (receivers) obtain a warranty, free from the exclusion of personal liability, that the receivers have been duly appointed as administrative receivers (where this is the case);
- consider mechanisms for mitigating risk of buying a pig in a poke—reduce price, escrow arrangements, deferred consideration.

8.3.5 Dealing with hedge funds

The issues when dealing with hedge funds are, in principle, no different from those encountered in any other counterparty relationship. But special guidance has been issued by the Basle Committee for banks dealing with hedge funds (referred to as 'highly leveraged institutions' or HLIs) since the near-collapse of Long Term Capital Management in 1998. The main points are:

- Before conducting business with HLIs, a bank should establish clear policies that govern its involvement consistent with its overall credit risk strategy and ensure that an adequate level of risk management is in place.
- A bank dealing with HLIs should use sound and well-defined credit standards which address the specific risks associated with HLIs. Banks should obtain comprehensive financial information about the HLI to understand its overall risk profile, such as firm-wide VaR and stress testing results, details of the risk measurement and management

systems it uses and information about its liquidity profile and its ability to meet margin calls in a crisis. In particular, the bank should investigate whether the HLI's repayment capacity is dependent on particular assumptions.

- Credit exposures on OTC derivatives positions should be measured and continuously monitored and the results incorporated into the decision-making process. Credit limits should be set; exposures should be grouped into realistic time horizons depending on the maturities of the potential exposures.
- Collateral, early termination and other contractual provisions are linked to credit quality and should relate to the HLI's ability to change its strategy or risk profile. Banks may seek to control credit risk pre-emptively. Collateral does not eliminate credit risk and may bring in liquidity, legal, custody and operational risks.

Most of these points are valid when dealing with any counterparty; what makes HLIs different is that their gearing wildly exaggerates any market fluctuation. This affects not only the profits or losses that the HLI makes but also its access to liquidity, its ability to close out its positions effectively and, ultimately, its solvency. The Basle paper points out that HLIs are unregulated, so that their leverage is not subject to prudential supervisory control and that it may be appropriate to get the HLI to post excess collateral to reflect the additional risk which is taken on if adequate financial information does not flow with sufficient frequency to enable effective credit risk monitoring.

REFERENCES

Regulatory guidance on unidentified principals

- FSA *Guide to Banking Supervisory Policy*, Chapter LE, Appendix 2.
- SFA Board Notice 511, SFA Rulebook Appendix 56.

Financial Law Panel guidance on fund managers

- Financial Law Panel *Fund Management and Market Transactions—A Practice Recommendation* (September 1995).

Financial Law Panel guidance on trustees

- Financial Law Panel *Financial Dealings with Trustees—A Preliminary Discussion Paper* (October 1997).

Basle guidance on hedge funds

- Bank for International Settlements *Sound Practices for Banks' Interaction with Highly Leveraged Institutions* (January 1999).

8.4 CUSTOMER COMPENSATION

8.4.1 Compensation schemes

Various schemes exist to compensate customers for losses suffered on the collapse of a regulated financial institution. Customers of investment firms (investors) and banks (depositors) are covered. The rules of the different schemes are complex, the exclusions are not uniform and the arrangements are undergoing reform. This section identifies some of the main features of the main schemes. Compensation is subject to EU Directives which determine the scope of the schemes. Participation in overseas schemes is sometimes available to firms doing cross-border business.

8.4.2 Investors' compensation

- Only 'private customers' may claim.
- Claims cover not only lost money and securities placed with an insolvent investment firm but other losses, which enables claims for bad investment advice to be brought.
- If the defaulting firm's liability is below £30,000, the full amount is paid; between £30,000 and £50,000, the sum paid is £30,000 plus 90 per cent of the excess over £30,000; over £50,000 the maximum payout of £48,000 is paid. Payments can be reduced if the compensation fund has insufficient resources in any year.
- Contributions to the fund are determined broadly by the nature and volume of investment business done by the contributing firm.

8.4.3 Depositors' compensation

- Anyone may claim, apart from banks and certain other excluded entities.
- Claims cover lost deposits only.
- Compensation is available directly to a customer where the deposit was placed by an investment firm in the form of a client account.
- The amount paid is 90 per cent of the first £20,000 in aggregate of deposits denominated in any EEA currency.
- Contributions to the fund are determined by the amount of eligible deposits taken by the firm.

8.4.4 Policyholders' compensation

- Who can claim and the level of compensation depend on the type of policy.
- For compulsory insurance, anyone can claim and 100 per cent is paid.
- For other types of insurance, only persons acting in a private capacity and partnerships of individuals can claim and 90 per cent is paid.
- There is no ceiling on the amount of compensation which is paid.

REFERENCES

EU Directives on Compensation
- Deposit Guarantee Directive 94/19/EC; Investor Compensation Directive 97/9/EC.

Investor compensation rules
- Financial Services Act 1986, s 54; Financial Services (Compensation of Investors) Rules 1994 (Securities and Investments Board).

Deposit compensation rules
- Banking Act 1987, ss 50–66.

Insurance compensation rules
- Policyholders Protection Acts 1975 and 1997.

8.5 HANDLING A COUNTERPARTY DEFAULT

8.5.1 Insolvency procedures

Liquidation/winding-up

The terms 'liquidation' and 'winding-up' are synonymous in English law. 'Bankruptcy' in England usually refers to insolvency of individuals rather than corporate entities.

Liquidation is primarily a remedy for unsecured creditors. The function of a liquidator is to realise the assets of an insolvent company and to distribute them to the persons entitled to the proceeds. His function is not to realise assets subject to valid security interests. Liquidation is also available to a solvent company as a method of terminating the venture carried on by the company and distributing the fruits to the company's shareholders. Liquidation can be initiated by the company itself or by a creditor.

If the company calls a shareholders' meeting which resolves to put the company into liquidation, this is called a 'voluntary' liquidation. Liquidation may also be initiated by a creditor: with this procedure a petition is presented to the court requesting that the company be wound up on the ground of its insolvency.

Receivership

Receivership is a remedy available only to a secured creditor. Often charge documentation contains express wording enabling the chargeholder to appoint a receiver if the grantor of the charge commits a default or fails to pay the sum secured by the charge when properly demanded. The function of a receiver is to realise the assets which have been charged and apply the proceeds to pay off the secured indebtedness. Where the receiver has been appointed over the whole of the company's assets and undertaking, he will usually wish to try to sell the company's business as a going concern. He will take over management of the company's business until a buyer can be found.

There are various types of receivership. An 'administrative receiver' is a receiver who has been appointed over all (or substantially all) of the company's assets and has been appointed by a person who has been given a floating charge by the company. If the receiver satisfies these conditions he will be an 'administrative' receiver and be able to exercise a series of additional statutory powers conferred by the Insolvency Act 1986 which are unavailable to other receivers.

The appointment of a receiver is a matter for the secured creditor. Once the right to appoint a receiver has arisen, which will almost invariably require some form of default or non-payment by the company which gave the charge, the receiver can be appointed by means of a simple document. There is no need to involve the court except in very unusual circumstances.

Administration

Administration is a procedure which can only be implemented in order to achieve one or more of the statutory purposes of an administration order. These are:

- the survival of the company and part or all of its business, as a going concern;
- the approval of a company voluntary arrangement (CVA);
- the sanction by the court of a scheme of arrangement (similar to a CVA); and

- a more advantageous realisation of the company's assets than would be achievable on a winding-up.

The first three objectives are designed to achieve a rescue of the company and the fourth may be capable of achieving a rescue of the company's business, so administration is often perceived to be a rehabilitative regime. The holder of a floating charge who is able to appoint an administrative receiver can veto an attempt to put the company into administration. Administration can only be initiated by a petition to the court. In theory the court will appoint a day on which to hear the administration petition; in practice the timetable in many administration cases is very much shorter, often with the hearing preceding the formal presentation of the petition.

An administration order (and an administration petition awaiting hearing) brings into force a moratorium preventing creditors from exercising their usual rights against the company unless the administrator consents or leave of the court is obtained. Leave is a matter for the court's discretion and whether it will be granted depends on the circumstances; however, if to give leave does not interfere with the purpose for which the administration order was granted and the person seeking leave is asserting a property right, leave is more likely to be given.

Company Voluntary Arrangements and Schemes of Arrangement

Company Voluntary Arrangements and Schemes of Arrangement ('schemes') are procedures whereby companies can compel their creditors to accept a compromise or composition in respect of their debts. Typically a composition will require creditors to accept less than 100p in the £ for their debt, or deferred payment over time, or a combination of both. In more complex CVAs and schemes different classes of creditors can be treated in different ways reflecting the relative strength of their positions. Both procedures require a meeting or meetings of creditors to be held and if a 75 per cent majority of creditors by value at each meeting approves the composition plan, the plan will bind all creditors. These procedures are useful primarily in binding ('cramming down') a minority of opposing creditors to accept a rescue plan which is acceptable to the majority.

8.5.2 Insolvency officers' powers

Various powers are given to insolvency office-holders to upset pre-insolvency transactions. These may require particular precautions. In addition, insolvency office-holders are not ashamed of taking points which are technical (such as lack of capacity) since there is no reputational risk for an insolvent company and their duty is to maximise the estate for the unpaid creditors. This means that the risk assessment of a transaction may change on insolvency for reasons unrelated to the credit of the counterparty: have you relied on the counterparty's commercial good sense and unwillingness to challenge received wisdom on any issue?

On the other hand, an insolvency office-holder has no general power to alter the terms of a transaction, so his power to cause difficulty for non-defaulting parties is limited.

- Liquidators A liquidator's powers are conferred by the Insolvency Act 1986. Slightly different powers and different controls on their exercise, arise depending on which type of liquidation is involved—for example, the power to run the company's business. From the solvent counterparty's viewpoint, the most important powers are those which entitle liquidators to attack transactions and the ability of liquidators simply to refuse to perform transactions (which often ends up with the same result). The most important attacks are described in the table. But do not ignore the potency of the liquidator's *power to do nothing*. With a solvent counterparty, downright refusal to perform will be met in the final analysis with threats of legal action. But if the counterparty is in liquidation, this is a meaningless threat: leave of the court will usually be required to begin proceedings and the chances are that the liquidator will not oppose them. The court will rarely order the liquidator to perform the contract and instead will award damages, which rank as an unsecured claim for a dividend alongside other creditors. A liquidator seeking to escape from a contractual obligation will thus only rarely have to use his statutory powers to do so.

- Administrators The most important effect of administration is the moratorium on creditors' remedies. This makes it unlawful to appoint a receiver or take other steps to enforce security, to repossess goods in the company's possession under hire-purchase or retention of title terms, to forfeit a lease, or to sue the company unless leave of the court or consent of the administrator is obtained. Like administrative receivers, administrators have a wide range of powers connected with management of the company, the power to examine the company's directors, the power to require utilities such as gas, telephone and electricity suppliers to continue to supply notwithstanding non-payment of their pre-administration accounts, the power to demand delivery up of the company's property and the power to sell assets which are the subject of security. Administrators also have a number of powers which are more like those available to liquidators, including the power to apply to set aside pre-administration transactions which are preferences or transactions at an undervalue.
- Receivers The primary source of a receiver's powers is the charge under which he was appointed. There are also limited powers (eg to collect rents and to create leases) which are conferred by the Law of Property Act 1925. An administrative receiver, however, has a wide range of additional powers under the Insolvency Act 1986. These powers include almost everything which is likely to be relevant to managing the company. An administrative receiver has additional powers (which cannot be conferred by contract), including the power to examine the company's directors, the power to require utilities such as gas, telephone and electricity suppliers to continue to supply notwithstanding non-payment of their pre-receivership accounts and the power to demand delivery up of the company's property. With leave of the court, an administrative receiver can sell property which is the subject of a third party's security interest.

REFERENCES

Insolvency office-holders' powers

- Insolvency Act 1986, Sch 1.
- *British Eagle International Air Lines v Air France* [1975] 1 WLR 758.

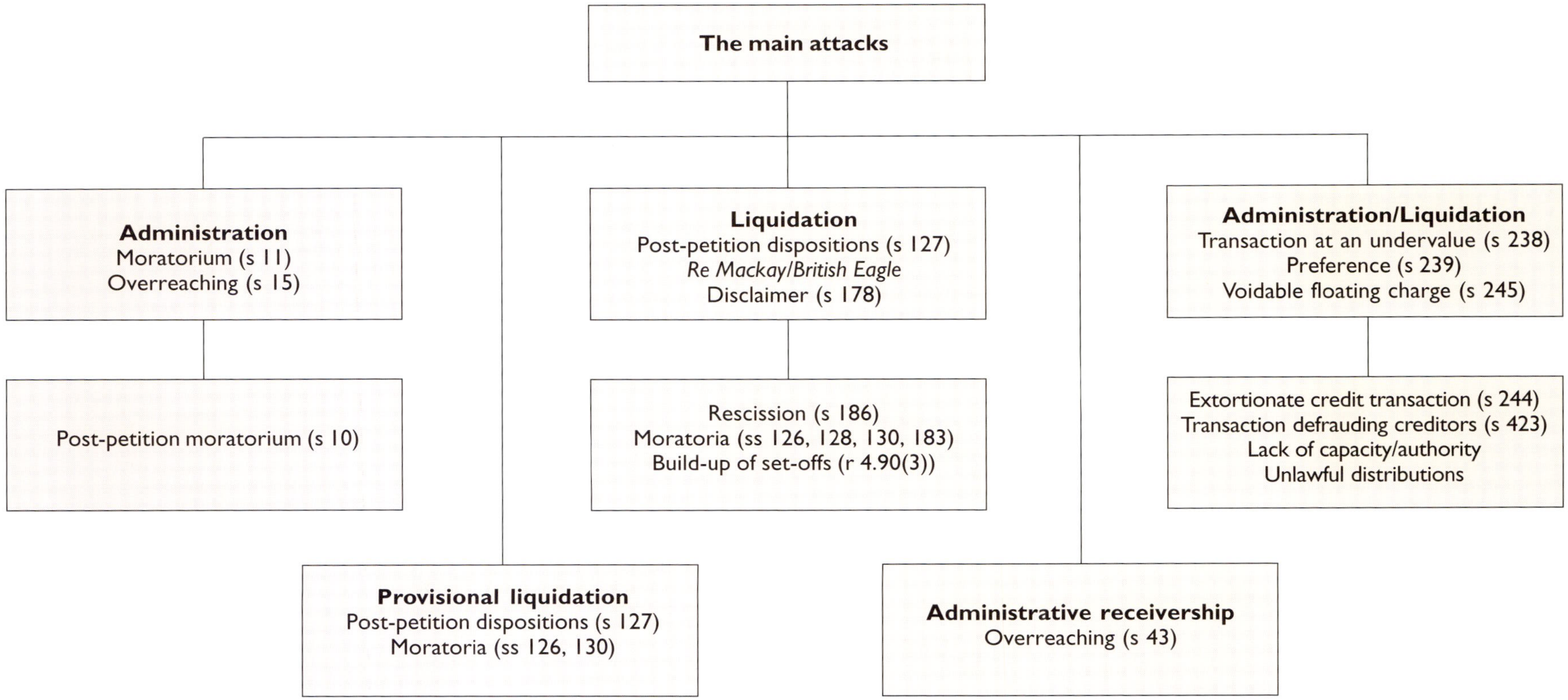

The insolvency office-holder's armoury

An insolvency office-holder's weapons depend on the regime under which he is appointed. Administrators and liquidators share some weapons, shown on the right-hand side of the diagram. Other weapons are specific to the type of insolvency procedure. The fire-power has been graded: the weapons in the upper box are generally more fearsome (at least to financial institutions) than those in the lower. Other procedures, such as provisional liquidation and administrative receivership, may be relevant, and these have different weaponry. The references to section numbers are to the Insolvency Act 1986.

COUNTERPARTY ISSUES

Insolvency Act 1986	Insolvency proceedings affected	Name of remedy	Circumstances from which attack might be made
s 238	Liquidation/Administration	Transaction at an undervalue	Here is £100 because you're a nice chap and I might go bust soon. (Generosity and liquidators don't mix. The liquidator might expect to see something resembling a bargain here.)
s 239	Liquidation/Administration	Preference	Here is the £100 I owe you in case I go bust tomorrow. (Good for you, at least till the liquidator finds out about it.)
s 244	Liquidation/Administration	Extortionate credit transaction	I will pay you interest at 100,000 bp over LIBOR. (Nothing wrong with that, of course. Well, not much apart from the interest rate.)
s 245	Liquidation/Administration	Voidable floating charge	I know I'm broke, so please take a floating charge as extra security for my outstanding loan. (More security for existing debts? The liquidator might think this is a bit off.)
s 423	Liquidation/Administration/ CVA /any "victim" can apply for an order	Transaction defrauding creditors	Here is £100 because you're a nice chap and I don't want my creditors to get it. (The creditors might think this is not such a good plan and apply to set things right.)
s 178	Liquidation	Disclaimer	I will take a lease of your house at only £100 a month but I will undertake full repairing obligations. (I expect my liquidator will think this is a lousy deal and try to get out of it.)
s 186	Liquidation	Statutory rescission	The deal is you supply me with goods at favourable prices on my order for 10 years. (You might not think this is such a good plan after I go bust and ask to be relieved of the bargain.)

ss 10, 11	Administration	Moratorium	Take a charge over this collateral. Incidentally, I am planning a formal reorganisation of my debts. (Tough about your ability to enforce it.)
ss 15, 43	Administration, Administrative receivership respectively	Overreaching	Take a charge over this collateral. (By the way, your power of sale might be exercised by my administrator/administrative receiver instead of you.)
s 175	Liquidation/Administration/ All types of receivership	Preferential debts	My employees will work for months without pay and I only pay the Inland Revenue and VAT-man on the final demand. (Bad luck for you as they'll get first pickings when the balloon goes up.)
ss 127	Liquidation	Post-petition dispositions	Here is £100 - you had better take it now as there is a winding-up petition against me. (Enjoy it while you can, the liquidator will want it back soon.)
s 130	Liquidation/Provisional liquidation	Moratorium	I don't feel like doing *that*. If you don't like my refusal, just try suing me. (Tough, eh, when you find you're not allowed to.)
Insolvency Rules 1986, r 4.90(3)	Liquidation	Build-up of set-offs	This is a good wheeze. I owe Fred £100. Fred will sell his claim against me for only £20. You owe me £100. If you buy Fred's claim, you could get a set-off and gain £80. PS: I have called a creditors' meeting for next week. (Oh, and because you know about that, you wont get the set-off after all.)
British Eagle/*re Mackay* cases	Liquidation	Forfeiture	Please take my car when I go bust. (Don't suppose the liquidator will think that's completely fair.)
Companies Act s 395	Liquidation/ Administration	Unregistered charge	As security, please take an assignment of my rights under this contract and a charge over the metal in this warehouse. (Your problem if you forgot about that Companies House registration stuff.)

8.5.3 Planning the strategy

As with any sort of risk event, it undoubtedly helps to have an emergency plan ready. With counterparty defaults no two are alike, but systems can be set up so that a prompt response can be put together and the maximum advantage can be retrieved (or minimum pain suffered) from the situation.

Use the early warning signals (missed payments, calls, settlement failures, exception reporting, staff sacked/walked out, slowdowns, odd trading patterns): do you have information flow systems which ensure that changes of pattern are reported to the credit team? (The wrong answer to this question is 'credit has no role after the decision to do business has been taken'.)

Lots of preparation can be done without jeopardising the counterparty relationship. Isolated legal entity collapses within a group of companies are unusual; so prepare for solvency problems to beset all companies in the same group. Even so, for every company to be afflicted in the same way is unusual, so different strategies may be needed for different companies in the counterparty's group.

Preparedness checklist

- Start with a clear understanding of the counterparty's group structure.
- Work out the transactional interrelationships—which companies are involved on our side, which on theirs.
- Work out where the offsets are and their timings. Don't forget that some insolvency procedures disallow set-offs across different legal entities (A owes me and I owe B; although A and B are in the same group, if B is in liquidation I cannot set off).
- Global arrangements—find out where the assets you want to grab/set-off against are located and which companies in the counterparty group are entitled to them: for example, if your group contains a bank which is holding a deposit, can this be used to mitigate your exposure?
- If possible, pre-arrange the offsetting exposures so that they arise in the right corporate entities.
- Work out the cash flow timings—where could the timing differences arise; bear in mind that close of business in Asia is different from close of business in America.
- Work out what is yours and whether you can get it, eg assets held by third parties, such as custody arrangements—will the third party allow you immediate access? Or if the asset is held by you, do you have rights over it?

Set up a war-room and *carry out a firedrill*. Things to consider are staff (who should have suitable authority to enable things to be done without question, even outside their usual area of involvement and who should have alternates in case of unavailability), information flow in a rapidly changing environment (email and bulletin boards?), appointing a taskforce controller, understanding what will happen and testing how it will work in practice.

Where counterparty solvency is questionable, how can you arrange your relationship with the counterparty so as to achieve (a) a continuing relationship if the signals have been misread but (b) avoidance of losses if the signals are right? Don't assume that no new business can be done, or that it is dangerous to take collateral or to receive a payment. Although insolvency officers can upset uncommercial or preferential transactions, often these powers do not preclude the provision of security by a company in financial difficulties. This may mean getting legal advice if the counterparty offers a real bargain on price or if collateral is to be made available.

Plan for mismatched timings, eg if they have to pay you several days before you pay them, you can usually withhold your own payment; but if the timings are the other way about, can you properly decline to pay until they reveal their hand? To delay without just cause may be unlawful and it may worsen the counterparty's problems. This strategy may incur you regulatory disapproval and there may be no defence if you are sued (even if by the time case comes to court their payment is due—but not if the counterparty is in liquidation). On the other hand it may be possible to get the counterparty to agree to a halfway-house such as an escrow arrangement, where a trusted third party holds the payment.

Close-out conundrums

- Can the transactions be closed out: is there a termination clause?
- Were they automatically terminated?
- Is it too late to terminate because the settlement process has begun?
- Is it economically advisable for transactions to be closed out?
- If exposures are closed out, how will this be done? Will a 'replacement cost' be calculated for the whole transaction? Or is the 'value' of each party's obligation assessed and set off?
- Will obligations due for future performance be accelerated or terminated?
- Is delivery of a security or other property necessary to collapse the relationship?
- Illegality vs default: if the circumstances which cause the counterparty's solvency problem make performance illegal as well as an event of default, does the contract machinery provide for a different procedure (and outcome) from pure insolvency?

8.5.4 Implementing the plan

At the very outset you need to establish which companies in the defaulter's group are in formal proceedings and which types of proceedings they are. You need to know this to work out what has been automatically terminated, where new exposures have arisen because the default leaves you unhedged and to prioritise work in implementing the contingency plan. You also need to check whether your credit support is affected—for example, if the parent company guarantor is insolvent.

Since the companies will be incorporated in various different countries, there can be sharp differences of policy and approach. For example, a proceeding going on in a country with a common law-based legal system may have an emphasis on trying to sell the business as a going concern; in other countries that may be unusual and a break-up and sell-off of assets may be more typical. Some countries appoint liquidators on a rota basis so the office-holder may have no experience of financial institution insolvency or its stock-in-trade.

Don't assume that the day one scenario will continue for long. Other companies in the group may take longer to implement formal insolvency proceedings because of court delays or other local factors. Also the procedure can switch: from provisional liquidation to full liquidation (Peregrine); from administration to sale to a new solvent parent (Barings); from administration to liquidation (other parts of Barings); from administration to an agreed workout (voluntary arrangement) (Chancery, Mount Banking Corp and various other small banks). A switch may have important consequences for:

- whether contracts are terminated;
- what remedies are available under contracts;

- the powers of the office-holder;
- the likelihood of payment of any sum owed;
- the bargaining power of the solvent party.

Getting confirmation of the office-holder's intentions may be necessary. In some cases there will be a press office which releases information periodically. Usually financial sector insolvencies unravel at lightning speed and it is impossible for the office-holder to set up effective information management systems which can keep up with developments. Rarely can insolvency office-holders be forced to supply information; and they will often be reluctant to compromise their bargaining position by giving away clues to strategic thinking.

But an administrator who proposes to sell a financial sector business will:

- need to act fast to preserve its value;
- need to obtain the approval of creditors or the court in order to do so;
- need to ensure that his plans are in the interest of creditors and therefore that his plans have broad appeal to creditors;
- need to give creditors an opportunity (which may be fleeting only) to comment on his plans, eg by responding to them in a court hearing;
- need to ensure that creditors with objections are ones with special interests which can safely be overridden for the common good.

These factors mean that administrators will usually wish to keep up some dialogue with creditors and counterparties. An office-holder who acts unfairly (in a manner which is unfairly prejudicial to the interests of a creditor or creditors) is at risk of being taken to court.

8.5.5 Default and its effect on contracts

The powers of liquidators, administrators and other insolvency office-holders are described at section 8.5.2. Applying these in practice, you will want to know:

- Can the office-holder force you to perform your obligations? Usually the answer is yes, subject to any valid termination right which you have already given yourself. An alternative (which is difficult to get to work) is to try to set up a 'repudiatory breach of contract' by the office-holder: if he breaches, then you can terminate. Until the time comes for the office-holder to perform it is usually unnecessary for the office-holder to confirm his readiness to perform on the due date. The mere fact that the company he is administering is insolvent is not enough, on its own, to establish a repudiatory breach. Office-holders can, and sometimes must, perform contracts.
- Can he cherry-pick? That is, can he select which contracts to perform and which to renege on? (Sometimes people think of this in terms of selective disclaimer—but it is not necessary for an office-holder to go through any special process of disclaiming a contract—all he has to do is not perform it. The solvent party can rarely force the office-holder to perform.) A defaulter may honour customer contracts but default on its house side positions. Exchange-traded positions may be dealt with under exchange or clearing house default rules and thus differently from OTC positions.

Information checklist

Things to consider upon counterparty default. This list is not exhaustive and is only a sample of items which might be included.

Counterparty structure

- Which company in the counterparty group is involved? Where is it incorporated?
- Which company in your own group is involved?
- Does the counterparty have assets? What kind?
- Does the counterparty deal on his own account, for customers, or for other group companies?
- Is 'client money' involved? Do any non-cash assets belong to third parties?
- Are there any guarantees and, if so, from whom? What are the guarantor's assets?
- What insolvency procedures are involved? (NB may be multiple procedures for single entity in different jurisdictions).

Transactions

- Types of transaction.
- Dates and copies of any applicable master agreements.
- Look out for cross-group set-off clauses and other bolt-ons.
- Governing law of transactions.
- Margin/security/external guarantees.
- Cash deposits, even if unrelated, and terms of business on which they are held.
- Any other relationships, eg letters of credit, guarantee facilities, travellers cheques.
- Trawl of non-UK branches.
- Loss-sharing provisions in syndicated transactions.

- Can he terminate contracts which you want to keep open? Not usually—but there might be automatic termination provisions which are triggered by the insolvency proceedings and in those cases it will be necessary to reach a special agreement with the office-holder to re-open the positions.
- Can the office-holder escape scot-free for breaches of contract? The office-holder will only rarely be personally liable for putting his company into a breach of contract. So the question is really what other remedies the solvent party has in such a case. In liquidation and administration you cannot sue to recover a debt or damages. Most of the time the only remedy is damages for breach, which can be proved for in a liquidation. (Proving means filing a claim.) If there is collateral or other credit support this may be the standard recourse. But do not forget the office-holder's commercial needs—if he is trying to preserve the business and sell it as a going concern, there may be pressure-points where the office-holder is willing to pay or perform in order to do so.
- Can you rely on a walkaway clause? (A walkaway clause is one which allows the solvent party to escape an obligation to pay the insolvent party, even though the insolvent party would remain liable in respect of an obligation which it owed.) Walkaway clauses are a rip-off on creditors of the insolvent party and give a windfall benefit to solvent counterparties. It is therefore unclear whether these clauses are enforceable under some legal systems and, for reasons presumably connected with depositor protection and systemic risk, they are frowned on by regulators—for example, under the rules relating to recognition of netting agreements for regulatory capital, walkaway clauses are unacceptable.

- Can you set up arrangements to enable you to be confident that the office-holder will perform where performance is promised by him? You might wish to set up an escrow arrangement where a trusted third party agrees to act as DvP agent for both parties.

9

Control of legal risk

9.1 THE NATURE OF LEGAL RISKS

There are legal risks in every facet of one's work. This book could have been called 'legal risks for financial institutions'. There are legal risks in every chapter. So there is no attempt here to set out a comprehensive checklist of legal risks—even the whole book does not try to achieve that. Convergence of legal, risk management and compliance functions means that classifying something as a legal risk may just be a means of deciding who owns the problem, rather than suggesting a technique for solving it.

This chapter looks at a few of the things which might be regarded as 'legal' risks because they are risks with 'legal' risk management solutions:

- documentation (see section 9.2);
- legal opinions (see section 9.3);
- governing law and which jurisdictions are relevant (see section 9.4);
- recharacterisation risk (see section 9.5);

Often legal risks cannot be tackled by 'legal' solutions (drafting, extra documentation, filings etc) but need a rethink from the transaction structuring viewpoint (get the counterparty to do the deal through an affiliate, use your Cayman branch, increase the price, check out the guy on the other end of the phone). This chapter cannot prescribe solutions of this type without a concrete situation to work on. But it can explain the issues which have to be tackled by the legal department.

9.2 DOCUMENTATION

9.2.1 Documentation as risk management?

To get the deal done you need to be led by the business not by the documents. Documentation can therefore get left till the last minute and it is all too easy to reach for a precedent, fill in the blanks and have done with it. Why is that bad?

The purpose of a document is to manage the risks. Amateur draftsmen are usually pretty awful at this, which is surprising. Contracts drafted by amateurs tend to be long recitals of history, what they want to achieve from the deal, but miss out the key things. Good contracts should at least cover:

- Obligations Which party shall do what, when and how. (It is no good saying 'The company shall be entitled to receive $1 million' unless the payer is identified. It does not always follow that the other party is the payer.)
- What-ifs Imagine the worst. (If all goes well, you may never look at the document again. Which implies that you will only need it if all goes badly. So the careful draftsman has to consider the things which may go wrong and their implications.) This means more obligations, or at least invocation of remedies . . .
- Remedies No obligation is worth anything unless you are prepared to stand up for yourself in the event of non-performance. A counterparty who will discuss remedies should not be thought of as a counterparty who is getting ready to renege. Consider the options: non-inception ('condition precedent'); termination; damages; non-renewal; forget the whole thing and start again ('rescission'); special arrangements agreed between the parties. English courts rarely award injunctions or specific performance (ie compel a party to perform) where damages would be an adequate remedy.

See also section 6.4.3 as to issues which may arise with inadequate documentation.

9.2.2 Clauses which don't always work

Sometimes one wants to achieve a particular result (a three-way set-off, for example) where it is known that there are circumstances where the courts would not give effect to the contract term needed. This can make people reluctant to include the clause. But it is quite rare for courts to strike down the whole agreement simply because you included a clause which doesn't always work. English courts allow unenforceable or ineffective provisions to be severed so long as the offensive part can be cut out without leaving the remainder meaningless—you may need to check under a variety of legal systems (see section 9.4 as to jurisdictions which may be relevant). If the clause is central to the agreement so that there is nothing of substance left, then the whole contract may fail.

9.3 LEGAL OPINIONS

What is the point of a legal opinion? Lawyers won't tell you 'there is no legal risk' any more than a market risk analyst will say there is no market risk. The reason for a legal opinion is to identify legal risks, but it is unlikely to control them. The controls have to come elsewhere (restructure or reprice the deal, or don't do it at all). Some firms regard the legal opinion as the solution to legal risks—they are credit-enhancing the deal with a lawyer's sign-off. The length of legal opinions reflects this, as lawyers try to include as qualifications all imaginable and several unimaginable situations where there might be a problem.

9.3.1 Basic architecture

The structure of a formal legal opinion differs according to its author. But, hidden amongst the verbiage, these features will normally be present:

- **Terms of reference** These set out the background against which counsel have been asked to opine, eg a description of the transaction or (where a generic opinion on a standard form document is required but counsel does not know the identity of the parties) the reasons for producing the opinion.
- **Assumptions** Assumptions emasculate opinions. The opinion does not apply if the matter has been assumed. Counsel will therefore assume all sorts of things to stop themselves getting into trouble. Some assumptions are hardly going to cause alarm unless fraud is going on (eg that the copy documents conform to originals or that the signatures are genuine). Others are more important (eg that the documents work under some other system of law). Assumptions should always be points of fact or foreign law. If counsel are uncertain on a point of their own law, the point should be dealt with as a qualification not an assumption.
- **The opinion itself** Counsel will keep this short and vague. Clients will want it long and thorough.
- **Qualifications** There will be various circumstances in which the opinion might be unreliable. There may also be particular legal risks mentioned by the client which counsel has been asked to address even though counsel considers that the risks do not arise. These points are generally addressed in qualifications. Qualifications are most helpful if they set out in full what the problem is, how serious it is and what steps can be taken to minimise the risk.

9.3.2 Danger zones

Here are some tips for reviewing legal opinions (and do review them, don't just file them).

- Ask why you are getting a legal opinion. It is usually to identify risks. If counsel didn't consider the risks you are seeking to understand, the opinion is useless. Always scrutinise the terms of reference and assumptions to check that counsel haven't assumed the whole problem doesn't exist.
- If an opinion is being obtained for regulatory compliance, check that the regulator's requirements have been met. The FSA has a long list of issues which must be covered in netting opinions. Netting opinions must generally be obtained 'in all relevant jurisdictions' and sometimes a side-letter confirming that all relevant jurisdictions have been covered in some way is needed. The jurisdictions which are relevant differ according to the risk. See further section 9.4.
- Sometimes a formal piece of written legal advice will be looked on as an opinion but will not contain a full list of assumptions and qualifications. In relying on it, it may be sensible to check what counsel assumed, particularly if the advice was given in relation to a different deal or a while ago.
- Assumptions should be checked where counsel give opinions on multiple issues. Often an assumption will be relevant to one part of the opinion but not to others. (For example, it should not be necessary to assume that the parties were solvent at the time of the transaction in order to opine on the effectiveness of a choice of law to govern a contract, even if it is necessary in relation to the binding nature of the obligations of the parties under the contract.) If an assumption is cutting down the scope and usefulness of the opinion, ask counsel to specify the parts of the opinion to which it relates.

- Legal opinions are far from comforting. They identify risks. What they rarely do is rank risks in categories of seriousness. Legal risks may not be deal-breakers. If counsel have identified a risk they can usually be pushed to indicate how serious a risk it is, even if they won't say so in the opinion. Ask counsel for an advisory side-letter on the manner of mitigating the risk (or confirmation of their advice that the risk is slender.) Counsel rarely have statistics so it is pointless to ask them 'is it a 50 per cent or a 5 per cent chance?'. But counsel do have information about the types of case that go before the court and should be willing to say 'to the best of our information there are no reported cases in this jurisdiction in which this argument has been raised'.
- Look out for bankruptcy qualifications (eg 'this opinion is subject to laws relating to insolvency, winding-up etc' or 'the rights of the parties may be affected if bankruptcy occurs'). Counsel traditionally used to include one of these in anything they wrote about. But opinions needed for counterparty and credit risk management purposes are useless with a bankruptcy qualification. You are most likely to need to enforce your netting or collateral agreements when a bankruptcy event occurs. Counsel dislike giving bankruptcy-proof opinions because contractual obligations are in danger of being invalidated for a whole range of reasons on bankruptcy.

9.4 WHICH JURISDICTIONS ARE RELEVANT?

9.4.1 The Ruritania problem

Who can tell whether you are at risk in some far-flung jurisdiction, let us say Ruritania? Unless you go to Ruritania and ask local counsel, you may never know. Most of the time we are happy to ignore Ruritania, because a Ruritanian court order is only a threat if:

- we are doing business in Ruritania which might be stopped;
- we have assets in Ruritania which might be seized;
- Ruritanian court orders on the issue in question might be enforced elsewhere, in a place where we would suffer real harm.

And most of the time we are willing to assume that the Ruritanian courts would not interfere unless Ruritanian interests are affected:

- if a Ruritanian entity is involved;
- if assets located in Ruritania are involved;
- if Ruritanian law has been selected to govern the relationship between the parties;
- if Ruritanian creditors might be prejudiced.

A slightly more scientific approach is to distinguish rights which have to be enforced by court action from self-help remedies (netting, collateral) where all we need to know is that we cannot be attacked afterwards.

Enforcement through the court

Where enforcement via the courts is concerned:

- If your counterparty wants your money, watch your back. The classic example of this is the Wells Fargo situation: Bank C took a deposit from Wells Fargo in the Philippines, where legal changes made it impossible for Bank C to pay. Wells Fargo sued Bank C in New York for recovery and won.
- If you want to force your counterparty to pay, cross-border enforcement is quite likely; but if you want an injunction or anything of that nature, cross-border enforcement is unlikely.

Self-help remedies

Self-help remedies like set-off and collateral are great, because you don't need the assistance of any authorities to get on with them. To test whether set-off and collateral are effective you need to work out how you might be attacked after the event:

- Where can you be sued? If only in Ruritania, do you care?
- Is there some other action which can be taken against you instead? (Such as regulatory action, commercial blackballing, exclusion from claiming in the counterparty's bankruptcy.)

Relevant jurisdictions	**Irrelevant jurisdictions**
– Places where you have • assets or property rights • regulatory or other business-critical licences • access to payment, settlement or other business systems • contractual rights • customers are places where you are particularly vulnerable	– Places where you have no such business-critical assets or activities – Places where there is no advantage to any party to take action (consider liquidators, tax authorities, counterparties trying to evade obligations) – Places whose judgments are not recognised in business-critical jurisdictions

REFERENCES

Wells Fargo case

– Wells Fargo Asia Ltd v Citibank NA (1991) 936 F 2d 723.

9.4.2 Function (and limits) of the governing law clause

Cross-border problems can often be simplified by using a governing law clause: this will identify the legal system by which the rights and liabilities of the parties will be determined and the contract will be interpreted. However:

- An express choice of law does not fix all cross-border legal problems. By choosing the law of X you do not cause all legal problems to be sorted by the law of X. So a choice of law clause cannot relocate property in jurisdiction X, cause the parties to be incorporated in jurisdiction X, or require the performance of the contractual obligations in jurisdiction X and all these places may be just as relevant in order to obtain enforceable rights under the contract.

- Courts may consider that a system of law was chosen improperly if it has nothing to do with the parties or the subject matter of the contract and the effect of the choice is to evade some rule of law which would apply if a more relevant system had been chosen.
- Courts may override the chosen system of law in other cases, eg where insolvency strikes, for policy reasons.

Do not confuse the governing law clause with the jurisdiction clause. The jurisdiction clause has the purpose of identifying the courts in which any disputes arising under the contract will be tried; the court in the place of trial may be obliged to apply the chosen governing law, except in relation to procedural matters.

9.4.3 Contracting over the Internet

Is the Internet special?

There are various issues when contracting over the Internet. Where contracts are based is a problem, considering the decentralised nature of Internet-based arrangements; but where the contract was *entered into* is often less relevant than where it is to be *performed*. Most Internet-related legal issues are just unusual manifestations of legal risks which are there anyway. So, what makes it special from the risk perspective?

- It is international, so you need to manage the legal risks on a cross-border basis—and so you need to know which jurisdictions are relevant.
- It is unpredictable, in that you don't know where your customer or counterparty is.

Which jurisdictions are relevant?

The approach is the same as for any other cross-border contract:

- select an appropriate governing law (simple to address); and
- check mandatory laws of other countries which override or supplement the contract.

As to mandatory rules of law:

- if the 'situation' has a close connection with the country; or
- where the contract is for supply of goods or services to a non-business consumer, if the consumer is solicited in the country of his habitual residence,

the laws of that country should be checked. Thus, the places to check are generally where the counterparty/customer is based (for consumer contracts: where the consumer is 'habitually resident') and where the performance of either party may occur.

But the picture is complicated by regulatory rules which may invalidate the contract if the firm making the contract is not duly authorised in all relevant jurisdictions. As to where regulatory licences are needed, see section 2.2.4.

When does the contract take effect?

Significance:

- duration of cooling-off periods;
- duration of contractual periods (interest calculations, etc).

English law model: the contract takes effect when the acceptance occurs. There is an academic debate about whether the 'postal acceptance rule' or the 'telecommunications contract rule' applies: if the former, acceptance happens when the acceptance letter is committed to the postal system; if the latter, it is instantaneous. Internet acceptances could fall under the postal acceptance rule because of potential delays and uncertainties in transmission.

'Battle of forms' issues could arise if the counterparty is a sophisticated Internet user—for example most firms now put disclaimers on their email and many firms purport to include standard terms into their websites.

Risk management: express provisions about acceptance should work, but communication of the *fact* of acceptance is needed at some stage.

9.5 RECHARACTERISATION RISK

9.5.1 What is recharacterisation?

Recharacterisation risk is the risk that a problem dealt with under one heading is considered by a court to have been misclassified, with the consequence that it has not been dealt with properly or at all. This is generally fine unless the problem was a legal one: who cares what a risk manager called something on the borderline between market and credit risk, so long as he dealt with it. In legal problems, the solution might be including a clause, or registering a document; failure to do so is the difference between total risk management and total failure.

Legal historians gain much amusement finding cases where judges had to rule on whether a goldfish was an 'article' or a bicycle was a 'carriage'. Most of the problems for financial sector firms occur when the law imposes a requirement (such as registration, payment of taxes, giving notice, use of particular clauses, using a notary) without which the entire legal relationship falls apart, with the consequence that you have no rights (in the final analysis, you cannot enforce or defend yourself through a court). Generally courts are reluctant to change what the parties thought they were doing. Proving that something is a sham or a fraud is hard work, but it is not impossible. More contentious are the cases where the parties were not trying to mislead anybody but were just guilty of wishful thinking: we know this is a digging implement, we understand the need for a tax on forks, but this four-pronged implement is so useful and has so many shovel-like characteristics that we will describe it in our documents as 'the Spade'.

9.5.2 Asset transfers and collateral

Recharacterisation problems arise most often in the financial sector:

- In securitisations: was the transfer of assets a 'true sale' or a secured loan in disguise?
- In collateral structures: was the collateral transferred outright or by way of charge/pledge/security interest?

- In security interests: was the security granted by way of fixed or floating charge?

Where the distinction is between outright transfer (sale) and security interest, consider the rights over the asset: was any part of the deal inconsistent with the absolute right of the transferee to *go out and destroy the asset if he felt like it*? Think, for example, of the right to get the self-same property back. Some incidents of ownership can be given up (eg risk on value depreciation/appreciation), but to go too far runs a recharacterisation risk.

Where the distinction is between fixed and floating charge, consider the control over the asset: was any part of the deal inconsistent with the right of the chargee to *control the disposal of the asset*? In discussions about floating charges, an awful lot of (misplaced) emphasis is placed on the ability to move property in and out from under the charge. *Only the chargor's right to move property out and to do things to it is relevant.* Some very minor degree of control (eg to make alterations to the property, such as physical alteration to machinery, or to exercise voting rights on shares) might be permitted without turning a fixed charge into a floating charge, but the more control which is yielded the higher the risk of recharacterisation.

Another risk arising in asset transfer cases is whether the property is ascertained: a contract to sell 5 of my 100 sheep may be ineffective to transfer property, or to create a fixed charge over them. In some cases it may not even create a floating charge—witness the Goldcorp case about bullion where the unallocated customers of the bullion depository had mere contractual rights and not even a floating charge.

These risks arise whatever the documentation said. So, if the parties practise something different from the innocent-looking documents, the courts may still recharacterise. And, as they are problems about property transfer, note that the jurisdictions which are relevant will include the place where the property is located.

REFERENCES

True sale v charge

– *Welsh Development Agency v Exfinco* [1992] BCLC 148.

Fixed v floating charge

– *Chase Manhattan Bank NA v Wong Tui San* (1993) 11 ACLC 3,112.

Goldcorp case

– *Re Goldcorp Exchange Ltd* [1995] 1 AC 74.

10

Systemic risk

10.1 SYSTEMIC RISK DESCRIBED

10.1.1 Description

The G30 Report on Global Institutions, National Supervision and Systemic Risk says:

> 'Systemic risk may be defined as the risk of a sudden, unanticipated event that would damage the financial system to such an extent that economic activity in the wider economy would suffer. To qualify as 'systemic', shocks must reverberate through and threaten the financial system, not just some small part of it. They may originate inside or outside the financial sector and may include the sudden failure of a major participant in the financial system; a technological breakdown at a critical stage of settlement of payments systems; or a political shock such as an invasion or the impositions of exchange controls in an important financial center. Such events can disrupt the normal functioning of financial markets by destroying the mutual trust that lubricates most financial transactions.'

IOSCO says that systemic risk

> 'refers to (1) the scenario that a disruption at a firm, in a market segment, or to a settlement system could cause a "domino effect" throughout the financial markets toppling one financial institution after another or (2) a "crisis of confidence" among investors, creating illiquid conditions in the marketplace. Systemic risk encompasses the risk that failure in one firm or segment of the market would trigger failure in segments of or throughout the entire financial markets.'

10.1.2 Species of systemic risk

In effect there are two types of systemic risk:

- **Contagion** Where 'serious disruption' (a coy description for insolvency or something which comes within a whisker of it) at a firm spreads to other firms.
- **Infrastructure defect** Where the pipework which links institutions together, such as payment or settlement systems, fails to perform.

An example of the first type is the near-collapse of Long Term Capital Management in 1998. Regulators feared the macroeconomic and market consequences of allowing LTCM to fail (see 'Long Term Capital Management'). An example of infrastructure nearly failing to perform is when Barings collapsed (remembering that Barings was allowed to fail) and the EBA ecu settlement system was unable without intervention to handle the consequences (see 'The EBA system and the Barings crisis').

Long Term Capital Management

LTCM was a highly-leveraged hedge fund. It was unregulated and its investors were wholesale market participants. Its trading strategy depended on (inter alia) an assumption that the interest on a US Treasury bill would move in parallel with the interest on an instrument of similar (albeit slightly inferior) quality. When the Russian economic crisis of mid-1998 unfolded, investors 'fled to quality', making US Treasury bills hard to come by and invalidating the assumptions about interest rate spreads. LTCM was in serious trouble by mid-September 1998.

The Chairman of the US Federal Reserve Board said that if LTCM's failure 'had triggered the seizing up of markets, substantial damage could have been inflicted on many market participants, including some not directly involved with the firm and could have potentially impaired the economies of many nations, including our own.'

Part of the problem was classic bad banking: banks had lent to LTCM to enable it to buy securities. The loans were collateralised by the securities which were thus bought. So the banks thought they were well secured. But when the markets dived, the value of the collateral fell in perfect correlation with the solvency of LTCM.

The Federal Reserve Board brokered a $3.65 billion refinancing plan for LTCM which was funded by LTCM's investors and counterparties. It was irrelevant that LTCM was not regulated by the Fed or that retail investors would not have been directly affected by its failure. Some members of senior management at UBS, a major investor in LTCM, left their jobs shortly afterwards.

The EBA system and the Barings crisis

The Ecu Banking Association's settlement system for payments denominated in ecu was, until shortly before the introduction of the euro, a daily net settlement system (see settlement risk, section 7.8). In other words the system would, at the end of the day, calculate the net payment in or out required of each participant, take in the payments from the net payers and distribute them to the net recipients.

When Barings collapsed, Barings was a net payer and failed to make its net payment in at the end of the day. There were two possible solutions:

1 deem all settlements that day to have failed.
2 somehow provide the missing ecus which Barings should have provided.

The EBA opted for solution 2 (not surprisingly). There are various ways of doing so, but in the absence of special legal protection there is a danger in increasing exposure to an insolvent entity even if the greater good of the system is being protected.

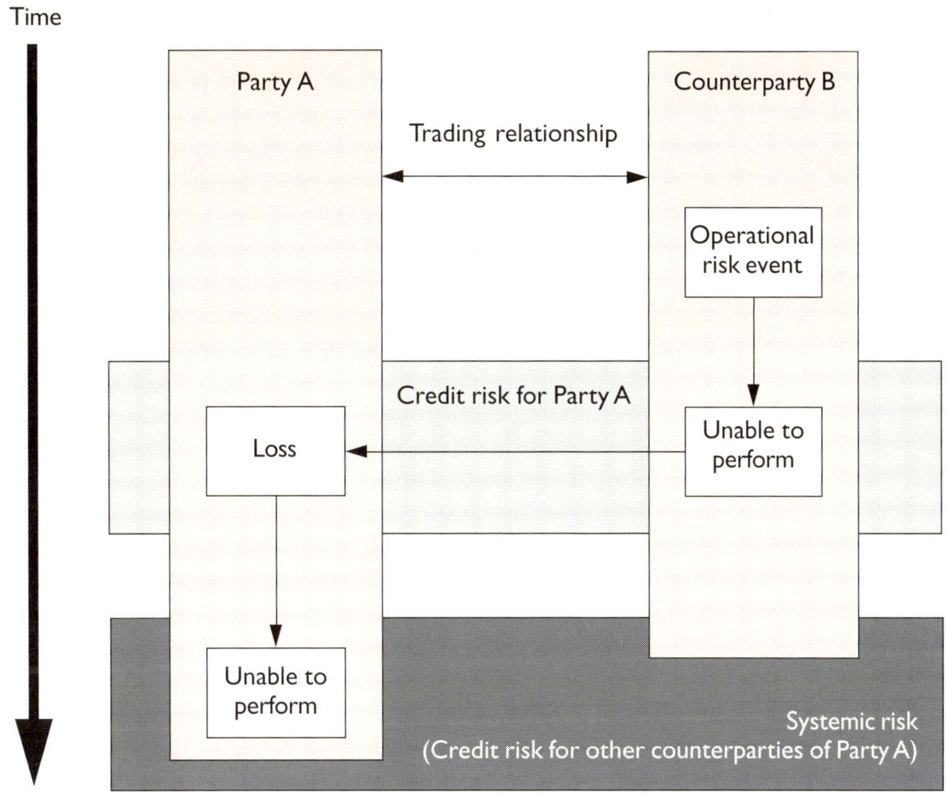

Relationship between operational, credit and system risks

Party A is trading with Counterparty B. B suffers a major operational risk event (say a trader in a far-flung place turns out to have invested zillions of client monies in companies who have patented machinery to turn moon-beams into silver). B finds that it cannot perform its obligations as a result. A is now itself in trouble if it has excessive exposure to B. When A suffers because of B's problem what was a local difficulty is now a systemic issue.

10.1.3 Operational or systemic risk?

Systemic risk and operational risk overlap substantially. Operational risk events are frequently the ultimate source of financial institution failures, which trigger market-wide events spreading beyond the failed institution itself. And the linkages, such as settlement systems, which can allow problems to spread out from a troubled institution are often categorised by firms as posing operational threats.

What distinguishes systemic risk from other operational risks is the means of managing it. It is rare for a firm to be able to take steps on its own to address systemic risk issues. A more concerted, industry-wide solution is usually called for. Regulators may also perceive that systemic risks are ones which do not normally feature in the decision-making processes of firms.

10.1.4 Regulation of systemic risk

The financial sector regulatory reforms in the UK left the Bank of England without its responsibilities for bank supervision and in control of the monetary stability of the UK economy. But they also left it with responsibility for management of systemic risk. This seems curious given that the link between monetary policy and systemic risks seems tenuous. As to the infrastructure with which systemic threats originate: with the exception of the CHAPS interbank payment system which of necessity is operated by the central bank, settlement systems are regulated by the Financial Services Authority. The firms themselves are also regulated by the FSA, so the case for moving systemic risk control across too seems very strong.

REFERENCES

G30 Report

– Group of 30 *Global Institutions, National Supervision and Systemic Risk* (1997).

10.2 RELEVANCE IN DAILY RISK MANAGEMENT

Why bother about systemic risk?

This stuff is obviously important but it is very tempting to imagine that it is not the function of regulated firms to worry about it: it is beyond their control—like market crashes, there are no sensible precautions that can be taken, and any risk events which do occur will be unravelled by regulators, governments or international action. IOSCO said, in May 1998, just before Long Term Capital Management was rescued, that 'although the domestic and international financial markets have withstood large firm losses as seen in the Barings and Daiwa cases, these isolated defaults occurred in the absence of significant market movement. Defaults of unprecedented nature and magnitude could occur in the event of heavy volatility across capital markets . . .' Within a few weeks, during a period of general instability in capital markets in Asia and Russia, LTCM had got into serious difficulties and a rescue was brokered by US regulators in order to avoid systemic consequences.

Systemic risk events have the potential to affect firms in various ways:

- If you are a counterparty of an institution which suffers serious disruption, you could be pushed over if your linkages with the institution are complex and substantial. Even if your direct exposures to the institution are well within large-exposure limits, there is a risk of a spiral (see box 'How a spiral works').
- You may also be called upon to participate in a bail-out on uncommercial terms for the greater good of the market.
- If you are a user of a settlement system which has to unwind or gets into difficulty, you may be called upon to bail the system out or suffer an unwind of all or some of the day's settlements.

How a spiral works

- Investor A takes a large position in a Ruritanian investment. Investor A recognises that the position is too large for it to be prudent to shoulder the entire economic risk in it, so off-loads some of the risk by sale, sub-participation, writing an option or some other derivative, or in some way entering into a relationship with Investor B.
- Investor B does a similar transaction with Investor C. Investor C combines its interest in the investment, acquired from Investor B, with various other similar exposures and repackages them as participations in a Ruritanian investment fund.
- Investor A, who specialises in Ruritania, is willing to increase its exposure in those investments so long as it has a good range of counterparties in the transactions which it undertakes. Investor A has no exposure to Investor C, so is willing to purchase participations in Investor C's fund.
- If the Ruritanian economy suffers a slide and Investor A gets into financial difficulties, each of Investors B and C could experience knock-on effects.

Various examples of spirals can be found in different markets. The best-known is the Lloyd's of London Excess-of-Loss Reinsurance Spiral which developed in the 1980s. More recently a spiral developed among investors in Russian Government debt.

The reason you need to know about systemic risk is that it is what turns someone else's counterparty risk event into everybody's credit or market risk problem. Firms need to know about systemic risk. Although it is a microscopic probability, if there were a risk event then the consequences could be calamitous. Regulators, particularly banking regulators, regard it as close to the top of their agenda. But management of systemic risk is not solely within the province of regulators: systemic risk originates in regulated firms. Good risk management includes awareness of systemic risk.

REFERENCES

IOSCO views on systemic risk

— IOSCO *Risk Management and Control—Guidance for Securities Firms and their Supervisors* (March 1998).

10.3 ORIGINS OF SYSTEMIC RISK

10.3.1 Is contagion a problem?

Does it matter if one firm pushes over another? Regulators believe so, in particular where a bank is concerned.

- Banks control peoples' livelihoods—imagine being unable to get your money out of the bank. And, what is more, they are the only source of loans for much of the economy.
- Banks' assets are illiquid but their liabilities can be called on demand. Managing this mismatch is difficult and it is not a problem faced by other types of financial institution.
- Bank difficulties lead to runs on deposits—depositors scrambling to get their money out before the collapse. Deposit runs can, regulators fear, be contagious.
- Banks are key participants in payment, clearing and settlement systems. Bank failures can spread via these media to other institutions, both banks and non-banks.

Investment and insurance firms are less prone to systemic risk, but it cannot be completely ruled out.

- Multifunctional groups of firms, which include banks as well as other types of institution, are particularly at risk. Intra-group firewalls are often ineffective owing to consolidated management, intra-group lending and so forth.
- Investment banks and other firms not active in retail deposit-taking business are as likely to be major participants in payment, clearing and settlement systems.
- Although investment firms' principal risk source is market risk, rather than credit risk, there can be events similar to a run on the bank: a fall in a market where the firm is not exposed can trigger a fall in the markets where it is.
- Some types of non-bank firm, such as certain funds, are prone to runs; in times of economic downturn, long-term investment strategies can be ruined with irreversible reputational cost.
- Consolidation and merger activity is not confined to the banking sector: all financial sub-sectors are finding activity becoming concentrated into the hands of a few global mega-players.

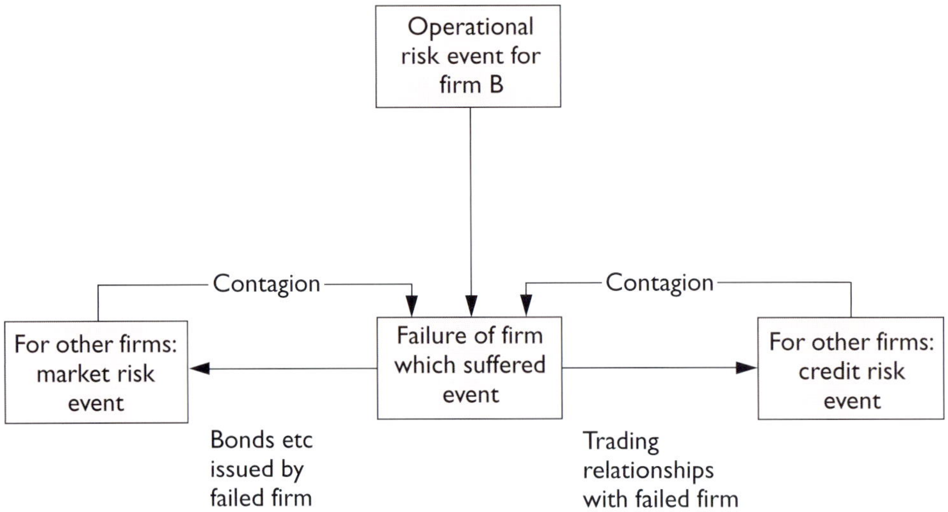

Contagion

Trouble at firm B may spread into the market in various ways. If B has issued bonds then these will plummet in price, potentially setting off market collapses and even (if investors in these bonds have managed their market risk badly) jeopardising their own existence. If B has simply engaged in trading with other firms, and cannot pay its debts, the issue is one of credit risk management by other market players. Either way, if B's failure triggers other failures, further failures may also be on the way. The 1987 stock market crash came very close to this kind of meltdown.

10.3.2 Sources of contagion

Institutions and markets are global. Behavioural patterns spread overnight from one part of the world to another. The same instruments are listed on exchanges in several countries, or derivatives are created which match their performance and can be dealt in wherever there is no suitable exchange. When there is a hiccup in the economy of one part of the world, or 'serious disruption' breaks out within a firm, the consequences can be felt elsewhere with awesome speed. This makes devising contingency plans extremely hard.

It is also wrong to look at the question of industry infrastructure as distinct from the problem of contagion. While the risk management solutions may be different, badly designed pipework can cause a containable problem to escalate. Settlement systems should be built to withstand the shock of a participant's collapse.

10.4 MANAGEMENT OF CONTAGION

10.4.1 Origin

Insolvency is obviously the key to contagion, the trigger which starts it off. Prevention of insolvency should prevent contagion. 'Insolvency' for these purposes includes illiquidity: it is no use having assets which cannot be converted into cash or other property for which the firm in difficulties faces demands. Operational risk has been the source of insolvency in many firms which have failed in recent years, thus management of operational risk is the starting-point for management of systemic risk.

The onset of insolvency can be accelerated by market practices, both good and bad. Where there is governmental or other encouragement to imprudent lending or investment activity (for example pressure to keep failing industries afloat), adverse economic conditions can reveal a much worse picture than might be expected if shareholder-imposed discipline were the sole motivator of corporate decision-making. Derivatives and other investment products with high gearing can have disproportionately bad effects. Economic downturns have other aggravating features. If liquidity is reducing because a contract is moving out of the money, it may be impossible to close out the position. A firm with a bad position can thus be forced into insolvency because of market conditions. Even prudent practices, like taking collateral, can aggravate a situation. Where there is a flight to quality, only certain types of collateral will be acceptable. To cover a position which is becoming ever further out of the money a firm must acquire yet more collateral at increasing cost, in order to avoid being put into default.

The other way of attacking contagion risk is to look at the linkages between firms and work out what causes the collapse of one to push others over. Linkages are predominantly of two types: contractual and infrastructural.

There is nothing inherent in a contractual relationship which means that the collapse of one party is going to cause the collapse of another. Management of large exposures should ensure that the risk of this is avoided. Of course it is possible to devise contractual arrangements which pass on the costs of 'serious disruption' to other participants in a market: any contract with a flavour of insurance will do this and therefore have a potentially systemic effect. Products such as total return swaps, guarantees, letters of credit and credit derivatives all have this flavour. As 'insurance' becomes a less and less useful term, all financial institutions need to consider the extent to which their contractual relationships with other firms expose them to risk if the other were to collapse. Furthermore, even in the absence of insurance, spirals can develop in markets where there are only a few players.

Contractual arrangements between firms are affected by regulatory policy. Regulatory interest in insurance-like products and in market behaviour which allows spirals to develop can be expected. The regulatory response to contagion is muddled. Guidance produced by the Basle Committee on dealing with highly leveraged institutions (hedge funds) after the near-collapse of LTCM comments on banks' practice of setting financial covenants, states that this is 'particularly relevant' and that covenants should be designed with a view to tightening credit limits as counterparty risk increases. On the other hand the guidance also warns against the use of 'sudden death' termination provisions which could have systemic implications. This seems to be saying—make sure you don't fail because your covenants are weak; but please don't make anyone else fail because your covenants are strong. The conclusion to be drawn (which is of course not spelt out) is that if the covenants are strong and the solvent parties use them, then the regulators will have to decide whether the ailing party is too big to be allowed to fail—ie that contractual provisions are a weak force in the fight against systemic risk.

Payment and settlement systems are an obvious linkage, where focused attempts at risk management might be feasible—see section 7.8.4.

Linkages can also be emotional rather than structural. Insolvency at one bank does not imply financial difficulties at another, yet it is received wisdom that a run on one bank will lead to a run on banks generally. This notion is deeply rooted in the history of banking problems in the previous century and the assumption by central banks of the role of lender of last resort. Clearly firms with no retail depositors are less likely to be subjected to this kind of problem; but the speed with which market disruption spread around countries in Asia in 1997–78 shows that emotional factors are not confined to the retail sector.

10.4.2 Too big to fail?

If one of the sources of systemic risk is contagion and regulators will step in to ensure that the collapse of one institution does not knock others over, then the consequence is an elite of major institutions which are too big to fail. Regulators do not like the idea that an institution is too big to fail—in other words that it must, at all cost, be rescued in the event of serious disruption at that institution. The reason is 'moral hazard'—there is no incentive at the firm to manage its risks well if it will be spared the ordinary consequences of failure, such as insolvency, disqualification, disciplinary action and the wrath of investors and unpaid creditors. Yet the efforts of regulators to co-ordinate a rescue of LTCM in 1998 show that support continues to be provided to institutions which 'ought' to have failed.

Other manifestations of moral hazard include:

- deposit insurance in respect of which the insured institution's premium is not related to the risk that the bank fails (as with the UK deposit protection scheme);
- disparity of treatment of failing institutions—leading to an elastic notion of which institutions are too big to fail.

Depositor, investor and policyholder compensation schemes are intended to limit the need to rescue financial institutions since they cap the social cost of financial sector failures. But the existence of the safety net does nothing to eliminate the moral hazard unless the costs become so high that peer pressure forces a delinquent firm to improve its standards. In practice the cost of the depositor and policyholder protection schemes in the UK are negligible relative to the turnover of contributors; the investor compensation scheme applies on quite different principles which makes an analysis of peer-pressure effects virtually impossible and of dubious relevance.

Firms do, however, have strong views on the approach of regulators to 'serious disruption' when it comes to light in one of their peers. If regulators allow small firms to go to the wall but require large or weakly capitalised ones, however badly run, to be rescued, questions of fairness are raised. Where a market has a reputation of distorting competition that can drive away business.

International financial activity tends to be concentrated among only a few financial institutions, which are relatively well-capitalised and based in countries where the regulatory system is relatively strict. On the other hand they deal with each other in the wholesale markets and their interrelationships would be virtually impossible to unravel. Such firms, particularly large international banks, are willing to take the issues seriously as they are most likely to suffer as a result of systemic risk events. Trends which put the matter on the agenda include the growth in size, volume, complexity and speed of transactions, consolidation of the financial sector into fewer hands and internationalisation of markets.

10.4.3 Historical and future approaches

Historically the approach to containment of systemic threats has been an ad hoc response such as the rescue of LTCM. As institutions become bigger one wonders whether this is likely to continue. Supervisors find it difficult to co-operate internationally in the event of even relatively minor shocks such as the collapse of Barings, because of cultural differences in regulatory approach and, of course, because regulation is still organised along national boundaries. To devise a rescue plan in the short time before a threat becomes a crisis may become impossible as the speed of transmission of shocks increases.

Entry into the club of the elite few institutions with unravellable interconnections by merger will be heavily scrutinised by financial regulators as well as competition authorities. Beyond that, self-interest seems a more likely model for management of contagion risk for the future.

Systemic risk remains a convenient excuse for additional regulation: the argument is that the supervisor alone is in a position to assess systemic risk and so firms should not resist rules which are founded on a fear of systemic risk events. But supervisors, who unlike firms are organised according to national boundaries, are less able to cope with systemic risk issues than once they were: payment and settlement systems, through which systemic shocks are transmitted, cross borders. Supervisory responses are ad hoc; contingency plans may not exist.

10.5 MANAGEMENT OF RISKS IN SETTLEMENT SYSTEMS

10.5.1 Regulatory management of crises

When a financial institution fails, there is usually an outcry of some sort. What is less easy to predict is whether the regulators, the central bank, or the Government will step in and aid the failing institution. The classic form of assistance is a liquidity facility to help a bank suffering a liquidity crisis and the danger that depositors will withdraw funds faster than the bank can convert its assets into cash (a run on the bank). If this form of assistance happens it will usually be effective to prevent a run on a bank if it takes place in secret; so there is plenty of opportunity for mystery.

Liquidity facilities of this type may be arranged or provided by the central bank—the 'lender of last resort'. Controversy surrounds how the lender of last resort concept will apply in the euro area of the EU given that flows of euro are not within the exclusive control of national central banks. The European System of Central Banks has been criticised for having no clear protocol for crisis management; the European Central Bank has countered that bank runs are unlikely in today's economy and that the institutions of the euro system would be able to react adequately if necessary.

10.5.2 Regulation of clearing and settlement systems

Given their strategic importance, it is odd that clearing and settlement systems do not generally require to be regulated. In the UK it is permitted (but not essential) for a clearing or settlement system to seek 'recognition' from the Financial Services Authority. The requirements for recognition as a clearing house are fourfold:

- a vaguely-defined financial resources requirement;
- arrangements for monitoring compliance with the clearing house's rules;
- provision of clearing services for an exchange (though this is to be abolished);
- being able and willing to promote and maintain high standards of integrity and fair dealing.

What is more, the law is so muddled that in the UK it has been possible to operate as a clearing house and to be regulated as a recognised investment exchange or as a settlement system for money market investments; and for CREST, the main equity settlement system, to be regulated as a recognised clearing house even though it carries out only minimal clearing functions.

In other countries there is a similar pattern. Industry infrastructure is either already under the direct control of the regulatory or governmental authorities or the central bank; to the extent that it is not it may be that an organisation providing a clearance or settlement system has sought regulation voluntarily rather than been compelled to maintain minimum standards.

10.5.3 International standards

International standards have, however, been discussed. The Basle Committee has laid down standards to be met by netting schemes, including multilateral netting systems (see 'the Lamfalussy standards', below). Other recommendations for safer clearing and settlement systems include:

- standards for IT and other back-up;
- standards for risk management systems;
- standards for financial backing.

The Lamfalussy standards

Minimum standards for the design and operation of cross-border and multi-currency netting and settlement schemes

I Netting schemes should have a well-founded legal basis under all relevant jurisdictions.

II Netting scheme participants should have a clear understanding of the impact of the particular scheme on each of the financial risks affected by the netting process.

III Multilateral netting systems should have clearly defined procedures for the management of credit risks and liquidity risks which specify the respective responsibilities of the netting provider and the participants. These procedures should also ensure that all parties have both the incentives and the capabilities to manage and contain each of the risks they bear and that limits are placed on the maximum level of credit exposure that can be produced by each participant.

IV Multilateral netting systems should, at a minimum, be capable of ensuring the timely completion of daily settlements in the event of an inability to settle by the participant with the largest single net-debit position.

V Multilateral netting systems should have objective and publicly disclosed criteria for admission which permit fair and open access.

VI All netting schemes should ensure the operational reliability of technical systems and the availability of back-up facilities capable of completing daily processing requirements.

The G30 has proposed various target standards for securities settlement systems. These include: trade comparison by T+1; moving securities to book-entry form; robust netting systems; DvP; settlement by T+3; and stock-lending to reduce fails. Several of these issues are examined in more detail in section 7.8.

After the collapse of Barings, the US Futures Industry Association issued various recommendations including recommendations for exchanges and clearing houses. These include:

- Mechanisms to protect exchange-member and customer property against the risk of dissipation as a result of broker activities. These should enable transfer or close out of positions and the return of customer property. The procedures should be pre-established and made known to market participants.
- Resources available to the exchange or clearing house should be sufficient to protect non-defaulting members and their customers against loss.
- Margining systems should be designed so as to preserve the integrity of the market and recognise timing issues related to margin, settlement and payment obligations.
- Margin should be collected from customers promptly. Where this is not done, clearing houses and exchanges should adjust their rules, eg by requiring additional collateral.
- Payments to the clearing house should be irrevocable and inwards payments should be (as nearly as is practical) simultaneous with outwards payments.
- Exchanges and clearing houses should publicise their market protection mechanisms, including sources of financial support and their financial statements.

For more on clearing and settlement systems, see sections 8.2.3 (discussion of counterparty relationships which can arise) and 7.8 (discussion of settlement risk).

REFERENCES

Lamfalussy standards

– Bank for International Settlements *Report of the Committee on Interbank Netting Schemes* (November 1990).

G30 views on settlement systems

– Group of 30 *Clearance and Settlement Systems in the World's Securities Markets* (March 1989).

FIA recommendations for exchanges etc

– Futures Industry Association Global Task Force on Financial Integrity *Financial Integrity Recommendations for Futures and Options Markets and Market Participants* (June 1995).

Index

All references are to page numbers

£ 120-00 CT 213 3/10/07